THE
ROAD TO
RAMADAN

THE
ROAD TO
RAMADAN

Mohamed Heikal

COLLINS
St James's Place, London
1975

William Collins Sons & Co Ltd
London · Glasgow · Sydney · Auckland
Toronto · Johannesburg

First published 1975
© Times Newspapers Ltd and Mohamed Heikal

ISBN 0 00 211653 7

Set in Monotype Times
Made and Printed in Great Britain by
William Collins Sons & Co Ltd Glasgow

Contents

ILLUSTRATIONS — 7

ACKNOWLEDGMENTS — 9

Chapter I   SURPRISE — 11

Chapter II   NASSER'S LAST STAND — 46

1. The Aftermath of Defeat — 46
2. Arab Contacts — 55
3. Enter the Palestinians — 62
4. The Libyan Coup — 68
5. Buying a Bomb — 76
6. The Rabat Summit — 77
7. Crisis in Moscow — 83
8. The Rogers Initiative — 90
9. The Second Moscow Visit — 93
10. Rogers Accepted — 95
11. The Cairo Conference — 98
12. The Death of Nasser — 103
13. The Funeral — 105

Chapter III   SADAT RIDES THE STORM — 114

1. First Diplomatic Contacts — 114
2. The Downfall of the Ali Sabri Group — 122
3. Palestinians and Sudanese — 139
4. Dinner at the Soviet Embassy — 143
5. The Randopolo Affair — 147
6. The Last Meeting with Rogers — 152
7. Into 1972 — 155

8. More Trouble with the Soviets   160
9. The Break   165
10. Libya   184
11. Relations with the USA   198
12. Pressures towards War   204

Chapter IV   WAR   207

Chapter V   A NUCLEAR ALERT   243

Chapter VI   A NEW TYPE OF WAR   257

Chapter VII   OIL   262

INDEX   279

Illustrations

The Author, at the front   *facing page* 48
Suez during the War of Attrition   48
Operational Headquarters   49
The Bar-Lev Line   49
Israeli Prisoners   64
Nasser Welcoming Podgorny   65
A Conference in Moscow   112
Nasser and Ghadaffi   112
Nasser's Body Lying in State   113
The Funeral of Nasser   113
King Hussein in Cairo   128
Podgorny at the High Dam   128
Yasser Arafat's First Call on Sadat   129
Sadat, Ghadaffi and Asad   129
A Summit Conference   144
General Ahmed Ismail   145
General Gamasy   145
General Fahmy   145
General Shazli   145
Inspecting Missile Sites   160
Crossing the Canal   160
Kissinger in Cairo   161

Foreword

In this book I have tried to give an honest report of things as I saw them during the October War of 1973 and in the six years that led up to it. I was of course far from being in a position to see everything. My analysis of events is therefore partial and may be mistaken, but I have done my best to give a true and candid picture. It has been my intention that this picture should not be a purely Egyptian one. I have preferred to draw it as far as I can from a wider Arab angle, and not to forget that the Arab world is only a part of the whole complex international scene.

Apart from any temporary gains or losses there may have been in the October War – the 'Ramadan War', – its outcome cast a shadow ahead on the inevitable next stage of the confrontation. The Arabs had shown their potential but failed to exploit it properly. The Israelis had been faced with their fundamental weakness, but turned away from it in horror and tried to pretend that it did not exist. The outside world concentrated its efforts on patching over the crisis rather than on attempting to get to the root of it. The main architect of the truce which succeeded the war, Henry Kissinger, saw it as essentially an exercise in relations between the two super-powers. The only conclusion to be drawn from all these missed opportunities and mutual incomprehension is that another war is inevitable.

Acknowledgments

I should like to thank General Hassan el Bedri, official historian to the Egyptian army; Dr Mustafa Khalil, former Deputy Prime Minister responsible for industries and mineral resources in Egypt; and Edward Hodgkin for help in preparation of my material; and many other friends for the assistance which they have given. I must also thank John Barry, whose knowledge of this period was invaluable in the final checking of facts and figures.

CHAPTER I

Surprise

On the morning of Wednesday 22 August 1973 eight Egyptian and six Syrian officers made their way one by one from the Officers Club in Alexandria to the headquarters of the Naval Command in the royal palace of Ras el-Tin. The Syrians had arrived from Damascus a day or two before, checking in separately and joining the crowd of Egyptians and officers from other Arab countries, as well as Russian technicians, who habitually used the club, particularly at that time of the year, the height of the summer holiday season. All wore civilian clothes, and there was no reason why they should have attracted any particular attention.

In a room at the Naval Command headquarters, the Minister of War, General Ahmed Ismail, seated himself in the middle of one side of a long table in the centre of the room; facing him was his opposite number, the Syrian Minister of Defence, General Mustafa Tlas. Flanking them were the senior officers for the two armed forces – the Chiefs of Staff, the Directors of Operations, the Directors of Intelligence, the Commanders of the Navy, of the Air Force and of Air Defence – but as in Syria these last two appointments were held by one officer there were only six of them against seven Egyptians. The fourteenth of those round the table was another Egyptian, General Bahieddin Nofal. His function explained the presence of the others: Nofal was Chief of Staff of the Federal Operational General Staff. In simpler terms, the men around that table were the military pinnacle of the joint Egyptian-Syrian command.

The purpose which brought them together was to put the finishing touches to the plan for a simultaneous attack on Israeli forces in occupied Egyptian Sinai and occupied Syrian

11

Golan some time during the autumn of that year. Planning for such an attack had started a long time ago – in one form or another from the immediate aftermath of the 1967 defeat. It had, inevitably, taken different forms according to the partner or partners with whom Egypt was expecting to operate, and this had only finally been determined with the setting up of the unified command of the armed forces of Egypt and Syria on 31 January 1973. Before that Libya had been an active partner in the planning, but when it became clear that President Ghadaffi of Libya had a fundamentally different concept from that of Egypt and Syria of the lines along which the attack should be conducted, the other two decided to continue their preparations without him.

The most stringent precautions were taken to ensure that no hint of what was in the wind should leak out. The room in which the fourteen officers met had been checked and re-checked over and over again for any possibility of bugging. No electronic devices of any sort were allowed in. No notes were to be taken except by one officer, General Abdul Ghani el-Gamasy, the Egyptian Director of Operations, who kept the minutes in pencil and subsequently made two copies only, one to be handed to the Egyptian Chief of Staff, General Saad el-Shazli, for President Anwar el-Sadat, and one to the Syrian Chief of Staff, General Yusuf Shakur, for President Hafez Asad of Syria. When they had left the conference room, none of the officers was allowed to communicate with another in writing or by telephone. Any exchange between them had to be made by word of mouth and by word of mouth alone.

For six days the meetings continued, for there were many points still to be settled even though the overall plan had been agreed as long ago as April. When the officers finally dispersed in August, a majority of the Syrians went back by ship from Alexandria to Latakia; the rest flew home. But in spite of their intensive deliberations two points remained unresolved when they broke up and there was no alternative but to pass these back to the two Presidents for a ruling. The two questions concerned the exact timing of the attack – the day and the hour: D-Day and H-Hour.

Two alternative periods for the attack had been put forward by the planners – between 7 and 11 September, and between 5 and 10 October. There had never been much enthusiasm for the first of these periods, but it was retained as an option in case there were strong political reasons, of which the planners were unaware, which might favour an early date. But one decision about timing on which they had agreed, virtually ruled out the September date: that there should be a countdown of twenty days. So in effect it would have to be an October war, though choosing the exact date was to be the responsibility of the Presidents. One more consideration affected the timing: a demand by the Syrians that they should have a special countdown of five days to give them time to discharge the refineries at Homs, which would be an almost certain target for the Israeli bombs once the fighting had started. As the Egyptians had learned during the War of Attrition, the damage bombs can do to an empty refinery is relatively small, but if the tank field is full destruction can be catastrophic. This Syrian request was agreed to, but was later to be a source of some misunderstanding.

As for the time when the battle should start, the Egyptians were in favour of the afternoon. This would mean their troops could attack across the Suez Canal with the sun behind them and in the eyes of the Israelis. They would have some hours of daylight for the crossing, followed by six hours of moonlight, during which the bridging of the canal should be completed, and a further six hours of total darkness in which the armour could be brought across. But the Syrians wanted to attack at first light, since they would be attacking westward and were no less anxious than the Egyptians to have the sun behind them. Several compromise proposals were put forward. The Egyptians, for example, said they were prepared to let the Syrians start at first light and to follow themselves in the afternoon. The Syrians objected that this would leave them alone in the battle for several hours and would destroy the element of simultaneous surprise on two fronts. Next the Egyptians suggested that they should start in the afternoon on D-Day and the Syrians open up at first light on D+1. The Syrians' objection to this was that not only would it too destroy part of the element of surprise, but it would be politically wrong because it would give the impression that they were lagging behind the Egyptians.

While the discussions had been going on in Alexandria President Sadat had been on a tour which took him to Saudi Arabia, Qatar and Syria. The first two stops were to a large extent part of the elaborate deception plan which had been mounted and were designed to give the impression that the President, like everybody else in Egypt, was simply going about his normal business. The Syrian visit had a much more serious purpose. Both Chiefs of Staff had left the planning meeting after the major decisions had been taken, leaving the details to their subordinates. Now General Tlas flew back to Damascus while President Sadat was there and gave him and President Asad an account of what had been settled in Alexandria as well as of the two points which had been left open. President Sadat and President Asad agreed that the September date should be ruled out and that the attack should take place some time during the period 5–10 October. In the afternoon of 27 August President Sadat arrived back in Cairo. He was met at the airport by General Ismail who gave him a more detailed briefing on the joint staff talks. He approved all that had been done except for the length of the countdown: twenty days, he thought, was too long; fifteen was more normal and should be sufficient. The adjustment was made.

Then followed in the first three days of September a series of meetings attended by those Egyptian officers who had been present at the Alexandria staff talks with the addition of the commanders of the two armies which were to attack across the canal. These had the situation explained to them, though they were given no dates and it was emphasized that none of the information might be passed on to anyone.

It was towards the end of one of these meetings on 3 September that General Shazli asked the Egyptian Army's Director of Intelligence, General Fuad Nassar, to give an assessment of the enemy's probable reaction to the attack. The assessment he gave was based on three sources: first, an intensive study which had been prepared following Israeli manoeuvres in May. These manoeuvres had clearly been designed as a warning to Egypt

14

following Egyptian concentrations in the area at the time, that if her forces attempted a crossing of the canal they would be annihilated. Secondly, on the known disposition of Israeli forces in Sinai at that moment; and thirdly, on the general intelligence background.

After General Nassar had made his statement General Shazli asked a question which led to a long and animated discussion. When, he asked, did the Intelligence estimate that the enemy would know about the Egyptian preparations? The answer he received was that the enemy was expected to know about them fifteen days in advance of the assault. In other words, immediately the countdown started the enemy would be in a position to move up his reserves.

This confronted the Egyptian command with a problem which at first seemed insoluble: if complete surprise was, as it appeared to be, impossible, the first troops across the canal would have to meet the full brunt not merely of Israel's regular armoured forces – that had always been foreseen – but of the mobilized Israeli reservists as well. Something might be done to speed up the bridging operations and so get the Egyptian armour across earlier than planned, but this was no real solution as bridges could be bombed and in any case it would not stop the infantry from being left for many hours alone and facing the risk – it might almost be called the certainty – of annihilation. It was not until about ten days later that the answer was found. To withstand the Israeli regular forces, the Egyptian command had always planned to equip the first assault waves with the best portable anti-aircraft and anti-tank missiles in the world, the Soviet Strellas and Molutkas (known to the West as SAM-7s and Saggers). The solution to this new threat was to equip the first 8000 shock troops, and the infantry divisions which went in immediately after them, with these missiles on a scale far in excess of anything previously contemplated. For this purpose the First Army – which was to remain west of the canal and not cross into Sinai in the first assault – was almost entirely stripped of its Strellas and Molutkas, which were handed over to the assault troops. It was this last-minute 'overdose' of weapons that enabled the infantry to hold out, and General Dayan was later to admit that it was not so much the novelty of the weapons that took the Israeli forces by surprise as the sheer numbers in which they were available to the Egyptians at the outset of the battle.

The suggestion was also put forward at this 3 September meeting that if the scope of the deception plan was enlarged it might be possible to cut down the period in which Israel would know of the Egyptian preparation from fifteen to four or five days. General Ismail thought this would be sufficient to ensure success, in view of the five to seven days estimated by the Egyptian command to be necessary for full mobilization in Israel, though he would naturally have preferred a still shorter period – say three days. Moreover, it was thought that on this occasion Israel's mobilization might take even longer in view of its coinciding with a time of feasts and holy days, culminating in the Day of Atonement (Yom Kippur), and the run-up to the Israeli general elections, due on 31 October.

As part of the deception plan it was decided that the final dispositions to the troops should be made under cover of preparations for the annual autumn manoeuvres, plans for which, under the code name of Liberation 23, had long ago been independently preparing. Israeli intelligence was bound to know all about this, for signals connected with the manoeuvres had already been filling the air. Accordingly, when the High Command went to the underground post known as Centre Number Ten, which was to be its operational headquarters for the campaign, it was, in the first place, with the maps for Liberation 23 that the walls of the command post were covered. It would be a comparatively simple matter to switch the troops actively engaged in Liberation 23 to their positions for the launch of Badr*, the code name for the joint Egyptian-Syrian assault.

The deception plan naturally covered a far wider field than this. Following the example of Montgomery before Alamein, studies for the deception plan had begun at the same time as, and proceeded parallel with, the operational plan, and covered all fields – military, diplomatic, and informational. The troops were moved up to the canal front by night and elements of them withdrawn ostentatiously by day (only, of course, to be moved

16

back again by night). A high sand rampart on the west bank of the Suez Canal, the construction of which started at the end of 1972 and cost £30 m., purported to be an additional protection against Israeli attack, but in fact helped to conceal the concentration of artillery and tanks. Egyptian and Syrian representatives at non-aligned conferences, the United Nations, and similar gatherings spoke in pacific terms (without, it must be added, knowing the purpose of the directive from which they spoke) while the Press and radio were encouraged to play up the concern of Egypt and Syria over the search for a peaceful solution to the Middle East conflict, and to refer with disapproval to the belligerent speeches and actions of the Palestinian Fedayin.

But successful though the deception plan proved to be, a great deal was owed to that fickle ally, General Luck. It would have been too much to hope for the good fortune which made Israeli public opinion at the beginning of October almost wholly absorbed in the Austrian Government's decision to close the immigrant camp at Schonau after members of the fedayin group Saiqa hijacked a train carrying Jewish emigrants from Russia. Another unlooked-for bonus was that in the spring of 1973 General Yariv, who was an exceptionally astute officer, had been replaced as Director of Military Intelligence in Israel by General Ze'ira, who had a rigid conviction that in no circumstances would Egypt be able to mount an attack. It was fortunate too that the Israelis drew wrong conclusions from the disastrous air battle over Damascus on 13 September in which they shot down thirteen Syrian planes. This led to a great deal of tension, and there were fears that the Syrians might be tempted to hit back and so exhaust themselves before the real battle started. They did in fact concentrate troops on their front, and Egypt moved troops forward too, but as part of Liberation 23. There was even an order for semi-mobilization, so that some Egyptian reservists could take part in Liberation 23, which was scheduled to last from 1 to 7 October. No doubt all the signals connected with the aftermath of the Syrian air battle were picked up by the Israelis and played a part in distracting their attention from the real threat. Another minor but significant and wholly unplanned coincidence was that at about this time an American company signed an agreement to build an oil pipeline with its southern terminal at Adabiyah on the Gulf of Suez, which would certainly be within the area of hostilities should the canal front be opened up. This was taken as a further indication that Egypt was expecting a long period of peace.

The Americans were to confess to Egypt afterwards that they had got hold of the plans for Badr in May, but did not believe them. Certainly, they were as surprised as anyone by the implementation of the plan. Certainly, too, they had in recent months been conducting increasingly intensive intelligence operations in Egypt, concentrating on the military. By September it was felt that the level of their espionage efforts had become intolerable. They could not use their own military personnel because diplomatic relations between Egypt and the USA had been broken off in 1967 and not resumed, but they worked through the military attachés of other countries, particularly one belonging to an Asian country. The Egyptian Intelligence people arranged an unfortunate accident for him – his car and another car were involved in a collision, there was a quarrel, he was beaten up and had to stay in hospital for several months. After this the head of the American interests section at the Spanish Embassy was declared persona non grata towards the end of September – though Egypt agreed that he might leave quietly, so as not to worsen relations publicly.

It was early in September that I myself was first let into the secret of the approaching battle. On Monday 10 September President Sadat asked me to come out and see him in his rest-house at Bourg al-Arab, near Alexandria. As I arrived he was just coming down the steps towards a brown Mercedes standing in front of the house. 'Come and sit beside me,' he said, getting into the driver's seat. This surprised me, because the President hardly ever drove himself. His guards tried to get into the back seat, but the President stopped them and told them to follow in other cars.

Normally the President went from his rest-house to a cabin on the sea shore, a drive of about five kilometres. This time I noticed that he was going in the opposite direction, along the desert road that leads to the oasis of King Mariut, on the way to Alamein, where there was another rest-house that the President was fond of. As we drove he started talking about war. We were passing through fields recently planted under a land reclamation scheme, and the President pointed towards them: 'Look at all this green – all this new life coming up. After we've finished our battle I think I'll settle down here, have a small ranch with horses and spend the rest of my life between the desert and the sea.'

Although, like many other people, I had at this time a feeling that there was something in the wind I had no idea exactly what we were to expect, or when. So I told the President that in that case I thought his retirement was still a long way off.

'Do you really think so?' he said. 'I suppose there must be a great many people who think we are never going to fight.'

'I think it is our destiny to fight,' I said.

'But there are others in the Arab world,' said the President, 'who would not agree with you, and who have lost hope of our ever fighting.' Then he added: 'By God, we are going to surprise them.' He looked at me, and said: 'I think you are going to be surprised too.'

'Why?' I asked.

'I'll tell you a secret,' said the President. 'Have you got strong nerves? Our battle will start about one month from now.'

I said: 'Mr President, why are you telling me this? Now I shan't be able to sleep.'

'I don't want you to sleep,' said Sadat, smiling. By now we had reached the rest-house at King Mariut. We sat on the veranda, where someone had arranged a lot of flowers as decoration. It seemed an incongruous setting for a talk about an imminent war. 'You've spoilt the day for me,' I complained. 'I feel as if there was a nightmare hanging over me.'

In front of the President as we sat were two black files. He gestured to one. 'Here you are,' he said. 'You are always accusing us of not applying technology, but the information in here shows how the last word in technology has been applied

19

to our plan.' This led him into a complete exposition of the coming operation. It was brilliantly done. For an hour he outlined with great clarity, and without once referring to his file, the thinking which lay behind it, as well as the problems which still remained to be solved.

This was our last chance, the President said. If we did not seize it we should have finally missed the bus. For one thing, Egypt was not going to receive any more arms than it already had so was at the peak of its military capacity. Again, from the international point of view Egypt had all the backing which had ever been dreamed of – among the Arab nations, the non-aligned, at the United Nations, and everywhere. People were beginning to say, 'What's the use of all the resolutions of support you have asked us for and we have given you? Nothing seems to happen. What are you waiting for?' Soon people would begin to lose interest. Then there was Egypt's economic situation. It would be impossible to survive the 'no peace, no war' situation much longer. Without a big injection of financial aid 1974 was going to bring a crisis. The only source of aid on the scale needed was some of the Arab countries and the Arabs were not going to give Egypt another penny unless there was some movement. On the home front, people were beginning to lose patience.

We talked about Egypt's internal problems for a while, and in the course of this talk the President came to two decisions, both of which were aimed at encouraging a climate of reconciliation. The first was to drop the charges outstanding in the courts against students involved in the 1972 demonstrations; the second was to reinstate the seventy to eighty writers and journalists who had been expelled from the Arab Socialist Union – and thereby been threatened with the loss of their jobs – earlier that year.

After this the discussion moved to some of the outstanding points on which the President had not yet made up his mind. The first of these was the casus belli – what was to be the trigger for the operation? One of the ideas that had been suggested to him was that an Egyptian submarine should fire on an Israeli tanker, but Sadat thought this foolish; the Israelis would be certain to react violently, and nobody could foretell the international fall-out from such an act.

The President was concerned about Egypt's information services and communications with the rest of the world. He was very conscious of the enormous advantages Israel enjoyed in getting its point of view heard outside. I told him my belief, which was that if we had something valid and reasonable to say, the world would listen to it and accept it, even if the only source for it was Cairo radio.

Another big unresolved problem was, who was to be told what, and when. What should the Soviets be told? The non-aligned leaders, particularly Tito and Mrs Gandhi? Western Europe, which meant principally Heath, Brandt, and Pompidou? Egypt's supporters in Africa and Asia? How was the situation at the United Nations to be handled? Obviously, after the first shot had been fired everyone could be put completely in the picture, but should any of them be told before the opening shot?

The most important decision was what to do about the Soviet Union. We discussed this for a long time, and finally it was decided that they should be told in advance. Later a letter for Brezhnev was drafted. Identical letters for Tito and Mrs Gandhi were prepared, and another identical three for Heath, Brandt and Pompidou, but the intention was that all these should only be sent after the outbreak of hostilities. As for the United Nations, it was assumed that the scenario would be: news of the fighting is received in New York; the Security Council is called; the Egyptian case is presented. So the office of Hafez Ismail, the Adviser to the President for National Security Affairs, was instructed to draw up notes for presentation to the Security Council and the General Assembly.

In the end none of these letters and notes were ever sent. In the rush and excitement of events of 6 October nobody remembered them. It proved much simpler to get hold of the ambassadors in Cairo and tell them whatever seemed appropriate at the time.

We turned to the likely Israeli response, and the President stressed his anger at what he called Israel's 'intolerable arro-

21

gance'. He picked up the second black file. 'This,' he said, 'is a dossier on Israeli intentions.' He pulled from it a report of a television interview given a month or so earlier by General Dayan, in which Dayan had made it quite clear that Israel was determined to build a new port and town at Yamit, on Egyptian territory bordering the Gaza Strip. Dayan had talked of this as a 'primary military defence line'. Egypt, his remarks showed beyond doubt, was to be presented with a *fait accompli*. 'Look at that,' said the President. 'If it was only for that one statement of Dayan's I think we should go to war.'

One wise decision which President Sadat had taken by then was that he was not going to the operational headquarters of the military command unless his presence there was specifically requested. As he said, the supreme commander of the country's armed forces was a civilian, and, remembering the disasters of 1967, he was determined that the professional soldiers should be left to run their own show. In 1967 the Commander-in-Chief, Field Marshal Amer, owed his appointment to political rather than military considerations, his own military training having stopped at the rank of major. This time the President would be with the command in the initial stages of the battle, to demonstrate that the political responsibility was his; but then he would leave them, and only come back if crucial decisions had to be made.

The President had also decided to set up a number of specialized committees. There was to be a foreign affairs committee, headed by Dr Mahmoud Fawzi, to maintain liaison with foreign governments and including a special section to deal with the foreign Press; a committee headed by Hussein el-Shafei, the Vice-President, and Mamduh Salem, Minister of the Interior, to deal with civil defence and relief; another committee headed by Sayed Marei, Assistant to the President, to ensure that the home front continued to function as normally as possible; and a committee headed by the Secretary General of the Arab League, Mahmoud Riad, intended to mobilize Arab public opinion, and in particular any actions contemplated against American interests.

The idea was that these committees would function in Tahra

Palace, which was to be the President's political command post. This had been built by a cousin of King Farouk, Mohammed Taher Pasha, and given by Farouk as a wedding present to his first wife, Queen Farida. After the Revolution it became a government guest-house. Nasser had been living there in the summer of 1956 when he announced the nationalization of the Suez Canal Company, because his own house at Manshiet al-Bekri was being repaired. When President Sadat decided to use it as his headquarters a lot of technological gadgets were installed – for example, to permit direct communication with the commanders in the field, President Asad in Damascus and President Ghadaffi in Tripoli – but none of these was used in the actual battle. Nor, for that matter, did any of the committees function as planned. For one thing, some of those who were supposed to take a leading part in them had overriding duties elsewhere, and, for another, the President came to the conclusion that too many committees on top of him would be more of a burden than a help.

On Monday 1 October, Major Abdel Salam Jalloud, the Prime Minister of Libya, came to see President Sadat. Jalloud had come to Cairo at the end of September with President Ghadaffi to attend the various commemorations of the anniversary of the death of President Nasser, but for some reason Ghadaffi elected to return home before the end of these. When President Sadat saw Jalloud that Monday morning, therefore, his ostensible purpose was to express his unhappiness at Ghadaffi's departure. But the President, without giving any details of the imminence or timing of the coming operation, also asked for the promised delivery of arms, including artillery and anti-aircraft missiles, to be speeded up. Jalloud said he would return to Libya at once to give these messages. To emphasize the urgency, the President got in touch with Jalloud again just as he was boarding his aircraft at three o'clock to go back to Benghazi. 'What we were speaking of this morning must come as quickly as possible,' he said. 'It's a matter of hours. Don't delay.' (Jalloud had to return once more to Cairo having delivered that message, but then the Libyan leaders were lucky in the matter of transport. The revolution had confiscated three

23

Mystere 20 private jets belonging to the royal family, and the leaders travelled in these in considerable comfort.)

I was with the President while he was talking to Jalloud. He was on the balcony outside the bedroom of his house in Giza. He was fasting, and was lying back in an armchair, wearing pyjamas and a brown dressing-gown. After Jalloud had left, the President said to me: 'I don't want to overplay my hand. But now we still have to be certain what exactly to do about the Russians.' We had already agreed that they would have to be told in advance, even if the terms used were vague; but the President was against giving them details of the timing. His reasoning was that, though he was sure they would not pass on any information to the Americans, once the fighting started and it came out that they had known all about it and had said nothing, they would be put in an awkward position. There was no need to embarrass them. Moreover, if for any reason the Russians did not want hostilities to break out at that time they might give a hint to the Americans. Alternatively, they might think they were doing Egypt a good turn if they approached the Americans and asked them to put pressure on the Israelis 'to behave'. Nobody was really clear how far the détente between the super-powers had gone or how it was working.

So the President decided that he would see the Soviet Ambassador, Vladimir Vinogradov, and give him a general warning that a breach of the ceasefire was likely but that on no account would he give him any precise information about dates. When he had explained this to me the President picked up the telephone and told his secretary to ask the Ambassador to come round at seven o'clock. When he came the President told Vinogradov that we could no longer put up with Israel's arrogance, and quoted Dayan's Yamit statement. 'It may be,' he went on, 'that we shall find ourselves obliged to move fast.' The Ambassador said what Soviet Ambassadors usually say: 'I will inform Moscow.' 'Please only tell Brezhnev,' said Sadat. Vinogradov said: 'I think that, without waiting for Brezhnev's reply, I know what he will say. He will say the decision is yours, and that as friends we will do everything we can to help you.' 'Tell Brezhnev,' said Sadat, 'that the coming days will be a real and practical test for the Soviet-Egyptian treaty.' At this point Vinogradov began taking notes.

After the President had talked to the Soviet Ambassador the question arose whether we should tell Dr Mohammed Hassan el-Zayyat, the Foreign Minister, who was in New York at the General Assembly. After some discussion it was decided to send no messages to him. One idea put forward was that a courier should be sent, so that he should not be completely taken by surprise when the fighting started. But this was rejected after the President had received a telegram from Zayyat on the 3rd in which he said that Kissinger had asked to see him on Friday the 5th for a discussion on the general situation. It was thought that if we sent a courier to Zayyat on the Wednesday, who would arrive in New York on the Thursday, this would mean that Zayyat would go to Kissinger knowing more or less what was about to happen, and this would be putting him under too much strain. So it was decided to keep him in the dark – and even to use him as an innocent source of deception. Naturally Zayyat was unhappy about this afterwards.

President Sadat now ordered a meeting the next day, Tuesday 2 October, of the National Security Council – a political body, which included, besides the President himself, the two Vice-Presidents, two Assistants to the President, the Vice-Prime Ministers, the Minister of War, the Director General of Intelligence, and usually the Director of Military Intelligence as well. At this meeting, which was held in the dining-room of the President's house in Giza at eight-thirty at night (this was in Ramadan, the month-long fast commemorating the first revelation of the Koran during which devout Moslems neither eat nor drink during the hours of daylight), the President explained that it might be necessary in the near future to break the ceasefire. He was asked what sort of battle he expected to result and said he thought it would be a limited battle. Some of those present tried to get him to define more precisely what he meant by a limited battle. Dr Mahmoud Fawzi, the Vice-President, produced the analogy of the Japanese samurai, who used to carry a long sword and a short sword. 'I think we are going to use our short sword,' he said.

The President was asked if he thought oil would become a weapon in the battle. His answer was that he did not think he could make any demands on the oil-producing Arab states in advance, but that once the fighting started any Egyptian requests to them would find a ready response. He spoke, too, about the international détente, pointing out that the two super-powers appeared to be reaching agreement on all subjects, including the Middle East, which made this the last chance for action.

The same day, 2 October, it was the turn of the military. The President called a meeting of the War Council, on which sit the Minister of War, the Chief of Staff, the Director of Operations, the Chiefs of the Air Force and Navy and the Heads of all Service Departments. Some of those present of course knew all – or almost all – of the plans for Badr, and the rest were aware that a count-down had started, though they did not know how or when hostilities would begin.

It was to this meeting of senior officers that President Sadat read out his directive for the battle. Just before the meeting started he had called a secretary into his office, told him to fetch a typewriter, and dictated the directive to him. The secretary could hardly believe his ears. After he had finished, the President thanked the secretary and gave him a raise.

The directive went over the efforts that had been made by Egypt to achieve a peaceful settlement of the Middle East problem and rehearsed many of the explanations the President had given me at the Mariut rest-house why, if there had to be a recourse to arms, it should be made now rather than later. Israel's strategy, he said, aimed at making all the world, including ourselves, believe that it was futile for the Arabs to try to challenge her, and that they would have to accept whatever terms for a settlement she wished to impose on them. But it was essential to prove this strategy wrong. 'I believe,' he said, 'that if the enemy's theory of the permanent superiority of its forces can be successfully challenged, both the short-term and the long-term repercussions will be incalculable. In the short term it should make possible a peaceful and honourable solution to the Middle East problem, and in the long term it will create a cumulative modification in the aggressive psychology of Zionism.'

In this second meeting the President asked if there was any indication of awareness in Israel of our moves and received two conflicting reports. The first was that General Gonen, Israeli G.O.C. Southern Command, had visited advance posts in Sinai that morning, which could be taken as a sign of apprehension. But the other report said that there was no change in the disposition of enemy troops, which pointed to a lack of awareness.

General Shazli, Egyptian Chief of Staff, added his view that we were a jump ahead of the Israelis. He said that, even if they became aware that evening of our intention to attack, their mobilization would not be complete before the attack started. He went into a detailed analysis of the forces Israel could mobilize on the first two days, which Sadat found reassuring. At Mariut, when I asked him whether he thought we could surprise the enemy, he had said: 'Strategically we can't, because of the very wide front on which we shall be attacking, but tactically we can.' In fact we were to surprise them both strategically and tactically.

As far as can be made out from the Agranat Commission, appointed by the Israeli Government to enquire into events leading up to the October war, there is no sign that, all the time these preparations were taking place, the Israelis had any inkling of Egypt's purpose. Yet, we now know, they were well informed at least about the preparations visible on the ground. It is strange to see how completely Israeli official thinking at all levels, civilian and military, was obsessed by the conviction that Egypt was not going to fight. Almost the only exception according to the Agranat Report was the warning given by General Dayan, the Minister of Defence, to the General Staff on 21 May: 'We, the Cabinet, say to the General Staff: Gentlemen, please prepare for war, those who are threatening to launch a war being Egypt and Syria . . . a renewal of war should be taken into account in the second half of this summer.'

But earlier in May Israel had been through a false alarm following the military meetings in Egypt at which (though of course this was something they could not know) the plan for Operation Badr was drawn up. They mobilized, unnecessarily, and this cost them a lot of money; after which they seem to have paid less attention to developments on the other side of the Canal.

Admittedly on 26 September General Dayan had gone north, following a warning by the commander on that front, General Itzhak Hoffi, that he was uneasy about the Syrian build-up, and authorized reinforcements of tanks and artillery. But he postponed further action until he had consulted the Prime Minister, Mrs Golda Meir. She was in Vienna, pleading with the Austrian Chancellor, Dr Kreisky, to reverse his decision to close down the camp in Austria for Jewish immigrants on their way from Russia to Israel. It was only late on this same day, Tuesday, that Mrs Meir returned to Israel from Vienna.

President Sadat referred in his directive to the activities of the Palestinian resistance organizations. It was on Monday 1 October that some officers of the resistance and about 120 other ranks had arrived in Cairo to take part in the battle. They came as the result of an invitation the President had given to Fateh a few weeks earlier, asking to see some of its senior officials. Sadat explained to Salah Khalaf (Abu Iyad) and Farouk Qadumi (Abu Lutf) that the situation was tense and that Egypt would be obliged to reactivate the canal front. But they were given the impression that what was contemplated was a renewal of the War of Attrition and that their function would probably be to take part in commando raids inside Sinai.

It was, incidentally, on the day of those two key meetings, 2 October, that there occurred one of those absurd and unforeseeable breaches of security which could have destroyed the remaining element of surprise. The Middle East News Agency sent out a news item to the effect that the Second and Third Armies – the two which were to launch the attack across the canal – had been put on a state of alert. This item should have appeared on a special restricted service which went only to a very small number of senior officials, but instead, owing to a mistake by the operator, it went out on the general service to all subscribers. There was a tremendous row, and the director of the agency was demoted. But in fact no harm was done.

The President spent the morning of Wednesday 3 October putting the finishing touches to the political and military plans and to the communiqués to be issued. Hafez Ismail, the President's Adviser on National Security Affairs, brought him drafts of the statements we were going to make at the UN and of the instructions to be sent to Zayyat in New York immediately the fighting started.

The same morning the problem of what should be the trigger for hostilities was solved. The atmosphere was one of mounting tension on all sides, and it was decided that there should be a claim that in the middle of all this the Israelis had launched an attack on Zafarana on the Red Sea. The political as well as the military timing was now clear. At 1330 hours on 6 October the normal broadcasting programme would be broken into with a news flash: 'It has just been reported that elements of Israel's armed forces have attacked our positions in Zafarana. This represents a most serious breach of the ceasefire, and the Security Council has been so informed.' Then normal programmes would be resumed, but at 1400 hours there would be a switch to military marches, which would continue for ten minutes. Then there would be an item about Egypt's reply to an enemy who pays no attention to the Security Council or to international opinion, followed by more martial music, till at 1430 hours the news bulletin would start with items about the Israeli attack, the Egyptian memorandum to the Security Council, and Egypt's response to the attack. Then ordinary news would follow, but after two items the announcer would break off to say: 'We have just received the following announcement: "A large-scale military operation has begun, and the Supreme Commander-in-Chief, President Anwar Sadat, has gone to army headquarters to take personal charge." ' This was, in effect, to be the first communiqué in the war.

The same day, Wednesday, General Nofal and General Ismail flew from Cairo to Damascus, the urgency of the situation obliging them to disregard a security rule that no two senior officers should travel on the same plane. Their journey had a double purpose – to inform the Syrians of the choice of the 6th for the launch of Badr, and to reach a final agreement on H-hour. General Nofal had approached General Ismail two days earlier, urging that the Syrians should be told at once about the choice of the 6th so that they could have the five days promised them for discharging the Homs refinery. General Ismail felt that this information was far too critical to be sent by the normal radio link, even in cipher. He was due to go to Damascus the following day, Tuesday, and suggested that General Nofal should accompany him. But as it turned out their journey had to be postponed a further day, until Wednesday.

In Damascus they met Generals Tlas and Shakur. When told about the timing of Badr, Shakur was upset. He protested that this was a violation of the undertaking that they were to have five complete days for emptying the Homs refineries. It was impossible, he said, for Syria to begin operations on the 6th: the attack must be postponed for two days. He was annoyed too about the MENA leak. General Ismail answered that any postponement would be extremely dangerous. Even if the Israelis did not pick up the MENA item they were bound at any moment to draw conclusions from the growing scale of Egyptian preparations on the canal front, since these could no longer be hidden. Our best hope, he said, was to attack as soon as possible; each day's delay would give the enemy another twenty-four hours for them to make good use of. The Syrian generals said that this was a disagreement that could only be resolved by President Asad.

On the question of H-hour General Shakur still wanted to start the Syrian attack at first light, while the Egyptians, who were trained in night fighting, which the Syrians were not, continued to argue in favour of attacking in the late afternoon. General Ismail tried to persuade General Shakur that dawn was exactly the time when the Israelis were most likely to expect an attack, and that, as far as the canal assault was concerned, it would be much better to wait until the sun was in the enemy's eyes – all the arguments, in fact, which had been urged before. General Nofal intervened at this point to say that if the Syrian air strikes planned against the airfields of Ramat David and Aqir took place too early in the morning the pilots might find their targets obscured by mist – as, indeed, reconnaissance later showed was the case on the morning of 6 October.

It was decided to carry this second point, the timing of H-hour, to President Asad also. When they saw the President both sides repeated their arguments, General Ismail stressing that if this chance was missed it would be a long time before action on both fronts could be coordinated again in such favourable circumstances. 'We are,' he said, 'taking a risk, but a calculated risk.' He suggested, as a compromise, that H-hour should be at two o'clock in the afternoon.

President Asad said that he did not want to cause any complications at the last moment. 'I accept the sixth,' he said. 'I accept starting at 1400 hours, which will give each of us some advantages.' General Shakur then said that Syrian enthusiasm for the battle had in no way been affected by the changes that had been made. 'If there is failure on the Egyptian front,' he said, 'it will be the end of the Arabs, which means the end of Syria. If there is failure on the Syrian front this would not be the end. It is on Egypt that all our hopes are pinned.'

President Asad asked the two commanders if they thought the Israelis would bomb cities, and whether we would do this if they did not. General Ismail's reply was that we were ready: 'If they bomb our cities we are ready to bomb theirs.' General Shakur said: 'My advice is that, for history's sake, we avoid bombing cities as far as we possibly can.' He then repeated his assurance that Syria would do anything in its power to ensure success on the Egyptian front: 'If Damascus falls it can be recaptured; if Cairo falls the whole Arab nation falls.'

It was decided that Ismail and Nofal should not again travel in the same plane, and that Nofal should return via Amman to give the Jordanians a veiled warning. He met the Jordanian Chief of Staff in Amman and told him that the Egyptian information was that the Israelis were mobilizing and might be planning something against Syria. He advised the Jordanians to declare a state of alert and be prepared for any eventualities. He also took the opportunity to agree new communications ciphers with Amman.

According to the Agranat Report it was exactly at the same

time on 3 October when General Ismail was in Damascus talking to President Asad that Golda Meir, now back from Vienna, called a meeting attended by Allon, Galili, Dayan, and Brigadier General Arye Shalev, standing in for the Director of Military Intelligence, General Ze'ira, who had flu. At this meeting Shalev gave an intelligence report which concluded that the possibility of an Egyptian-Syrian attack seemed remote since there had been no change in the Arabs' apparent assessment of the balance of forces in Sinai. None of those present disagreed with this assessment. At the end of the meeting Golda Meir decided that security of the borders should be put on the agenda for the regular Cabinet meeting due on 7 October.

When General Ismail came back to Cairo on Wednesday night he called a meeting of senior officers at which he reported on his Damascus talks and asked if there was any sign that the enemy sensed what was going on. He was told there was nothing positive to report, but all the same he gave another order aimed at strengthening the deception picture – some of the reservists called up in September for the Liberation 23 manoeuvres were to be sent home so that by the 6th they would be back at their place of work.

Another touch to the deception plan involved the newspaper, *Al Ahram*. A small news item was given to its military correspondent which said that the Commander-in-Chief had opened a list for those officers who wanted to go on the small pilgrimage (*Umra*). When I saw this item I understood what it meant. I telephoned to General Ismail and told him: 'All right, that means we are going to be liars. But for your sake I will accept it.' Then, since it was known that the Israelis got an early copy of the paper each day via Cyprus and studied it carefully, the paper was asked to put in another item saying that the Minister of Defence was preparing for his meeting with the visiting Rumanian Minister of Defence on 8 October. The item had been written by Military Intelligence and it was agreed that it should appear under the byline of *Al Ahram*'s military correspondent, who also wrote another piece about the Israelis escalating the situation on the northern front, warning them that they were playing with fire because Egypt could not stand

32

idly by, etcetera. This was all part of the general atmosphere of thickening the plot without giving anything away that might be of real use to the enemy.

General Ismail also gave orders that the progress of the Liberation 23 manoeuvres be adjusted to the requirements of an escalating situation on the northern front, because by that time there was a great deal of talk in the Press everywhere about the tension following the Syrian air battle and to have taken no such action might have aroused suspicion. He asked Intelligence to give him an estimate of the forces Israel could spare for the Jordanian front in two possible circumstances – either if Jordan joined in the battle, or if it merely put its armed forces in a state of alert.

By now there was nobody in Egypt who could escape the impression that something was impending, though there was still no sign that the Israelis knew anything. This seemed incredible to us, for again there were obvious clues that Israel might have been expected to seize on. For example, there was a certain chemical which was to be sprayed on to the troops' clothing as a protection against burning from napalm (a terrible number of men had been burned to death by napalm in 1967, which the Israelis used indiscriminately on the retreating and disorganized hosts in Sinai). Once this chemical had been applied to combat uniforms they could never be used again, so it would never be issued for an exercise. Yet it was issued early on the morning of the 6th. The Israelis, as the Egyptian authorities were well aware, had an effective espionage organization known as Mitkal, made up of Arabic-speaking – mostly Egyptian – Jews who were infiltrated into the Canal area and equipped for transmitting information back to Israel. For a short period, they had even managed to set up a permanent radio station east of the canal. They must have reported these preparations, and it should have given the Israeli High Command at least six hours' warning. Tactical missiles were also moved on to their launching pads at dawn on the 6th, and this was another mistake which should have been picked up and provided a warning. So, for that matter, ought the air evacuation of Russian families from Egypt in the early hours of Friday.

Several military attachés saw bridging equipment moving from the back road by Cairo airport to the Suez road. More serious, some senior official of the Egyptian civil airline felt so convinced that the situation was building up to a point at which Israel might repeat its pre-emptive air strike of 1967 that he sent out an order over telex to all his planes abroad telling them to stay where they were. Also, as Cairo airport is near a military base, he cancelled all flights and ordered it to be evacuated by his planes, including several new Boeings for whose safety he was justifiably concerned. So hundreds of passengers turned up at the airport to find no planes available for them. When General Ismail heard of this he was annoyed and told the Minister of Civil Aviation to see that all planes carried out their normal flights. But by then six or seven hours had passed. This action by the manager of the airline was – though of course he could not know it – completely contrary to the general deception plan which was that officers who had been invited to parties should continue to attend them, soldiers should go on swimming in the Canal right up to the last minute, and so on.

On Thursday 4 October President Sadat was just preparing to move from his Giza house to Tahra Palace when the Soviet Ambassador asked to see him urgently. He came round at 7 p.m. bringing with him Brezhnev's answer to the President's message of Monday. As expected, Brezhnev expressed the view that the decision when to fight must be for Sadat alone to take, and added that the Soviet Union would give him the support of a friend. But Brezhnev also asked for permission to withdraw Russian civilian advisers and their families from Egypt. The President was puzzled by this request but reluctantly agreed to it and took the opportunity to press for the speedy delivery of some equipment which had been ordered but not delivered.

After seeing the Ambassador, Sadat left for Tahra Palace where he changed into uniform. He had a final meeting with the Deputy Prime Ministers, the Ministers of War and Interior and Hafez Ismail. It was at this meeting that it was found necessary to make radical changes in the special committees which it had been intended to set up to help the President. First of all there was a message from Ismail Fahmy, who had gone to Vienna to see Chancellor Kreisky the day before, 3 October, saying that Kreisky had asked him to stay on because he wanted to see him again on Friday afternoon: should he come back or stay? Sadat told him not to cancel this meeting because a change of plan might cause comment. So neither the Minister of Foreign Affairs nor his stand-in on the foreign affairs committee was going to be in Cairo on the 6th. Then it was decided to scrap the committee for internal affairs and substitute a working group made up entirely from within the Cabinet, and headed by the Deputy Prime Minister, Abdul Qader Hatem. Sayed Marei was switched from the home front to looking after contacts with the Arabs, and Aziz Sidqi, who had been Minister for Industry for several years and had good relations with the labour movement, was to concern himself with the problem of American installations in the Middle East. It was hoped that the oil-producing countries would co-operate by putting pressure on the Americans, but should these hopes not be realized it might become necessary to think of other ways of exerting pressure.

One of the President's main preoccupations during his first few hours in Tahra Palace was Brezhnev's answer as reported by Vinogradov. The first part had been what he expected – the Russians left the decision for breaking the ceasefire to him. What puzzled him was the second part – their request to be allowed to withdraw the Russian civilian advisers and their families. What did this mean? Did it imply foreboding about the outcome of the battle? Or did it reflect some aspect of the global balance of power, and if so might it be that the Russians were not going to give us the help we were expecting? The President eventually went to bed at four o'clock in the morning of Friday 5 October.

Now Centre Number Ten was completely sealed off from the outside world. Anybody allowed in had to stay there – there was no going out again, since pretty well everyone by now was aware of the timing of the battle as well as of its aims. Nobody slept much that night at Centre Number Ten or Centre Number Three, the substitute command post set up in case anything happened to Centre Number Ten. Everyone was asking 'Do the

Israelis know?' At about 9.30 a.m. two Israeli planes were sent up for air reconnaissance and photography. They did not enter Egyptian air space because their cameras could operate from within Sinai. We picked up the pulses of their electronic reconnaissance and everyone was convinced that by now the Israelis must at least know about the presence of bridging and crossing equipment near the canal. It now seems that the Israelis had even run an earlier reconnaissance the previous evening. Nor did it seem possible that they could be unaware that between two and seven in the morning six enormous Tupolev planes had landed to pick up the advisers and their families and had taken off again. As tension grew Korans could be seen on many officers' desks.

During this Thursday/Friday night the Israelis were receiving an increasing volume of information about our troop movements but, as the Agranat Report shows, they were still unable to believe exactly what was going on. At the same time that Sadat was going to sleep Dayan was being woken up, after which he had discussions with General Elazar, the Chief of Staff. They decided to go together to Golda Meir's house asking General Ze'ira, the DMI, to accompany them. They briefed her, and Elazar said he might be obliged to put the armed forces on a state of highest alert. Though not then asking for mobilization he was proposing to cancel leave in the air force and armoured units. He would concentrate armour on both fronts. Golda Meir decided to call a Cabinet meeting for the afternoon, which would give all ministers time to attend, but she then came to the conclusion that the situation demanded greater urgency and instead called a meeting of her inner cabinet shortly before noon. Those present were Bar-Lev, Dayan, Hazani, Peres, Galili, Hilleh, the Chief of Staff and the DMI, whose appreciation was that 'we are not facing a total war'. Elazar supported this appreciation. It was agreed not to order mobilization until more evidence of enemy intentions was available.

On Friday 5 October Dr Zayyat had meetings with three of the Western Foreign Ministers who were in New York – Kissinger, Jobert and Douglas-Home. Kissinger told him that he had not yet begun consideration of the Middle East file but that the Egyptians should prepare for its being opened after the Israeli elections. He hoped, he said, to be able to look at it before the end of the year. Jobert told him he was sorry that Egypt had to go on bringing up the same problem at the UN year after year, but there was no hope of a change unless the Egyptians themselves did something. Douglas-Home told him he saw no new factor in the situation. He thought the Egyptians should try to negotiate with the Israelis after their election was out of the way.

Zayyat was depressed by these three conversations and quite forgot that he had been invited to a party to be given that evening in his honour in the apartment of Egypt's permanent representative at the UN, Dr Ismet Abdul Meguid. He was rung up and reminded of it, and went round. But he told his hostess he could see no reason for a party. 'I can't think what you can be celebrating tonight,' he said, 'unless it's Yom Kippur.'

Back at Centre Number Ten in the afternoon of Friday a moving scene initiated by General Ismail was enacted in the presence of President Sadat. All those in the Centre were asked to take an oath on the Koran: 'We pledge to God on this Koran that each of us will give his utmost, even to the last breath in his body, to fulfil the mission with which he is entrusted.'

That night Ashraf Ghorbal, Press Counsellor to the President, came to my flat and we sat together in my study revising the last details of the communiqués and memoranda that would soon be needed. We were also waiting for news from Zayyat about how his meeting with Kissinger had gone off, but that was delayed.

It was at 4 a.m. on the morning of that Saturday 6 October, that Dayan received a telephone call at his home giving him the news that Israeli Intelligence now believed that an attack on Yom Kippur must be definitely expected, but Intelligence gave the time when it would start four hours lat̲ – at 1800 hours instead of 1400 hours. Dayan consulted with the Chief of Staff, General Elazar, whose recommendation was that total mobilization should be ordered so that preparations could be made for large-scale counter-attacks after the enemy's initial assault had been contained. Dayan, on the other hand, wanted only forces

37

sufficient for defensive action to be mobilized. A delay of some hours ensued while the Prime Minister's decision on full mobilization was awaited. The order was not given until mid-morning, after the idea of a pre-emptive strike had been discussed and rejected. Agranat says this decision was taken for political reasons, but any attempt at a pre-emptive strike against Egypt would have come up against the missile wall. It would have been militarily useless as well as politically risky. It could have had no effect on Egypt's plan of attack. Golda Meir called the American Ambassador to her office at 10.30 and had a cabinet meeting at twelve. It was while the cabinet was still in session that the first news of the Egyptian attack came through.

Eban, the Israeli Foreign Minister, had to be contacted in New York on the open telex line at about 11.30 (there is a closed cyclophone between the Ministry of Foreign Affairs in Jerusalem and the Israeli Embassy in Washington, but as Eban was attending the General Assembly and sleeping in a New York hotel this could not be used). He was told to talk to Kissinger, ask to see Nixon, and get Nixon to contact Brezhnev on the hot-line and tell him that they had evidence the Egyptians were about to attack. If this was a result of reports in the world Press about Israeli troop concentrations, he could give Brezhnev an assurance that Israel had no intention of attacking. Brezhnev should pass this message on to President Sadat. Eban was told that every minute was important.

At 11.30 a.m. (Saturday) President Sadat called the Soviet Ambassador to Tahra Palace because he was still worried about Soviet intentions. The planes were coming in to pick up civilians but were not bringing in any supplies. 'You have been very quick about your civilians,' he said, 'but not so quick about the stuff I asked for.' He too said that every minute was important. Later, when I asked Vinogradov whether he had understood from this conversation what was afoot, he said he had gathered that some sort of operation was about to start but not that it was only two hours off. Anyhow, he at once got through to Brezhnev on the special telephone link between the Soviet embassy in Cairo and Moscow, established when the Soviet air defence system was set up in 1970.

Golda Meir, meanwhile, had seen the American Ambassador who immediately tried to get in touch with the White House and the C.I.A. He also tried to wake up Kissinger, who had in fact been woken by one of his assistants with the news that the State Department Situation Room was reporting signs of trouble. Then Eban wanted to talk to him urgently. So he spoke to Eban at about 07.00 (13.00 Cairo time) and, after receiving some confirmation of developments from the C.I.A. and the Pentagon, contacted Zayyat, who was also staying in New York, and told him that Eban had just spoken to him and said Israel had information that Egypt was going to attack. Perhaps this was due to a misunderstanding which could be cleared up. 'If you think Israel is going to attack you I can assure you that it is not. Can you pass this message on to President Sadat right away?' Zayyat asked how he was expected to pass it on, as he had no way of contacting Cairo. Kissinger said: 'I'll ask my office to arrange a White House line to be given to you right now.' This was done; and the call to Cairo was put through at once.

By 13.25 Cairo time Zayyat was talking to Hafez Ismail – the President himself could not be reached. Zayyat passed on the Kissinger message and Hafez Ismail told him that it was not Egypt that was attacking Israel but Israel that was attacking Egypt in the Gulf of Suez. Zayyat then called Kissinger back and reported what he had been told by Hafez Ismail. Kissinger said he had no information but would check and be in touch with him later. Five minutes later, at 13.30 hours, we gave out the news of the Zafarana raid over the radio. At 13.35 Hafez Ismail had another call – this time from Vinogradov who asked if he could see President Sadat. The President was unwilling to see him in case he would say something aimed at stopping the attack, now less than half an hour off. So Vinogradov was told that the President was away. Vinogradov told Hafez Ismail that Israel had spoken to the Americans complaining that we were planning an attack on them. He was told that it was Israel who was attacking us. All this shows the speed of communications in a modern crisis. In half an hour Kissinger had spoken to Eban, Zayyat and Moscow; Zayyat and Moscow had talked to Cairo.

After President Sadat had seen Vinogradov at 11.30 that Saturday morning he went at 12.30 to Centre Number Ten. The atmosphere there was very different from what it had been the day before when the oath of service had been taken. Then the maps on the walls had been those for Liberation 23; now they were those for Badr. The President was now wearing his uniform as Supreme Commander of the Armed Forces.

In Tel Aviv General Ze'ira had a meeting with Golda Meir, after which he called a Press Conference to brief Israeli war correspondents. While he was discussing the position on the canal front the director of his office came in and gave him a card. He looked at it and said: 'They tell me a war may be starting at any minute,' and went on with his briefing. After a while another card was brought in. The general looked at it, left the room, came back, and said: 'Gentlemen, the meeting is ended.' As the correspondents went down in the lift in the Ministry of Defence the air raid sirens were sounding.

At five minutes past two the first news of the battle started coming in to Centre Number Ten. President Sadat and Ahmed Ismail listened with astonishment. It seemed as though what they were watching was a training exercise: 'Mission accomplished . . . mission accomplished.' It all sounded too good to be true. At 3.30 President Sadat called up Vinogradov. The first person with whom he wanted to share his delight was the ambassador – partly no doubt to reassure him, partly to prepare him for the demands for replacement of equipment that were bound not to be long delayed. Vinogradov told me later that he was having lunch alone on the upper floor of the embassy when the servant told him that the President was on the line. He was surprised at this because there had for some time been a special telephone link between the Presidency and the embassy, and this call had apparently come through on the ordinary line. 'Are you sure it is the President?' he asked. He was told it certainly was. So he took the call and heard a voice say in Arabic '*Es-Safir?* [the ambassador?]' 'Yes, I am the ambassador.' 'The President would like to talk to you.' Sadat was laughing: 'Vinogradov, my boys are riding on the Bar-Lev line: We've crossed the canal! I want you to telephone our friends in Moscow and tell them my sons are on the eastern bank of the canal.' Vinogradov said: 'All my congratulations, Mr President.' President Sadat: 'Here is General Ismail beside me. He wants to have a word with you because there are so many things he needs from you to finish the job.'

President Sadat gave the telephone to Ahmed Ismail who reported that the first wave had crossed safely, that many of the strong points on the Bar-Lev Line had been taken and that practically the whole line was now neutralized.

The delight of the President and Commander in Chief and the astonishment of the ambassador were hardly to be wondered at. All military experts, including Soviet ones, used to emphasize the hazards of an assault across the canal, the difficulty of troops storming the rampart of the Bar-Lev Line, exposed to crossfire and strafing from the air, as well as the probable use of napalm in the canal. The Egyptian command had been prepared for 26,000 casualties in this initial attack. So when it was all accomplished so quickly and painlessly everyone felt as if they were in a dream. Vinogradov hastily called a conference with the two generals on the staff of the embassy to help him prepare a report for Moscow.

There was a delay in getting the Third Army across the canal owing to trouble with the bridging equipment. This worried President Sadat but he felt that he should leave the military command to sort things out, so he came back to Tahra Palace. By then the news that, after only three hours of fighting, the Bar-Lev Line had been stormed and neutralized was going round the world, and the President was bombarded with calls from the leaders of other Arab countries. First came President Ahmed Hassan el-Bakr of Iraq, some of whose pilots, flying Hawker Hunters, had taken part in the first sorties. Then came King Hussein of Jordan, President Boumedienne of Algeria and President Bourguiba of Tunisia. All offered their warmest congratulations and wanted to know in what way they could help.

Eleven hours after the battle started we received a coded telegram from Dr Zayyat in New York. He reported that Kissinger had gone back to Washington and that he had called

Zayyat from there and made several points. First, Kissinger said that after their talk on 5 October he had been optimistic that they could jointly begin a new and effective effort to reach a settlement, but the day's events had come as a complete surprise and he was afraid that if the fighting did not stop in a reasonable time things would get out of hand. Second, the Americans' assessment – though this could of course be wrong – was that it was the Egyptians who had started the fighting. Third, the Americans calculated that if the fighting went on it would end in an Israeli victory, and that a massive Israeli counter-attack was probable at any time within the next 48 hours. Fourth, if this did happen he wanted to assure Egypt that the United States would not allow Israel to occupy any more territory. Fifth, Kissinger had questioned Zayyat about the idea of a Security Council resolution for a ceasefire with a return to the lines occupied by both sides before the fighting started. Sixth, he thought any debate in the General Assembly when it reassembled on Monday could only complicate matters.

Zayyat said his answer had been: First, he had gained the impression from what Kissinger told him at their meeting on the 5th that Israel was completely satisfied with its ability to prolong the ceasefire indefinitely and had no intention of making any change in the status quo. Kissinger had told him that the United States was unable to force Israel to accept the sort of settlement that would be acceptable to Egypt. So, whatever the outcome of the day's events, and whatever their origins might turn out to have been, it was clear that the Suez Canal could no longer be regarded as an impenetrable barrier, or the ceasefire as a permanent institution. Second, an Arab return to the lines occupied before the fighting started would mean for Egypt a retreat behind the Suez Canal and would be unacceptable to us. This was something, said Zayyat, he would not dare even to suggest to Cairo. It would be more appropriate to link a new ceasefire with a return to pre-June 1967 lines rather than the pre-October 6th line. Third, he had no instructions from Cairo relating to the raising of the matter before the Security Council or the General Assembly. But if he (Kissinger) had any reasonable proposals to make they would of course be forwarded to

Cairo. Fourth, Zayyat added that Kissinger had said he understood Zayyat's remarks, but he wanted to say something that
the Egyptians should think hard about. The events of the day
were very important (then Zayyat's telegram quoted Kissinger
in English): 'You have made a strong point, but I hope that you
will not behave so as to let matters get out of your control.'
Finally Kissinger said he would contact Zayyat again the next
day.

How did it happen that the Israelis were completely surprised,
strategically as well as tactically? In my opinion the Israelis
completely misunderstood history. The difference between myth
and history – and this is one of the pitfalls of Zionism, which is
liable to confuse the two – is that in myth you are dealing with
something fixed, static, past, whereas history is a changing
process. If you think in terms of myth you find yourself dealing
with states not people. Zionism is the prisoner of its mythology –
Masada and all the rest.

The Israelis completely underestimated the balance of power
between the Arabs and Israel. A military or political balance
between the 100 million Arabs and the 3 million Israelis cannot
be kept for ever. Perhaps the Soviet Union and China – 300
million to 800 million – can preserve a balance of a sort in spite
of the disparity of numbers, but a ratio of 100 to 3 is absurd.
With modern technology the population gap becomes even
more significant. Take, for example, the Strella (SAM-7) which
played so big a part in the October War. This is a small and
comparatively simple weapon which can be carried and fired by
one man and operated without a great deal of technical knowledge. Yet it was fatal to the Israeli military aircraft. What the
Israelis did not appreciate was that of the 800,000 Egyptians
under arms no fewer than 110,000 were graduates of universities
or institutes of higher education. One of the steps taken by
Nasser when he was rebuilding the army after 1967 was to give
an order that any tank commander or officer responsible for
electronic equipment must be a graduate of either an engineering
or a technical school. So Egypt had begun to match Israel in the
quality of its troops, while having of course far greater potential
in quantity.

An incident from the early days of the fighting illustrates this change in the balance between the two sides. General Husni Mubarak, Commander of the Air Force, was at the Mansoura base when there was a dog fight overhead in which an Israeli plane was shot down. It seemed to him that the Israeli pilot had not shown much skill and, as he had landed not far away, asked to see him. When he was brought they talked together in English. 'What has happened to the standards in your air force?' he asked. The answer was, 'It's not us. I think you've changed.'

It is true that there had been a great ferment in Egyptian society in the years between 1967 and 1973, but this was largely because we were not fighting. As Nasser once told Brezhnev, 'We have our troubles on the internal front, but once the first shot is fired these troubles will disappear.' The Israelis misinterpreted what was going on inside Egypt. They forgot that a society can be apparently in ferment and yet sections of it can be unaffected. This applied to the army in Egypt, which was given its own specific mission to fulfill.

During these years the Israeli Army underwent a marked change. It took up static defence lines instead of relying on mobility. There is always a danger that victory will sap the quality of an army, and after 1967 arrogance made the Israeli Army blind to what was happening in front of its nose. It assumed that it could not be challenged and that it had the power to cope with any attack. This can be seen in the intelligence reports coming in almost up to the moment when the battle started. Moreover, the Israeli forces were apparently unaware that on the Friday night there were already eight commando patrols operating inside Sinai, while other patrols were active in the canal itself, cutting the pipes by which it had been planning to flood the canal with napalm.

Israeli generals also became too mixed up in politics and spent too much time in public and social life. There was a time when Israeli generals used to live spartan lives, but then the world started hearing of Dayan's collection of antiquities, of his marital troubles, of generals with their big cars and big cigars. Disillusion with this sort of behaviour is reflected in contemporary Israeli poetry.

Surprise

Israel's building of the Bar-Lev line was a victory for politics over strategy. Until the end of 1967 the Israeli Army had a plan by which they could meet an Egyptian attack by retreating to the passes, but they preferred to dig in on the canal because they wanted, as Dayan said, to be buzzing all the time in the ears of Nasser and the Egyptian people. They forgot that it was not their genius but our failure that handed them victory in 1967 on a plate.

The Israelis were taken by surprise although the evidence was there before their eyes if they had been prepared to see and understand. They never appreciated that, ironically enough, Egypt's main problem in planning had been to match the element of surprise with which Israel had so successfully brought off the sudden dawn air strike of 5 June 1967.

On one occasion General Abdel Munim Riad, who was Chief of Staff after the 1967 defeat and one of the best generals Egypt produced, was discussing the problem of surprise with Nasser. He said: 'The mere fact that we start an attack at all will be the most important element of surprise.' This was proved abundantly true six years later.

CHAPTER II
Nasser's Last Stand

1. THE AFTERMATH OF DEFEAT

General Riad's conversation with Nasser came towards the end of a chapter in Egypt's history which began after the June war of 1967. That defeat had been a complete surprise to everybody. It may be that Egypt had not expected victory, but nobody had been prepared for defeat on such a shattering scale. Everybody was shocked, including the Russians; the Israelis were jubilant; the Arab world was in a state of total confusion; Nasser was left in the midst of the wreckage, trying to salve something out of it.

His first thought was that he must look to what remained of Egypt's defences. At this time he was receiving a great many warnings to the effect that the Israelis regarded what they had achieved as unfinished business, particularly after the events of 9 and 10 June when, following Nasser's speech of resignation, people all over the Arab world went on to the streets imploring him to stay on. That was a political victory for Nasser, though of course it could not compensate for the military defeat.

But Nasser now felt he had a mandate to try to reorganize the home front and to rally the ranks in the Arab countries. He saw his future strategy as falling into three phases: to begin with he would have to be purely on the defensive; then he could move to active deterrence; and finally would come liberation of what had been lost.

The start had to be made on the army, for that was the key to everything else, and the army could only be rebuilt with the help of the Russians. Immediately after the war, at the end of June 1967, the Soviet President Podgorny came to Egypt to see what had happened, bringing with him Marshal Matvei Zakharov,

Chief of Staff of the Soviet Army. Inevitably the Russians regarded Egypt's defeat as to some extent their defeat also, and Nasser encouraged this attitude because he thought it would lead to greater Russian involvement in the Middle East which was the only way in which American superiority in that area could be offset. It was Nasser's firm belief that at that time Israel was being used by the Americans as an instrument by which they could impose a new order on the Middle East.

However, Podgorny's visit did not go well. For one thing the Russians were naturally angry that some of their most sophisticated arms had been captured by the Israelis and handed over to the Americans. They also thought Egyptian demands for new armaments were excessive. On their side, the Egyptian command complained that the range of MiGs and Sukhoys available to them was very limited, and were demanding long-range fighter-bombers. Podgorny defended the MiGs and Sukhoys, whereupon Nasser said: 'Very well then, in this first, defensive phase, I am prepared to leave the entire air defence of Egypt to the Soviet Union.'

There was also some misunderstanding over Russian demands for facilities for their fleet. Podgorny began by asking for a command post in Alexandria for Soviet ships in the Mediterranean. This fitted in with Nasser's thinking because he had come to the conclusion it was to the advantage of the whole non-aligned world for Russia's naval presence in the Mediterranean to be strengthened. He hoped that some sort of parity might be reached between the Soviet fleet and the American Sixth fleet. By this means the Mediterranean would cease to be an American lake, and if, bearing in mind the claim once made by Eshkol that the American navy in the Mediterranean was Israel's strategic reserve, Egypt and other Arab governments tried at a later date to urge a reduction in America's naval strength there, they would have some cards in their hands. Balanced reduction by both super-powers would have some attraction for the Americans, whereas as long as they enjoyed a virtual monopoly there was no inducement for them to cut down.

At a second meeting during his visit, however, Podgorny

asked for a command post and a repair shop in Alexandria, and then proposed that both these should be guarded by Russian marines. Next he suggested that the whole area – command post, repair shop, and quarters for the guards – should be handed over to them. All this was under discussion when, at yet another meeting in Kubba Palace, Podgorny asked for permission to raise the Red Flag over the area allocated to them. At this Nasser lost his temper. 'This is just imperialism,' he said. 'It means we shall be giving you a base.' Podgorny backed down, but the damage had been done.

Nasser was, in fact, pursuing two contradictory policies. He was trying to make the Russians see Egypt's defeat as their defeat and to increase their aid to Egypt, even to the extent of taking over, temporarily at least, Egypt's air defences; but at the same time was telling them 'no base, no Red Flag'.

It was while our relations with the Soviets were thus strained that Presidents Aref of Iraq and Boumedienne of Algeria went to Moscow on 17 July 1967, to plead for more help for the Arab cause. Brezhnev told them that the Soviet Union was doing what it could to rebuild Arab defences. 'I assure you,' he said, 'that here in Moscow I have spent sleepless nights because of the warnings we keep on receiving that Israel is planning to cross the Suez Canal. It would obviously not be easy for them to do this because of our support for the Arabs and because of world public opinion, but all the same they might at any moment make a quick dash towards Cairo, which would bring the whole world to the brink of catastrophe.' He gave the two Presidents figures of the aid that had been going to Egypt. 'In two weeks,' he said, 'we have sent fifteen shiploads of material, amounting to forty-eight thousand tons, as well as one thousand five hundred technicians.' Again, the atmosphere in these meetings was not good.

But of course the rebuilding of the army was not just a question of getting more aid from Russia. The whole officer corps had to be recast from top to bottom, and in this task three men were principally involved. First there was the new Commander-in-Chief, General Mohammed Fawzi. He was not an imaginative man, but he had the deserved reputation of a strict

The author, centre facing the camera, beside a captured Israeli tank with Gen. Saada, Commander of the 2nd Army.

Suez at the time of evacuation, a victim of 'No Peace, No War'.

A group at Operational Headquarters (Centre Number 10).
From the reader's right: Gen. Gemasy, Gen. Ahmed Ismail, President Sadat,
Gen. Shazli, Gen. Nasser and Gen. Magdoub.

The Egyptian flag flying over the Bar Lev Line.

disciplinarian – too strict, perhaps, for he rode roughshod over all human considerations. Nasser called him 'the cruel disciplinarian', but his qualities were what was needed to pull together an army demoralized by incompetence and favouritism during the time of Field-Marshal Amer. His successors reaped the harvest of what Fawzi sowed.

Nasser always said the General Fawzi was not the commander he would choose to fight the war. He said that for a war he wanted a Montgomery and not a Rommel, and the man he had in mind for that purpose was the second of the three, General Abdel Munim Riad, whom he appointed Chief of Staff. General Riad was the opposite of General Fawzi: humorous and sociable – he was a bachelor and something of a *bon viveur* – he won the respect and affection of his subordinates in a matter of minutes. He was mistrusted by some of Nasser's closest aides, who feared that his undoubted popularity in the army might give him political ambitions. It was also held against him that he had been seconded to command the Jordanian Army during the run-up to the June War and had allowed himself to be taken in by King Hussein. But Nasser believed Riad understood modern warfare: he had trained in air defence and become a missiles expert and an instructor in radar and anti-aircraft gunnery. As for his political ambitions, Nasser's only comment was: 'If he is efficient and can command in battle, and if he can win the battle, I am ready to give him my job without waiting for him to stage a coup d'état – and he would be perfectly entitled to have it. He can take over, I don't mind.' And, beyond all doubt, Riad was a fine soldier, one of the best Egypt has produced. A tour of duty in the United Arab Command had given him a grasp of the overall strategy necessary to the Arab world. He was one of the rare Arab generals to understand the importance of mobility. He had breadth of vision – he would come to my home and relax over a couple of whiskies and his talk would range far beyond the usual military preoccupations. Above all, he was obsessed by the need to fight. I remember his coming to my home one day and saying: 'I have no use for all this talk of a peaceful solution. The army must fight. If the army is not given a chance to fight, all our men will become slaves, and all our women prostitutes.' It was a tragedy for Egypt that he was killed in an Israeli artillery barrage on the canal front in March 1969 – though it was typical of a man never happy sitting behind a desk that he should have been where the action was.

The third man who should share the credit for the reconstruction of the Egyptian army after the 1967 disaster is President Nasser himself, who devoted a large amount of his time to the army and its problems. He got rid of a great many incompetent officers and encouraged promising ones. He showed a gift for spotting talent. He would have meetings with five of six officers at a time, at the end of which he would recommend those whom he thought suitable for promotion. Also to his credit was the decision for the first time to hold manoeuvres at divisional level, in which two armies faced each other at more or less full strength. Some senior officers complained about the expense of these manoeuvres. Nasser's answer was simply: 'Defeat is more costly.'

Marshal Zakharov had arrived with Podgorny and then stayed in Egypt to take charge of all aspects of Russian assistance in reconstructing the armed forces. He was an extraordinary figure. To disguise his presence in Egypt, Zakharov did not wear his field-marshal's uniform; instead, he adopted a civilian suit and black beret. The beret hid his bald head, but his stocky frame and his face – not unlike that of the Western film director, John Huston – were still instantly recognizable, of course. The authorities had to censor hundreds of photographs of that period, because Zakharov seemed to be everywhere. Without his uniform, naturally, Zakharov did not look so impressive, and it was a strange sight when this 'civilian' bawled out some terrified colonel. At close quarters, Zakharov was overpowering: his voice was very loud and he would punctuate his remarks with fearsome digs and slaps, even kicks.

It would be an exaggeration to say that he was popular in Egypt, though Nasser respected him greatly and he had a good, teasing relationship with Riad. But Zakharov's presence in Egypt was undoubtedly a big Russian concession, and Zakharov never really troubled to hide his opinion that he was doing

Egypt a favour. He was also unrelentingly harsh – he bullied everyone without mercy. Nasser had said to him: 'I want to know what really happened,' and Zakharov blasted practically everyone and everything connected with the war. When Egyptian officers broached the topic of fresh arms, Zakharov shouted them down: 'Arms? What do you need more arms for? To deliver these to the Israelis too? What you need is training, training. Then we will see about arms.'

But even Zakharov found that he could not do the task by himself. He complained to President Nasser that if he was to get quick results – and everyone was still thinking in terms of a possible resumption of the war by Israel – he would need more training advisers rather than the few hundred he had at that time. Nasser said he was ready to accept advisers even at brigade level. So each brigade commander had a Soviet adviser allotted to him, and eventually there were 1,500 attached to the army. Inevitably these foreign advisers were the source of some friction, but Nasser insisted that no questions of prestige or false pride should be allowed to interfere with their work. The Egyptians, he said, had to learn.

Nasser asked General Fawzi, General Riad, Marshal Zakharov, and General Lashinkov, the first head of the permanent Russian Military Mission established in Egypt in the wake of Podgorny's visit, to report to him when Egypt's defences were ready. One day he said jokingly to Marshal Zakharov: 'You are under arrest here until your work is finished.' But this was not really a joke, as was shown when a day came when Zakharov said he wanted to go to Moscow to see his family. Nasser told him: 'My order stands. You are not going to leave Egypt.' So Zakharov did not go – or, at least, he was allowed to return to Moscow only for a few days in July, to present the Soviet Ministry of Defence and the Chiefs of Staff with a first account of what had happened in the war and his assessment of Egypt's needs in its aftermath. Then he returned and stayed in Egypt until one day at the end of October or beginning of November – it was just a few days before the vote in the Security Council which passed Resolution 242 – he went to Nasser with the three other generals and told him categorically: 'Mr President, I think

51

that Egypt can now stand up to anything Israel can deliver. I have no fears for the Egyptian front. The defences are perfectly all right.'

Although the armed forces were the first object of Nasser's concern, he was obliged to give urgent attention to the economy, which was in a terrible state. On top of the losses caused by the war and the closure of the Suez Canal, Egypt was suffering from the burden of the Yemen campaign and from the after-effects of the successful five-year plans and the expenditure of huge sums on the High Dam, all of which projects had still to become productive. Nasser called a number of joint meetings of the High Executive Committee of the Socialist Union and the Cabinet at which the whole question of what had gone wrong and what should be done was thrashed out. The problem was how to prevent the whole development programme from grinding to a halt, and to escape this a big injection of capital was needed, otherwise there might not be enough to pay even for essential wheat imports, because the Russians were concentrating all their efforts on military supplies and we could not ask them for wheat as well.

Then came the Khartum conference at the end of August. This was a great political success for Nasser. There must have been about 500,000 people who turned out to meet him on his journey from the airport to the city and to cheer him as rapturously as ever. (*Newsweek* devoted a cover story to him called 'Hail to the Conquered!') King Feisal, who arrived immediately after him, found no crowds left to greet him. The only slogans shouted at his party were, 'Go with Nasser! Work with Nasser!'

The conference was much more of a success than Nasser had expected. A formula for bringing the fighting in the Yemen to an end was concocted and the oil-producing countries agreed that, instead of cutting back their oil supplies to the West as advocates of the 'oil weapon' had been urging, they would give financial support to the countries which had suffered from Israeli aggression – which meant in the first instance to Egypt and Jordan, since Syria was not represented at Khartum. King Feisal opened the bidding with an offer of £50 million – a generous gesture calculated to take the pressure off both the oil-producing countries and the oil companies.

Egyptian engineers had been building bunkers to protect the new planes the Russians were sending against another surprise attack by Israel. After testing out various designs with heavy bombs they had found one which seemed to be effective. The new Commander of the Air Force, General Madhkour Abul Ezz was extremely energetic in building new airfields, all with their protective bunkers, as well as silos for the SAM-2s – which had been in Egypt, though unused, even during the June War. He even widened the Cairo-Alexandria road so that it could be used as an emergency landing strip. All this engineering work set Egypt back £100 million before the end of 1967 – which meant that the entire amount promised by King Feisal and the others at Khartum was spent within less than half a year and on a single project.

Khartum had convinced Nasser that Arab summits might have a part to play in implementing a policy that had already been agreed elsewhere, but that they could never initiate policy. Nor was organization of a second front for the next round, already agreed by the planners to be essential, something that could be prepared through a summit.

Parallel with these military preparations Nasser was looking at the possibilities for a peaceful settlement, though from the outset he had little hopes of one. During the negotiations which led up to the passing of UN Resolution 242 22 November 1967, several interesting points emerged. First, Arthur Goldberg, the American representative at UN, gave Mahmoud Riad, then the Egyptian Foreign Minister, assurances that the wording of the Resolution meant that Israel would have to withdraw from *all* the territories occupied during the war, provided we were willing to end the state of war. Second, and in direct contradiction to these assurances and President Johnson's five points, the course of events indicated that there was a tacit understanding between the United States and Israel that the Arabs were not to be allowed to escape from direct negotiations and that Israel's designs on some of the occupied territories were being condoned. This was more or less admitted by Joseph Sisco, the

American Assistant Secretary of State dealing with the Middle East, in one telegram which he sent to Mahmoud Riad, in which he said: 'You cannot insist on *all* the territories and expect to have peace.' From the start it was clear that the territories which Israel was coveting included Sharm el-Sheikh, Gaza, Jerusalem, some parts of the West Bank, and the Golan Heights.

Nasser was always sceptical about Resolution 242. At one of his regular meetings with senior army commanders, which took place on 25 November, only three days after the passing of the Resolution, he said to them: 'Let me tell you a few facts. Everything you hear us say about the UN Resolution is not meant for you, and has nothing to do with you. If you look at what the Israelis are doing in the occupied territories it is perfectly obvious that they are never going to evacuate these areas unless they are made to do so. Please remember what I have said before – what has been taken by force can only be recovered by force. This is not rhetoric: I mean it. And listen to this: I have asked the Soviet Union to let us have bridging equipment, and I have told them I want this as a loan, not a gift or a deal, because after we have crossed the canal I am going to hand back the bridges, so that those who have crossed will have no way of getting back. If I were Levi Eshkol or Moshe Dayan I would do the same as they are doing; they want to expand and now they think they have the chance to expand. I don't see that even if they wanted to they could withdraw, because they have fed their people with too many hopes and promises. What they are saying now will inevitably harden into official policy and they will become bound by it. So you don't need to pay any attention to anything I may say in public about a peaceful solution.'

It has to be said that Israel's actions and attitudes at this time were introducing a new element into the Arab-Israel struggle. Earlier the Egyptian people had been involved with Israel either because of the Palestinians, as in 1948, or because the Syrians seemed to be threatened, as in 1967 (in 1956 the main enemy had been the British and French). Israel made the great mistake in 1967 of emphasizing the conflict as one between itself and Egypt, as Egypt. The way in which they treated the Egyptian wounded and prisoners; the way in which they projected their victory to the world; the way in which they subsequently behaved as if they had a right to land their forces anywhere in Egypt they liked – all these were calculated to impose the maximum humiliation on their defeated enemy. They rubbed our noses in our defeat and showed over and over again what intense pleasure it gave them to do this.

To avoid giving the Israelis any excuse for restarting the battle there had to be an order forbidding all shooting on the canal front from the Egyptian side. This was very hard, because Israeli snipers were active and their planes were bombing civilian as well as military targets. In fact it was so unwelcome an order that General Fawzi refused to issue it over his own name and passed the responsibility on to Nasser as supreme commander of the armed forces. Some troops were in fact court-martialled for disobeying the order.

After a while Israeli bombing became so relentless that in October 1967 Nasser decided to evacuate the three canal cities, Port Said, Ismailia and Suez. As a result more than 400,000 refugees from the Canal Zone flooded into Cairo and the rest of Egypt. Israeli tactics clearly showed that they intended to stay indefinitely on the banks of the canal. The Israelis seemed to have a particular hatred for Egypt's irrigation system. Several attempts were made to bomb Nag Hammadi, an important transformer station in Upper Egypt, and to lay mines in the Barrage below Cairo. Lines of barrels as a protection against floating mines had to be laid above the bridges on the Nile and main canals, at a cost of £7 million (they are, at the end of 1974, still there). This threat to the irrigation system touched the deepest instincts of the Egyptians.

2. ARAB CONTACTS

By November, then, the first phase which Nasser had outlined in June, the purely defensive phase, was at an end. The armed forces had been reconstructed; their equipment and infrastructure were more or less complete; the economy had revived;

it was time to think of the next phase – reactivating the front. This did not, of course, mean Egypt's taking the offensive – that would have to come later, as would plans for the second front which, it was now agreed, must be an essential concomitant of any strike by Egypt. But preparations for both could begin. For the reasons he had given the army commanders, Nasser was convinced that the front must not be allowed to freeze: that, he thought, would be the end of everything. When he received Zakharov's assurance, therefore, Nasser turned his thought to a reactivation of the front and instructed General Fawzi to begin the planning of what was to become known as the War of Attrition.

Meanwhile it was the search for a peaceful solution which was making most of the headlines, though as Nasser told King Hussein on 13 January 1968, he had already lost hope in the Jarring mission. His attitude was, broadly speaking, that if somehow a satisfactory solution could be produced, that, naturally, would be fine. We should also aim at convincing world public opinion of our good intentions. This was something to which Israel had always paid great attention and which we had neglected – to our cost. But the main point of continuing negotiations, as he saw it, was to convince the Russians that there was no diplomatic solution and to get them more and more involved.

Through 1968, the Russians were beginning to have direct contact with the Americans over the Middle East. We were not unaware of these: on three occasions in 1968 – on official visits to Moscow in April and July and at the United Nations through October – Mahmoud Riad had been able to discuss Soviet thinking. Finally, the Soviet Foreign Minister Gromyko came to Cairo towards the end of December to ask us what our attitude towards such bilateral talks would be. Mahmoud Riad, then the Foreign Minister, was rather unhappy at the prospect, because he felt that all negotiations ought to be channelled through the UN. He asked Gromyko what was wrong with Jarring, who had been made U Thant's special representative for the Middle East in November 1967, and got a very Stalinist answer: 'There is nothing wrong with Jarring, except that he has no navies in the sea and no missiles in the air.' Riad was not impressed by this answer and saw Nasser before his second meeting with Gromyko to try to get his support for insisting that Jarring should be encouraged to go on with his mission. But Nasser said: 'No. I agree with the Russians. Let us look at it from a realistic point of view. Jarring isn't going to solve anything. If he does appear to have produced a solution, this would only be because something had been arranged behind the scenes between the two super-powers. I want the Russians to be in daily touch with us so that they can see the impossibility of a diplomatic solution: that way they will increase their help to us.'

Another reason why Nasser was not averse to all the diplomatic coming and going was that it helped to buy time, and this was a commodity whose value he was coming more and more to appreciate. At his 25 November meeting with the army commanders he told them that they would have to look forward to five years of concentrated training. At first, he said, he had been thinking in terms of months; now he had come to the conclusion that, with a miracle, they could mount an offensive in three years, but that all the facts pointed to five years as a more realistic estimate. It was after this that General Riad instructed a planning group to prepare the first of many training exercises – Liberation 1 – the object of which was an assault across the canal and the establishment of a bridgehead on the eastern bank.

At the beginning of 1968 Nasser was concentrating almost exclusively on three aspects of policy – the armed forces, Egyptian-Soviet relations, and Arab relations insofar as they concerned his search for a partner or partners in a second front, or the eastern front as it was called. These subjects he kept in his own hands; all the rest he left to others.

One of the first meetings with an Arab head of state which had a bearing on the second front problem was that with King Hussein of Jordan on 13 January 1968. After giving his opinion that a diplomatic solution would never come to anything, Nasser said the question they all had to ask themselves was why the 100 million Arabs were still divided, with few effective links between them. What worried him particularly was that he had no real contacts with Syria. 'We are,' he said, 'all still living in a state of frustration and nervous reaction following the June defeat.' King Hussein had just come from Saudi Arabia and said he had the impression that the Saudis were not prepared to go on giving cash support to the Arab states – as agreed at Khartum – for ever. He also said he was worried because Eshkol (then Prime Minister of Israel) had tried to send him a letter via Jarring. He had refused it, but his guess was that Jarring was under strong pressure from Israel to get all the Arab states to send secret representatives to Cyprus to meet an Israeli representative in Jarring's presence. He said he had told Jarring this was outside the scope of his mission.

King Hussein also said that, shortly before the last time Jarring visited Amman, he had seen Eban (Foreign Minister of Israel) and asked him to define exactly what it was that Israel wanted. Eban had proceeded to give Jarring a long lecture on the origins of the 1967 War, followed by Israel's interpretation of Resolution 242. He obviously regarded the Resolution as no more than an agenda for a number of subjects which would have to be settled by direct negotiations. Jarring asked for a list of these subjects in writing, and Eban gave it him. The list covered: (1) Political and legal problems; (2) The establishment of permanent, secure frontiers; (3) 'Human issues'; (4) Economic cultural and technological co-operation; (5) The Holy Places and access to them. When King Hussein had read this list Nasser turned to Mahmoud Riad, who was present, and said, 'Is this what Jarring told us too?' Riad said, 'Yes, except for one change. Instead of number three on the Jordan list our number three was "opening the Suez Canal to navigation for ships of all nations without discrimination".'

King Hussein was to some extent acting as an intermediary, because there had been no direct contact between Egypt and Saudi Arabia after Khartum: the Saudis paid their financial contribution, but that was all. Apart from other difficulties, the Saudis were afraid that the Egyptians were evacuating the Yemen only for it to be taken over by the Russians. There had been a plane shot down near Sanaa a month before, and the Saudis had made a big issue of it, claiming that the pilot was a

Russian – but this was just because he had a white face; in fact he was a Syrian. Another source of misunderstanding was ex-King Saud, who was living in Egypt. At Khartum Nasser had invited King Feisal to visit Cairo, but King Feisal was unwilling to do this as long as his brother was there. Nasser's attitude was that Saud was a political refugee and so he could not turn him out of the country. To make matters worse the exiled king was living in a house which King Feisal considered his property, and when some Egyptian officials were sent, at Feisal's request, to ask him to leave, Saud burst into tears and said it was impossible for him to do so.

The next of Nasser's Arab visitors, in February 1968, was President Abdul Rahman Aref of Iraq, who was on his way back from seeing De Gaulle. Nasser had encouraged the Iraqis to sound out the French as suppliers of arms. Though the Soviet Union must always, he knew, be the country on which Egypt would have to rely for essential supplies, there might be gaps which other countries could fill, and in the Mirage the French had a fighter-bomber which suited Egyptian needs. The Soviet Union had for several years been relying on intermediate and long-range missiles and had only recently begun to think of the requirements for a limited war fought with conventional arms. President Aref reported greater success than he had expected. De Gaulle had obviously greatly impressed him, and when asked for planes had at once said 'We are ready'. Aref got the impression that De Gaulle did not always like to speak freely in front of his Ministers. It was when he was saying goodbye to Aref on the steps of the Elysée Palace that he became most expansive. 'Defeat,' he had said (speaking from experience), 'need not mean demoralization.' And then he added; 'You know that we are backing you, even if you want the French Army.'

Apart from Nasser's Arab visitors there were a great many would-be mediators in and out of Cairo around this time. Nahum Goldmann (President of the World Zionist Organization) tried to contact Nasser through Marshal Tito, but after an exchange of two letters on each side between Goldmann and the Marshal it was clear that this was leading nowhere. A more serious attempt was made by the Rumanians, who alone among the eastern bloc countries had not broken off relations with Israel in 1967. In fact, when Gideon Rafael of the Israeli Foreign Office had been staying in Bucharest for weeks on end, having brought messages with him that his Government was interested in contacts with Egypt, the Rumanian Deputy Foreign Minister, Gheorgiu Macovescu, came to Cairo in June 1968. Nasser was careful not to rebuff him because he felt that the Rumanians probably represented a point of view that was more common in the eastern bloc than was generally admitted. So eventually Nasser told the Deputy Foreign Minister: 'All right, what I want you to get for me from the Israelis is a map showing what they think the final frontiers of Israel should be.' He heard no more from the Rumanians after that.

Haile Selassie's attempt at mediation was more or less the same story. The Emperor was sympathetic, saying that he too had once lost his country and that when he was in exile the Italians had offered him $3 million and four palaces if he would abdicate. He was also directly involved in the Arab-Israel dispute because he had documents which proved that at one time President Truman had offered the Israelis as a homeland parts of Ethiopia. Nasser put the same proposition to him; 'You are going to see Abba Eban in Ethiopia in a few days,' he said – this was in June 1969. 'Get me a map of what they think the final frontiers of Israel should be.' Again no more was heard.

The main military problem confronting Nasser and his advisers at this time, when the War of Attrition was first beginning, was how to hold a bridgehead on the other side of the Suez Canal. Operating under the plans code-named Liberation 1 and Liberation 2, commando patrols had succeeded in crossing the canal and staying in Sinai for up to twenty-four hours before returning. The Russian Military Mission was of the opinion that these patrols ought to be kept there longer, but Nasser's view was that without missile cover anything bigger than hit-and-run raids would be certain of annihilation. Egypt had, in short, to face the fact that in the air Israel had gained a considerable lead and there was no quick means of catching up except by building a system of air defence.

We knew from intelligence reports that Israel had about fifty crack pilots and crews who were transferred from one front to another and from one mission to another and whose feats helped to build up the legend of Israeli invincibility in the air. This legend was in itself an effective deterrent, but we were to learn during the October war that the general level of the Israeli air force was by no means as high as that of this small élite group.

It being clearly impossible for us to achieve superiority – or even equality – in the air we were obliged to look around for alternatives. So it was that once again we came to pay more and more attention to the idea of a second front. But nothing much came out of these meetings. The main trouble was the conflict between Syria and Iraq. The Baath Party was in power in Syria and there were Baathists in the Iraq Government; but the President, Abdul Rahman Aref, was not a Baathist. And even after a coup d'état by Baathists had ousted Aref, the two brands of Baathists quarrelled with each other as violently as ever.

Temperamental differences between individuals and governments were responsible for much wasted time at meetings which were supposed to be discussing strategy: nothing much came out of such meetings towards a second front. They produced a great deal of paper but, as Nasser once complained: 'I seem to have seen and signed a vast number of documents, but what has been the result of it all?' What particularly worried him was whether there was any Arab officer who was capable of commanding the combined armies on the eastern front. He thought we had officers capable of commanding a brigade or even a division, but commanding an army required abilities of a different order and he could not see where such abilities were to be found. He was continually warning senior officers against the dangers of taking things easy, of neglecting the pace of modern war. The Arab armies, he felt, were over-extended and still governed by a defensive mentality. Political considerations governed military strategy, instead of the other way round.

Nasser had encouraged President Aref to go to France. He said: 'Even if the French attitude was not as favourable as it is, we should have to pretend it was, because we need a bridge to the West'. He encouraged the Iraqis too to try to get Mirage planes. In the same way, when King Hussein talked at their

61

January 1968 meeting of asking Russia for arms (being disappointed with what he was getting from the United States and Britain), Nasser told him not to. He said it would be wrong for Israel to be equipped solely with Western arms and the Arabs solely with Russians arms. 'Take British arms if you can get them,' was his advice to the King.

3. ENTER THE PALESTINIANS

By 1968 the strain of events was beginning to tell on Nasser's health. He had been suffering from diabetes for several years, and now he began to have attacks of severe pain. In July he went to the Soviet Union, mainly to talk about delays in arms deliveries and to urge once again the need for a fighter-bomber capable of matching Israel's American Phantoms, but he took the opportunity for a checkup at the Bervikha Hospital. As before, he preferred not to be treated as an official guest but stayed at one of the big guest houses on Lenin Hills overlooking the Moskva River. The journey was significant in another respect because he took Yasser Arafat, leader of the Palestine Liberation Organization (PLO), with him. It was the first time Arafat had been to Moscow.

The Fateh Group had first got in touch with the Egyptian authorities some time in 1966. At that time our Intelligence was responsible for all underground activities and all dissident movements in the Arab world, and unfortunately they were convinced that Fateh was an offshoot of the Muslim Brotherhood, which had been outlawed since the attempt on Nasser's life in 1954. So nothing came of these first contacts. Khalid el-Hassan (Abul Said) who had arrived in Cairo as representative of Fateh, came to see me and tried to explain what Fateh stood for, but suspicion of the movement was so strong that no approach to Nasser or Field-Marshal Amer was possible. However, by 1967 Nasser was beginning to think of ways and means of activating a second front, and Fateh had begun to make a name for itself with some limited military operations, so the prospect looked more hopeful. Farouk Qadumi (Abu

Lutf) came to Cairo and was later joined by Salah Khalaf (Abu Iyad), but they still found nobody except myself who was ready to meet them. I took them to see Nasser and it was arranged that Yasser Arafat should join them and that we should all have a further meeting.

An appointment was duly made, but our Intelligence had still not changed their views on Fateh, and on the morning of the day for which the meeting had been fixed I received a telephone call from one of Nasser's aides saying, 'We don't want to disturb the President, but we feel we should tell you that we are not satisfied about the intentions of the three men who are due to go with you this afternoon to see him. Please inform them that, before seeing the President, they will have to submit to being searched and, if necessary, disarmed.' I said: 'For heaven's sake leave this to me. Don't search anybody.'

The three Palestinians came to my office from the Fateh 'safe house' in the centre of Cairo where they always stayed and I drove them on to Nasser's. On the way I tried to tackle the subject in as tactful a manner as I could. 'What's this hanging here?' I said to Yasser Arafat, who was sitting in the front seat beside me, 'A revolver? My God, you'll scare everybody. Abu Iyad, have you got a revolver too?' Arafat said he would feel completely naked without a revolver, and Abu Iyad said it was impossible for him to move without one. 'What about you, Abu Lutf?' I asked. 'No' said Abu Lutf, 'I haven't got one: I'm a civilian.' When we had reached Nasser's house and were waiting in the lobby, Nasser's secretary came up, whispering to me that the presidential guards must be allowed to impound the men's revolvers. I told him to keep away. Eventually, to my intense relief, as we got up to go into Nasser's office Arafat and Abu Iyad spontaneously took off their revolver belts and left them on a chair.

Nasser started off the meeting by saying: 'According to a message our Intelligence people received from Kuwait, you three came here to assassinate me.' They all protested that this must be an attempt by somebody to drive a wedge between Egypt and Fateh. Nasser then explained his point of view towards the Palestinian resistance. He said he saw no reason for any contradiction between them and us. We had accepted the Security Council Resolution 242 because, though he had little hope of its producing anything, if it was properly carried out it would meet the requirements of Egypt, Syria and Jordan. But he could see that it would not meet the requirements of the Palestinians. 'You have every right not to accept it,' he said. 'There is no reason why you should not publicly oppose the Resolution because it is not designed for you.'

Nasser went on to say that one of our problems had been the absence of a Palestinian element in the struggle. 'I would be more than glad,' he said, 'if you could represent the Palestinian people and the Palestinian will to resist, politically by your presence and militarily by your actions.' He said Fateh ought to be completely independent of all Arab governments, though it should co-ordinate with them. 'But why not be our Stern? Why not be our Begin? You must be our irresponsible arm. On this basis we will give you all the help we can.'

The meeting went off well, and after it the Egyptian authorities started to co-operate with Fateh as well as helping in the training and equipping of its members. The Jordanians were not happy about this development. Two planes which arrived in Amman were discovered to contain arms destined for the Fedayin and King Hussein sent Bahjat el-Talhouni, then his Prime Minister, to Cairo more than once to complain about the assistance Egypt was providing.

Israel made a series of raids on Fedayin bases in Jordan and the Fedayin were trying to buy arms in Western Europe. Their leaders had read in *Aviation Week* about an anti-aircraft rocket called 'Red-Eye', capable of being carried by one man (the American counterpart of the Russian Strella which was to play so important a part in the 1973 war) and they wanted that. I suggested to Nasser that, as the Fedayin's arms requirements seemed to be getting beyond the range of what Egypt could easily supply, the best plan would be to introduce them to the Russians so that they could conduct their own negotiations.

Thus it was that Arafat went with Nasser to Moscow in July 1968. He travelled on an Egyptian passport under the name of Muhsin Amin, and was listed as one of the technicians in the

Israeli prisoners-of-war.

President Nasser welcomes President Podgorny to Cairo.

party. The plane in which we travelled was a Soviet one, because the Russians thought there was a real risk of an Egyptian plane being attacked by the Israelis over the Mediterranean. Nasser was in great pain through the journey, which lasted five hours, particularly in his legs and thighs, and spent the whole time lying down. As we were nearing Moscow I pointed out to him that Arafat had had no chance of speaking to him during the trip, and suggested that I should bring him along for a quarter of an hour or so before we landed so that they could discuss plans. Nasser agreed, and after he had got dressed I brought Arafat to him. The descent had begun by then and we ran into some turbulence. Arafat turned rather green, but made tremendous efforts to control himself so that he should not appear at a disadvantage on his arrival in Moscow.

The first day, 4 July, was mostly spent in discussing the usual problem of arms supply. The Soviets had some complaints that not enough co-operation was being given to their advisers in Egypt, but we managed to make a new agreement about payment for the advisers, worked out in sterling. After lunch Nasser introduced Yasser Arafat to Kosygin, Brezhnev and Podgorny. Next day they asked Arafat to come to the building of the Central Committee, where he met Kyril Mazurov, who was responsible for National Liberation Movements, as well as two generals. Mazurov was well suited to his task: he came from Byelorussia, which gave him sympathy towards small peoples caught in a wider struggle; and having first risen to prominence in the Soviet resistance movement during World War Two, he could appreciate Arafat's technical problems too. Arafat gave the Russians some idea of the aims of the Fedayin, their strength and their requirements.

Then on the morning of the third day Nasser went into hospital. Anwar Sadat, who was a member of our delegation, went to the hospital with him. I remember that I spent the morning in our Embassy writing an article, and there met General Abdel Munim Riad, who was drawing up lists of arms requirements. We went back to Nasser's house on Lenin Hills at about one o'clock, to find that Nasser was back from the hospital and had sent a message that he would like to see me. I went in, expecting to find him in the garden, because before going to the hospital Nasser had promised to meet Yasser Arafat and myself in the garden of his house overlooking the Moskva River, where the trees were covered with cherries. It was the first time he had ever seen cherries growing on trees and he said: 'When I come back from the hospital we'll all pick some more cherries to have for our lunch.' But I was told he was not in the garden but in his room, so I went upstairs. On the way I ran into Anwar Sadat and asked him how the President was, what did the hospital think was wrong with him? Sadat said everything was all right: 'Just some rheumatism.' He went with me into Nasser's room.

We found Nasser lying on his bed in his pyjamas, obviously in very severe pain. 'What's this?' I asked. 'Don't tell me this is rheumatism.' Nasser looked at Sadat and said: 'Anwar, I think you had better tell Mohamed the truth.' 'What's wrong?' I asked. Sadat said: 'It's nothing dangerous. It's hardening of the arteries in the legs, caused by too much sugar, by diabetes. But they say it can be cured by mineral treatment in Tskhaltubo.' 'Anwar and I talked about this on our way from the hospital,' Nasser put in, 'and they think I should have this treatment, otherwise the thing could be dangerous.'

At this moment General Riad, whom Nasser had sent for too, knocked at the door and came in. He sat beside me on the President's bed – Sadat was in a chair – and the President told him about his illness. So now there were four of us who knew. General Riad was almost in tears, though he tried to conceal them. 'Anyhow,' said Nasser, doing his best to reassure us, 'they tell me it's not dangerous, if I have the proper treatment. So I'll go back to Cairo for the July Twenty-third celebrations, and then immediately afterwards go to Tskhaltubo. They say it ought only to take about a month.' Then he said he did not want any lunch: he was tired, and asked us to draw the curtains.

The three of us went out. Sadat went to have a rest, and General Riad and I walked into the garden. The General was terribly worried. 'If anything happened to him,' he said, 'it would be an absolute catastrophe. Nobody else can do the things he is doing. To think that all the time he has been making this effort he was in all that pain: I never realized it.'

So we came back from Moscow and Nasser told the National Assembly that he was going for a course of treatment to Tskhaltubo. For the first time the country realized that there was something wrong with the President's health.

Doctor Evgeny Chazov, the Soviet Deputy Minister of Health, who was treating Nasser, thought that if he continued his treatment for several years the condition could eventually be cleared up. The President was due to go to Tskhaltubo for a month's cure from July, but this had to be postponed until September because the War of Attrition was already hotting up. It was the time of Israel's deep penetration raids into Egypt: Nag Hammadi and our whole irrigation system became their target.

It was in 1969 that the Russians started equipping us with portable Strella rockets (SAM-7s) against low-flying aircraft and with Grad armoured cars fitted with several rocket launchers. The first list of promised deliveries was brought to Cairo in January 1969 by Alexander Shelepin, a member of the Politburo, and when Nasser saw him he told him that, although we always needed more from the Russians, they must not think we failed to appreciate what they did give us. 'I always tell my Arab friends and our own Egyptian people,' he said, 'that, even if the Russians are slow, in the end they give us what we want. That is the most important thing; and that is what makes them different from the Americans. King Hussein went many times to see President Johnson to ask him for arms. He never got a single plane. You may sometimes be exasperating people to deal with, but in the end you do deliver.' The actual deliveries of Strellas came towards the end of 1969. The first Strellas were fairly primitive and also misfired on early trials; but the later types were extremely effective.

When September 1969 came, it was time for an important meeting in Cairo of the governments of what are known as the 'confrontation states', attended by representatives of Syria, Jordan and Iraq as well as by President Nimeiry of the Sudan, who had come to power by a coup d'état in May – President

67

Boumedienne of Algeria joined the conference a little later. These confrontation meetings had a curious effect in some other Arab countries, which were not directly involved but felt somehow jealous of being left out. It was, for example, while this meeting was going on that King Hassan of Morocco launched his idea of a new Arab 'Summit'. Nasser made, in passing, a light-hearted reference to this sort of attitude when he addressed one of the sessions of the conference. 'We would like everybody to be here,' he said, 'but I can't be sure what is going to happen when all of us get together. There always seem to be a lot of leakages and the oddest conflicts of personality arise. For instance not long ago I met President Bourguiba and we were talking about quite serious political questions when suddenly he looked at me and said; "Why are you tall while I am short?" I was baffled by this question. I said I didn't know the answer and that he had better consult God. I think we really have enough unsolved problems already without adding new ones to them.'

The first session was on 1 September, and at it General Fawzi read an important report on the political and military situation which had been prepared by the Chiefs of Staff of the confrontation countries. The report concluded that, with proper co-ordination between the armies concerned (which of course assumed the active creation of a second front), we ought to be ready for battle within eighteen months.

4. THE LIBYAN COUP

It was while King Hussein was addressing this first session that the first news was brought to President Nasser of a coup in Libya against King Idris. This was somewhat embarrassing because King Hussein enjoyed close relations with King Idris, and now inevitably the 'progressive' States would feel that the removal of one king might be the prelude to the removal of another.

As soon as the news was made public all the delegates began to discuss its significance. Nasser tactfully paid a tribute to King Idris. 'I remember,' he said, 'one occasion when we were in urgent need of money to buy arms. I sent Hassan Sabri el-Kholi to see the King, and he promised to give us £20 million straight away on only one condition – that we should return to him a *subha* (rosary) which had been given by one of his ancestors to Al Azhar mosque and which he thought was still hanging there. I told Hassan el-Kholi to go to Al Azhar and collect the *subha* and take it to the King. Which he did.'

Everyone was naturally speculating as to who the authors of the coup might be. Were they Baathists, were they Nasserites, or what? The first clue to their identity came from the radio monitor at *Al Ahram*. One of their early communiqués said that their aims were 'freedom, socialism and unity'. This showed that they were not Baathists, because the Baath slogan has always been 'unity, socialism, freedom'. Though the order may not appear important it does symbolize the ideological split between Nasser and the Baath, his point of view being that you cannot have unity unless you are free, so that freedom must come first. Anyway, when I heard the monitoring report I spoke to Nasser in Kubba Palace and told him that it looked as if the revolutionaries were close to us in their thinking. At about the same time the Revolutionary Council sent an emissary, Adam el-Hawaz, to get in touch with the Egyptian Consulate in Benghazi with the message that they wanted to see somebody from Egypt. They were asked whom they wanted to see. It seemed that apart from President Nasser himself the only name they could remember on the spur of the moment was mine, because of my articles in *Al Ahram*. So Nasser called me up and said: 'The people in Benghazi seem to want you, so you'd better go off tonight.'

A special plane was arranged and the three of us in the delegation – a military liaison officer from General Fawzi's staff, a political intelligence liaison officer, and myself – set off for Benghazi. It was a most unpleasant journey. Al Adem airfield was still controlled by the British, and as we approached it the pilot reported that he had received a signal asking who he was, who his passengers were, and what was his destination. He asked for instructions, but there were none that could be given to him, so he stalled with Al Adem control and climbed high.

Fortunately this worked, for we heard nothing more. When we reached Benghazi the airport was in complete darkness. Then a few landing lights were switched on, revealing armoured cars drawn up on both sides of the runway. As I stepped out of the plane I was greeted by Mustafa Kharubi, who, as I learned later, was a member of the Revolutionary Council. When I told him who I was he began embracing me and weeping. 'I can't believe my eyes,' he said.

We went together to our consulate, and he began to tell me all about the Revolution. 'We are all believers in Nasser,' he said. I asked him who was their leader. 'You will see him tonight before you go,' he answered. (I had arranged to fly back the next morning). 'You can't imagine how pure he is.' I asked what rank he held. Kharubi said: 'His rank is lower than mine because he was punished. He was a captain like me, but he was reduced to first lieutenant.'

At about two o'clock in the morning Muammar Ghadaffi came into the consulate. It was quite a shock to me to see how young he was and I began to think that perhaps I had been tricked and that this man could not be the leader of a successful revolution. But once he started to talk I revised my views. He spoke eloquently on many subjects, and then suddenly said that he and his brother officers wanted union with Egypt. They were ready for unity, he said. He emphasized that he had been following everything that had been happening in the Arab world, and he knew that Nasser was looking for a second front with Israel. 'But,' said Ghadaffi, 'he is forgetting depth. Libya represents depth. We have hundreds of miles of Mediterranean coastline; we have the airfields; we have the money; we have everything! Tell President Nasser we made this revolution for him. He can take everything of ours and add it to the rest of the Arab world's resources to be used for the battle.'

I was taken aback by this offer. When I got back to Cairo I found a message waiting for me at the airport with the news that the President wanted to see me immediately. I had taken a photographer on the plane with me because I know Nasser's habit of studying all the photographs he could lay hands on of any new person he was going to have dealings with. I had assured Ghadaffi, who had not wanted pictures of him to appear, that these would be for Nasser's eyes only, and now sent the photographer off to get them developed while I went to Nasser's house.

'Well?' said Nasser, as I came in.

'It's a catastrophe,' I told him.

'Why? Are they against Egypt?'

'Far from it. The problem is that they are shockingly innocent – scandalously pure. They are your men and they want unity with you.'

Nasser was as astonished by this news as I had been. He made me go over and over again every detail of my journey and of my meetings with Ghadaffi and the others. What were they wearing? How did the rest treat Ghadaffi? Did I get the impression that he was really in command? When I mentioned that Ghadaffi had been unshaven Nasser seized on this: 'Yes, yes,' he exclaimed. 'You are right to tell me all that sort of detail.' But as I had only been eighteen hours in Benghazi altogether – one sleepless night and a bit of the following morning – there were many questions Nasser put to me that I was unable to answer at that stage.

Next day a telegram came from Benghazi. The emissaries in the plane with me – apart from the photographer, the military liaison officer and the political intelligence liaison officer – had stayed behind. They were now reporting that a warning had been received from West Germany – Libya had close relations with Bonn because Germany took a large amount of Libyan oil – that the West Germans were helping the Turks to mount an expedition by sea which would have the aim of reinstating King Idris. The King had been on holiday in Turkey when the coup took place, and the idea apparently was that he could be brought back in the same way that the Emperor Haile Selassie had been restored in 1960 when he was out of the country at the time of the coup against him by his son, Prince Asfa Wassen. This naturally caused Nasser some anxiety because he was much concerned at this time with the problem of depth for the defence of Egypt, and it was of the utmost importance to give the Libyan revolution time to consolidate. After he had read the telegram Nasser went to the telephone and called General Fawzi. 'Fawzi,' he said, 'I want you to calm things down on the canal front [this was at a time when the War of Attrition was at its height] and prepare for action in the West.' I can imagine General Fawzi's consternation at this order, but in fact that night an armoured brigade was moved to Mersa Matruh, and two destroyers and several submarines were sent there from Alexandria.

The Cairo confrontation meeting produced no concrete results. Instead of adopting the report presented by General Fawzi, it was decided that the same participants should meet again the following March to finalize their plans. But, as can be imagined, when the meeting broke up the main thought in everybody's mind was how the Libyan revolution was going to work out.

President Nimeiry had special hopes of co-operation between the two youngest revolutionary nations in the Arab world, particularly in view of the Sudan's difficult economic problems. In November he paid his first visit to Moscow, and on the way back he passed through Cairo and gave a report on his journey. Apparently his meetings with the Soviet leaders had been a great success. They had shown much interest in the Sudanese revolution and still more in the Libyan – Libya being of course a bigger international prize because of its oil and strategic position. Kosygin warned him that the Sudan would come under heavy pressure from the West which would refuse to accept its 'loss'. Brezhnev asked him how much benefit the Sudan had got from its earlier Russian loan (granted before Nimeiry seized power). Nimeiry said that some of the factories built with the loan had been faultily sited and were not working properly. 'Well,' said Brezhnev, 'one of our difficulties is that some countries we have given aid to spent the money on building football stadiums when many other things were more urgently needed.' He seemed especially interested in China's penetration of Africa. When Nimeiry said that as far as the Sudan was concerned no penetration had taken place, Brezhnev nodded his head and said, 'Very good.'

The Israelis reacted to the Libyan revolution, which they

72

rightly regarded as encouragement for Egypt, in their customary manner. On 9 September, six days after the Cairo conference had ended, they staged a highly publicized raid on Zafarana, a post on the coast of the Red Sea. They landed several tanks and amphibious vehicles and took a great many photographs of what they called 'the invasion of Egypt'. The day this happened Nasser was attending army exercises in the desert near the Cairo-Suez Road. When the news of the Israeli raid reached him he asked General Fawzi – who was with him – for details, but Fawzi said that all he knew about it was what was coming out of the news agencies. Nasser left the manoeuvres and came back to Cairo.

He rang me up and asked to be given all the agency reports. Then he tried the army and intelligence people but nobody could tell him anything – where the Israelis were or what they were doing – or even give any confirmation that the raid had taken place. Nasser was extremely upset. The last time he telephoned to me, between six and seven in the evening, he complained that we were still apparently behaving in 'the 1967 way'.

The next day, late on the evening of 10 September, I was summoned to the President's house. There I found Anwar Sadat, Sharawy Gomaa, General Fawzi, Sami Sharaf, and Amin Huwaidi. Sadat told me that Nasser was going away for a month's vacation and that in his absence business was to be handled by a committee, presided over by Sadat himself and with the other five of us as members. 'I don't understand what's happening,' I said, 'Is the President going abroad? He was talking to me yesterday and said nothing about it.' Sadat said: 'No, he's not going abroad. He will be staying in the country.' I still could not understand what was happening. 'I'm sorry,' I said, 'but I can't agree to anything until I have seen him.' Somebody said, 'He's got flu.' 'What do you mean?' I asked. 'Flu which takes a month? For my part, I'm afraid I can't take part in anything until I know exactly where I stand and where the President is going to be. It's different for you. You are all members of the Government. Sharawy is Minister of the Interior, Sami is Secretary to the President for Information,

General Fawzi is Commander of the Army, Amin Huwaidi is Head of Intelligence, but I have no official position. How am I supposed to fit in?' 'Don't be obstinate, Mohamed,' said Sadat.

We were all gathered in Sami Sharaf's office, which was in a building just across the road from the President's house. It was night time and we could see that the light was on in Nasser's room. 'Very well, then,' said Sadat, after a pause. 'I'll go and see what can be done.' Fifteen minutes later he came back. 'The President will see you,' he said, 'and tell you personally what it is he wants you to do.' So I went with Sadat across to Nasser's house and up the long flight to the first floor, where I found Nasser sitting in a chair eating some of his favourite white cheese. He was very pale and was unshaven, which was most unusual. 'What is all this?' I asked him. 'It's flu,' he said. 'I think I must rest. All the doctors tell me I must rest and stay in bed.' 'But why do you want me to join this committee?' I asked. He said: 'You know how I react to things. All the others are officials, but you know the way my mind works, and so I want you to be in this committee.' I said: 'But this is quite different. Talking things over with you is one thing, but talking them over with others is something completely different.' 'Do it for me,' he said. 'All right,' I said. 'For you I will do it with pleasure.'

As we were preparing to leave I said to Nasser: 'Is there anything else?' He said: 'It's a heart attack.' I said: 'A heart attack?' He said: 'They tell me it's not serious.' When we went out of the room I asked Sadat who had seen him, and he told me the name of the doctor. 'But shouldn't we get a foreign specialist to see him?' I asked. Sadat said the difficulty was that if we got anyone from America or Britain the Israelis would know about it immediately and it would be in all the newspapers. 'Why don't we get someone from the Soviet Union?' I suggested. He thought that was a good idea, and got in touch with the Soviet Ambassador.

Within a few hours Doctor Chazov had been flown to Cairo in a special plane from Moscow. After he had seen Nasser he gave his verdict: there could be no Tskhaltubo (Nasser had just been preparing to go to his second cure there); his heart would not be able to stand up to the mineral treatment. Instead he would have to adhere to a strict regime. For at least six weeks he would have to stay in bed; he should see no one and be spared all worries and tensions. Also, he should stop smoking completely. Nasser looked at the professor and said: 'You are depriving me of two things, one which I love and one which I cannot avoid. Cigarettes used to be my love, but tension was my life.' Nasser followed the strict regime for three days. After three days he was at the end of the telephone again getting everybody on the move.

But he was still more ill than he cared to admit. Chazov stayed in Cairo for ten days, though his visit was kept secret until Nasser was more or less well again. Meanwhile, to explain the President's lack of public appearances, it was announced that he had flu. His ministers did try to shield him from work: the Jordanian Prime Minister, for example, was in Cairo at the time and pleaded that he would be 'dismissed' if he returned to King Hussein without having seen President Nasser. Finally, he was allowed to see the President – asleep. But it was no good: Chazov's six weeks were forgotten and Nasser was back at work by the last week of September.

Pressure for a summit conference of all Arab states continued to be strong in certain quarters, though Algeria and Syria were against the idea. Kuwait and Saudi Arabia too were against it, and King Feisal sent a message to Cairo stating that he was only willing to attend such a conference 'provided the UAR declares openly that it has abandoned all efforts to achieve a peaceful solution, is withdrawing its co-operation with the mission of Dr Jarring and its acceptance of Resolution 242, and is prepared immediately to declare a Jihad.' This was asking rather a lot.

The problem with King Feisal was always that he thought the religious bond, Islam, should be the framework for political action in the Arab world. But Islam extended over countries such as Pakistan and Indonesia, and President Nasser asked what role *they* had to play in the struggle against Israel. Nasser's view was that Arabism and Arab nationalism were the more realistic context for political action: hence, an Arab, as opposed to Islamic, summit was a more suitable forum. The dispute was never resolved.

5. BUYING A BOMB

Shortly after this Muammar Ghadaffi paid his first visit to Cairo. He had several meetings with Nasser, and it became plain that his knowledge of current affairs was largely derived from reading the newspapers, though he was anxious to learn. Two things stood out: first, his dependence on Nasser's guidance for his understanding of Arab politics and his reliance on the Egyptian revolutionary experience as a model for Libya; and second, the extremely simplistic way in which he looked at the problems of war and peace.

On one occasion when Nasser was outlining to him the relative strengths of the Arabs and Israel in tanks, aircraft, and so on, Ghadaffi burst in: 'No, no: we should go straight to an overall war and liquidate Israel.' Nasser said patiently that this was impossible: the international situation would not allow us to do it. Neither the Russians nor the Americans would permit a situation that might lead to nuclear war.

Ghadaffi asked: 'Do the Israelis have nuclear bombs?' Nasser said this was a strong probability. 'Have *we* got nuclear bombs?' Nasser said 'No, we have not.'

Two or three months later the second man in Libya, Major Jalloud, paid a surprise visit to Egypt and came to see Nasser. He said his visit was to be kept secret and that the only purpose of it was to consult the President. Nasser asked him what he was to be consulted about. Jalloud said: 'We are going to buy an atomic bomb.' Nasser asked him where they were going to buy it. Jalloud said that they knew the Americans and Russians would be unwilling to sell them but that maybe the Chinese would. Nasser said that as far as he knew atomic bombs were never for sale. 'Oh,' said Jalloud. 'We don't want a big atomic bomb, just a tactical one. We contacted the Chinese and said we wanted someone to go there and pay them a visit, and they said they would welcome us. So I am going.'

Jalloud set off incognito, changing his Libyan passport for an Egyptian one, and travelling to Peking via Pakistan and India.

The Chinese did not know what the visit was all about, but a meeting was arranged with Chou En-Lai. At this meeting the Deputy Chairman of the Revolutionary Council of Libya explained that he had come to Peking on a very important matter. 'China,' he said, 'is the pride of all Asian countries. You have done a great deal to help the backward countries, and have proved to the world that you are just as strong as the West. So we from Libya have come to you for help. We have no wish to be a burden to you, and we know that these things cost a lot of money – we want to buy an atomic bomb.' Chou En-Lai was very polite. He explained with perfect Chinese courtesy that atomic bombs were not for sale, and that while China would of course be delighted to help over research as, in fact, China had some years before agreed to help Egypt, the actual production of nuclear weapons would have to be done by the Libyans themselves; every nation must practice self-reliance, etc. So Major Jalloud came back empty-handed.

6. THE RABAT SUMMIT

Eventually it was decided that preparation for an Arab, as opposed to Islamic, summit should go ahead and King Hassan's invitation to hold it in Rabat in December 1969 was accepted. Nasser asked King Feisal to call in at Cairo on his way to Rabat because he felt that the success or failure of the conference would largely depend on whether Egypt and Saudi Arabia could find any common ground. Saudi Arabia disliked the close relations which Egypt enjoyed with the Soviet Union, while we stood in continuing need of Saudi Arabian financial aid, particularly in helping over the rapid procurement of arms. But when President Nasser and King Feisal met a new complication cropped up. There had been an abortive coup in the Saudi Air Force, following which a number of pilots had been executed. Few outside Saudi Arabia knew what had happened. Whatever trials there had been had not been in public. News of the affair had merely leaked in June 1969; and it was later said that the ringleaders, having concerted plans abroad, had returned to the country – only to be picked up at the airport. When he met Nasser, however, King Feisal's story was that the rebel officers had connections with Egypt: he mentioned Sami Sharaf by name as being involved. Nasser told him that if any Egyptian was accused of subversive activities in his country he was ready to send him for trial in Saudi Arabia. 'It doesn't matter who he is,' the President said, 'whether he is one of my close assistants or even my secretary – you can try him. I want relations between our two countries to be good.'

'God give you long life,' said King Feisal. 'I do not know the exact outcome of our investigations, but certainly some of the plotters did mention Sami Sharaf's name. It seems that they are communists. We do not have any communists, thank God, in Saudi Arabia. Our country is an Islamic country. Our people live and die according to their traditional beliefs. We have no contact with the communist world, diplomatic or otherwise. But unfortunately young people from our country who go abroad to get educated come back with communistic ideas. The worst centre for spreading communism is the American University of Beirut.' Nasser said that Egyptians who go to the AUB or the University of Cairo did not seem to turn into communists. 'No, no,' said the King. 'Just take a look at everything that has happened in the Arab world and at the sort of people who graduated from the AUB. After the First World War it was Paris which was the chief hatching ground for communists – men like Salah Bitar, Akram Hourani, and Michel Aflak came from Paris. But after the Second World War the centre of the poison moved to the AUB.' Nasser tried to get back to the accusations against Sami Sharaf. 'Have you any proof of his involvement?' he asked. 'I admit that before nineteen sixty-seven we may have been working against you, but after the Khartum conference I gave orders that all such operations should cease.' Nasser told the King that one of his problems was that people outside Egypt sometimes claimed to be acting in his name without any authority to do so. King Feisal said: 'Your real problem, God save your life and make it long, is that everything that is printed in *Al Ahram* is believed to come directly from you.' 'I talked to Heikal yesterday,' said

Nasser. 'I told him that he was creating a lot of trouble for us in Saudi Arabia and all he said was, "What do you want me to do – close the paper down?" I don't have anything at all to do with *Al Ahram* myself,' Nasser added, 'Heikal is my friend, but I don't tell him what to write. He wouldn't accept instructions if I gave them to him. As you know, he's much too obstinate for that.'

Nasser then brought the conversation round to questions of finance. He said that Egypt needed additional help. King Feisal said that Saudi Arabia was going through an extremely difficult period. Its reserves of foreign currency were almost at an end. They might be faced soon with the alternative of borrowing from the IMF or stopping their aid to friendly countries. He blamed his difficulties on the sabotage of Tapline – 'done by your friends, George Habash and the rest, who work in league with the Zionists and are trying to bankrupt us.'

So Nasser and King Feisal went to Rabat without any real basis of understanding with each other. It turned out to be one of the strangest summit conferences ever held. The centre of attraction, naturally enough, was Muammar Ghadaffi, since it was his first public appearance on the international stage. King Hassan presided over the conference, and at the opening session the Chief of the Royal Cabinet came up to the King, kissed his hand, and told him that the proceedings were ready to start. All the kings and presidents were waiting in the adjoining room, and a look of horror spread over the face of Ghadaffi. 'My God,' he cried. 'Did you see what I saw? This man,' pointing at the Chief of the Royal Cabinet, 'kissed the hand of Hassan. Does hand kissing still go on in the Arab world? Do we still stick to these relics of feudalism and slavery? How are we ever going to liberate Palestine if we still kiss hands?' There was a good deal of embarrassment at this outburst, and Nasser tried to calm him down.

At this first session the heads of state once again heard a report on preparations for the battle from General Fawzi. Once again Ghadaffi interrupted, 'Is it wise,' he asked, 'to tell all these secrets in front of everybody sitting here? One of them is certain to go and tell the Israelis.' As the proceedings got under way he caused more raised eyebrows by addressing the conference president as 'Brother Hassan' and King Feisal as 'Brother Feisal'. Nasser used to call the King 'Brother King Feisal', but Ghadaffi stuck to plain 'Brother'. King Feisal gave Nasser a look as if to say 'What are you going to do about your friend?'

One day there was something of a crisis at one of the sessions and Ghadaffi stalked out of the conference hall and into the corridor where I was sitting. He came and sat beside me. Someone came past and greeted me. 'Who is that?' asked Ghadaffi. I told him that it was General Oufkir – 'Don't you know him?' Ghadaffi exploded: 'Oufkir: that's the man who murdered Ben Barka.'* I agreed that Oufkir had been suspected of being involved in the assassination. 'No,' said Ghadaffi. 'He killed him all right. He's a murderer. How can he be allowed in here among all of us? The police must be given orders to arrest him.' I pointed out that Oufkir was himself Minister of the Interior and thus controlled the police. Then someone else I knew passed. 'Do you recognize him?' I asked Ghadaffi. 'He is the man responsible for that big private deal with an arms firm and an oil company, in which he took a large commission. You probably remember the scandal.' Almost before Ghadaffi had recovered from this new shock Dulaimi, one of Oufkir's assistants, came by and was pointed out. Ghadaffi went straight off to see Nasser. 'At this conference,' he complained, 'we are surrounded by thieves and conspirators and spies. No good can come of such a gathering. It would be better for us not to be here. I'm going home tomorrow.'

King Hassan heard of Ghadaffi's threat to walk out of the conference. He passed a note to Nasser: 'Brother Excellency, the President of Libya has ordered his plane to be ready straight away and he is planning to leave. His abrupt departure before the conference closes will be interpreted as meaning that the conference is in a crisis. Please do all you can to persuade the President of Libya to remain until the conference ends.' Nasser did as he was bidden and Ghadaffi stayed to the end.

However, Ghadaffi asked Nasser to stop off in Libya on his

*The Moroccan leader who disappeared in Paris in October 1965. General Oufkir was convicted by a French court of complicity in his disappearance.

way back to Cairo and he agreed to do this. He had a tremendous reception from the crowds everywhere. Later he received a message from Brezhnev: 'Doctor Chazov has heard the news that you spent five hours standing up in a Jeep and followed this up by making a speech lasting an hour. This is absolutely contrary to his instructions and a grave danger to your health.'

President Nimeiry came to Libya with Nasser, and the three Presidents signed what was called the 'Tripoli Pact', which envisaged a complete union of their countries. This represented in a way one half of the military equation which Nasser had been trying to work out for the past two years: how to weigh up the rival advantages of an active second front and of greater depth. Libya and the Sudan offered Egypt depth; a federation would consolidate this. They held out other advantages too. Ghadaffi had expressed his willingness to buy Russian arms on Egypt's behalf.

A month after the Libyan revolution, when the new regime's relationship with Egypt was still a matter for conjecture in the rest of the world, the Americans had offered Ghadaffi Phantoms and the French had offered him Mirages. But Nasser sent me over to Ghadaffi with a note saying he did not want Libya to buy any arms on Egypt's behalf for the time being. If he could get Phantoms, he said, that would be excellent – though he did not think the Americans were really prepared to supply them. He should try to get Mirages from France, particularly now that the deal arranged with Iraq appeared to have fallen through. On their side the Sudanese were in a position to offer us facilities in their northern airfields, which were outside the range o Israeli bombers.

Another consideration which made Nasser at this time pay more attention to the concept of depth was the disarray among some of our potential allies in the second front. The quarrel between King Hussein and the Fedayin was growing in intensity. We maintained good relations with the Fedayin, and when the Israelis raided their bases inside Jordan they asked us to supply them with anti-tank guns. I took two of their leaders, Abu Lutf and Abu Iyad, to see the Soviet Ambassador and two days later we got a message that the Soviets were prepared to give the

Fedayin ten anti-tank guns: how should they be delivered? The Fedayin suggested that to speed things up the guns should be supplied from Egyptian stocks, and that the ten new guns should be sent to Egypt as replacements. Nasser gave orders for this to be done.

Soon there was more help forthcoming. When Yasser Arafat was in Moscow with Nasser he had seen Mazurov and discussed arms supplies. Mazurov gave no immediate undertaking, but two or three weeks after we got back Ambassador Vinogradov brought Nasser a letter in which it was stated that the Soviet Central Committee, on Nasser's recommendation, had decided to give the Palestine resistance movement arms worth $500,000.

By the time Nasser returned to Cairo from Libya some of President Nimeiry's ministers were already beginning to have cold feet about the implications of the Tripoli Pact, and in consequence the original idea of a federation between the three countries was watered down to a loose confederation. Even so, had it survived, this would have been a step in the right direction.

All this time the Israelis had been stepping up their programme of subjecting Nasser, and his Government, and the Egyptian people, to the maximum humiliation: the aim was to make us appear totally impotent, and so bring about the collapse of the regime and the disruption of the proposed union with Libya and the Sudan. While the Rabat conference was still in session they landed on the Red Sea coast of Egypt and carried off a complete radar installation. Later their planes made frequent raids in depth, including the attacks on Abu Zaabal and on the school at Bahr el-Bakkar, which resulted in heavy loss of life. We were trying to establish our missile sites in a 30-kilometre strip west of the Suez Canal where the army was concentrated, and where our army commanders were convinced, the fate of the Middle East would eventually be decided. But as we worked, the Israelis bombed. No praise can be too high for the civilian engineers and workers who laboured on the missile sites. They worked in close co-operation with, and under the supervision of the army, but they were daily exposed to ruthless enemy attacks. No fewer than 4,000 of them were killed. From the end of 1969 to the middle of 1970, when the new Russian missiles were installed, they made a superhuman effort against heavy odds. I believe that this was the finest hour of the ordinary working man in Egypt.

It was in these circumstances that Nasser decided to go on a secret visit to Moscow to thrash out the whole question of Egypt's air defences with the Soviet leaders.

7. CRISIS IN MOSCOW

He was ill – an attack of flu on top of all his other complaints – and had been warned of the extreme cold in Moscow at that time of year. Nevertheless, he felt that he was bound to go, and so early in the morning of Thursday 22 January 1970, we went on board a special Soviet plane which was waiting in the military part of Cairo Airport.

There was something gloomy about this large plane with only a few people in it – the crew up in front, four or five guards, a couple of doctors, and besides Nasser only General Fawzi and myself, and two Russians, Sergei Vinogradov, the Ambassador in Cairo and General Katyshkin, who had succeeded General Lashinkov as head of the Soviet Military Mission in Egypt, after Lashinkov suffered a minor heart attack and had to be hospitalized in Cairo.

We reached Moscow airport between 9.30 and 10.00. The plane taxied to the end of the tarmac, and when we got out we found Podgorny and Kosygin waiting with a single guard to greet us. A fleet of the usual black, curtained cars took us to Villa Number One on Lenin Hills, one of the houses available for official visitors. Near the villa is a stadium with a Health Centre in it which is often used by government officials and contains rooms for massage and exercise, a swimming-pool, and so on, as well as a big reception hall. This was only a short drive away for the Egyptian party, and it was decided to hold our talks there.

Podgorny and Kosygin asked us whether we would like to rest and start talks the next day, but Nasser said he would prefer to get down to business straight away. So the first meeting was

83

fixed for the same afternoon – by now Murad Ghaleb, the Egyptian ambassador in Moscow, had joined the party.

Nasser opened this meeting with an explanation of the reasons which had brought him to Moscow. The fate of the whole Middle East, he said, was going to be decided in the strip of land about thirty kilometres either side of the Suez Canal. Israel's deep penetration raids and low-flying attacks on the interior of Egypt seemed designed with two objects in mind: first, they were intended to forestall all attempts by Egypt to build up a missile wall which could cover an attack across the Canal; and second, they were aimed at breaking the morale of the home front. Israel had failed to force Egypt into surrender in 1967, but was determined to do so now.

Nasser said that the whole of Egypt felt unprotected – naked. Many hundreds of civilian workers as well as troops had been killed. He said he had always believed that Israel's advantage in the air must be matched by some equivalent advantage on the Egyptian side, and that for the immediate future this could only be in air defence. He spoke firmly, but I could see that he was tense.

Brezhnev began to defend the SAM-2s, with which Egypt was already equipped. Nasser said he had nothing against the SAM-2s except that they were not effective against aircraft flying below 500 metres and not particularly effective between 500 and 1,000 metres. The Russians' own technicians in Egypt could bear witness to this. (SAM-2s had actually been installed in Egypt before the 1967 War but, in the surprise of the Israeli air-strike, they were never fired. When Zakharov gave his assurance about Egypt's defences, therefore, nobody in Cairo knew – perhaps the Russians themselves did not know – the SAM-2's limitations; certainly, nobody dreamed that the Israelis, with the help of American electronics, would find the answer to the missiles so swiftly.) Nasser told Brezhnev that he wanted to be able to protect Cairo, Alexandria, and other vulnerable areas as well as the canal front. He particularly stressed the importance of Alexandria, because now that Port Said was out of action and the Red Sea virtually closed it was Egypt's only port, taking the whole of her maritime traffic. If the Israelis bombed Alexandria, said Nasser, Egypt would be under a blockade.

The discussions went on, becoming heated at times, and it looked as though there might be a complete deadlock. But this danger was averted when Brezhnev admitted that the SAM-3 would meet Egypt's need and that they were prepared to let Egypt have them. 'Our friend Nasser,' said Brezhnev, 'always gets what he wants.'

After this the discussion moved on to the quantities of SAM-3s that would be needed, but it was decided to postpone further consideration of this aspect until the following day, when General Fawzi and Marshal Grechko would have had a chance to get together and consider the areas that would have to be defended. So we left these two, together with General Katyshkin and some other experts, working on this.

Early the next morning General Fawzi came to Nasser's bedroom to brief him. He had brought with him to Moscow a list of areas that would have to be defended. These included, besides the Canal front, Cairo, Alexandria, and Aswan, industrial centres such as Mahalla Kubra, Kafr el-Dawar, Shibin el-Kom, Shubra el-Kheima, and Helwan. It was clear that the crews needed to man all these sites simply did not exist in Egypt. Nasser asked Fawzi about the possibility of switching crews from SAM-2 sites, but probably by then a new idea was beginning to form in his mind.

The two full delegations met again in the Health Centre at ten o'clock. Brezhnev began by saying that the decision which had been reached the day before presented many difficulties; the targets which Egypt wanted defended were so vast. Obviously Grechko had briefed Brezhnev on these just as Fawzi had briefed Nasser, and for the first time Brezhnev appreciated the full extent of Egypt's needs. Nasser pointed out that Egypt had crews trained on SAM-2s and suggested that some of these might be switched straight away to SAM-3s. But he was told that it would take at least six months for SAM-2 crews to be able to operate SAM-3s and that their training should preferably be carried out in the Soviet Union. So it looked as if there was going to be a gap of at least six months during which Egypt would continue to be exposed to low-flying Israeli attacks – in which, indeed, Egypt would be worse off than ever, since some of the crews at present manning SAM-2s would be away in the Soviet Union being trained on SAM-3s. During this dangerous period Egypt would be exposed to both low-level and high-level attack by Israeli aircraft.

Then Nasser produced his bombshell. The only way to bridge this gap, he said, would be for the Russians to give Egypt the necessary crews. Brezhnev and the rest were not prepared for this demand. Nasser said he appreciated that what he was asking was a hard thing for them to comply with, but he said it was the only solution he could see. He could not allow the army to be destroyed or civilian morale to collapse. Egypt had stuck it out for three years and were not going to surrender now. The hopes of the entire Arab world depended on the decisions we were making today. Nasser said he was not asking that Soviet crews should be placed in the front line. Egypt would go on manning the sites on the canal; what he was asking of his hosts was that they should undertake the manning of the sites in the interior.

Grechko had a word with Brezhnev, and then Brezhnev said that the problem was not just one of crews; missiles were only part of a complicated defence system requiring aircraft as well. 'All right,' said Nasser, 'send the planes too.' Brezhnev said that this would be a step with serious international implications. It would provide all the making of a crisis between the Soviet Union and the United States. Nasser asked him: 'Why is it the Americans can always escalate their support whereas we sometimes behave as if we were scared . . .' Brezhnev interrupted him: 'We are not scared of anybody. We are the strongest power on earth. But you must understand that this will involve a considerable risk, and I don't know that we are justified in taking it. We must weigh up our position.' Nasser said: 'As far as my own position goes I have made the necessary calculations. Let me be quite frank with you. If we do not get what I am asking for everybody will assume that the only solution is in the hands of the Americans. We have never seen the Americans backward in helping the Israelis. But Egypt is an anti-imperialist outpost in the Middle East, if Egypt falls to American-Israeli force the whole Arab world will fall. We are not asking you to fight for us – we want to keep our independence. But as far as I can see, you are not prepared to help us in the same way that America helps Israel. This means that there is only one course open to me: I shall go back to Egypt and I shall tell the people the truth. I shall tell them that the time has come for me to step down and hand over to a pro-American President. If I cannot save them, somebody else will have to do it. That is my final word.'

Nasser's words electrified the room. At once Brezhnev got to his feet and said: 'Comrade Nasser, don't talk like this. You are the leader . . .' Nasser interrupted: 'I am a leader who is bombed every day in his own country, whose army is exposed and whose people are naked. I have the courage to tell our people the unfortunate truth – that, whether they like it or not, the Americans are masters of the world. I am not going to be the one who surrenders to the Americans. Someone else will come in my place who will have to do it.'

There were outcries on the Russian side: 'Please let us talk things over. What is it you really want? Give us another day and we will see what can be done.' Nasser said he could not wait another day, so the Russians proposed a break of ten minutes while they talked among themselves. The Egyptian delegation went into the garden. 'So,' I said to the President, 'we are on the brink?' Nasser said: 'No, I was not indulging in brinkmanship. What I said represents my honest conviction. I should be deceiving the people if I behaved otherwise. We have been training an army, but now the Israelis are using tactics we are not equipped to face – raids in depth, and raids against civilians. When children are killed and when soldiers die because they have no defence the whole situation is changed.'

The Soviets decided that the sending of their own crews to man the SAM-3 sites in Egypt was such a critical step that it should be put before the whole Politburo. Its members were summoned from wherever in the country they happened to be, and one by one they began arriving in their big black cars with the curtains drawn. For the first time in peace time twelve

Soviet marshals were brought in to share the deliberations of the Politburo.

We went back to Villa Number One for lunch. Our next meeting had been fixed for six o'clock. As soon as we came into the room it was clear that a decision had been reached. Brezhnev made the opening statement. 'Comrade Nasser,' he said, 'the Soviet Union has today taken a decision fraught with grave consequences. It is a decision unlike any we have ever taken before. It will need your help in carrying out, and it will call for restraint on your part.' Then we were told the number of SAM-3 batteries they were going to give us and the positions in which they would be placed, and the number of men who would come with them. Eighty Soviet aircraft were going to be sent, preceded by four high-altitude supersonic reconnaissance planes – X500s the Russians called them, though the West now knows them as MiG-25s. About 1800 Egyptians were to come to the Soviet Union for six months' training.

We could all sense the changed atmosphere in this meeting – the marshals and politicians on the whole enthusiastic about the decision, but among some of them, particularly Kosygin, the confirmed pessimist, enthusiasm tempered with uneasiness.

Nasser spoke in reply. He realized the historic nature of the decision, and was grateful for it. Egypt would not gamble with what was being given her; on the contrary, it was his intention to play things down as much as possible, because his main aim was to concentrate on training the armed forces. He could promise that with the help which was now to come we should be able to complete our preparations for the battle. 'I only want your crews to be here for a limited time,' he told the Russians. 'I don't want them to be in Egypt when the battle starts. But the intervening period is going to be a very difficult one, and they will help us to bridge it. If the Israelis had been allowed to go on sapping the morale of the public and of the Army they would have been able to come and take whatever they pleased. We could never again have held our heads high.'

At one point Brezhnev left his place in the middle of the opposite side of the table and came round and sat beside me. 'Gospodin Heikal,' he said, 'all this is secret.' I said of course I knew it was secret. 'But it is important,' said Brezhnev, 'that it should stay secret for a long time. Of course one day the Americans and the Israelis are bound to know, but before that happens, we come to your domain. How can we present it to the world? I want you to work out a scheme so that we can face the campaign they are certain to wage against us – against both Egypt and the Soviet Union.' I said: 'Mr Secretary; it is up to the statesmen to make the big decisions. We can always find ways and means by which we can present their decisions to the world.'

That was typical of Brezhnev; he was brilliant at public relations. He was, I suppose you would say, a showy man: his words and his actions were all those of a man who enjoyed power, enjoyed exercising his authority, and enjoyed showing his strength. His dress seemed to emphasize his status: his clothes were, for a Russian leader, well cut and he was the only one of the Russian hierarchy who obviously took care of his suits and looked after his appearance. Even his jokes – and he was full of jokes – showed his power. 'Don't let Gromyko deceive you,' he called across to Mahmoud Riad at one point, 'he is full of deceit.' And, like Khrushchev, Brezhnev seemed to have an inexhaustible store of Russian anecdotes and proverbs to illustrate any point.

All these were tools he used to achieve his end – and so too was his action in getting up, walking round the table and consulting me personally on the presentation of this momentous Russian decision. I was trying to get up as he spoke but he stood too close over me, and I was flattered – who would not have been? – by the gesture; yet at the same time I could see how Brezhnev used such means to exercise his sway.

When we got back to Cairo an obvious first priority was to prepare the sites for the new missiles, and it was here that the civilians continued to make such a heroic contribution. But the programme was costly in money as well as in lives. Egypt was desperately short of cement, which became a commodity more precious than gold, because this was the year when the High Dam was due to be finished, and the government in effect found itself committed to building two High Dams simultaneously, one at Aswan and one for the missiles. When it came to the allocation of cement the missiles had to have priority.

By the beginning of April the first Russian reconnaissance planes arrived and were installed in the air bases at Janaklis and Beni Suef, both in the desert not far from Alexandria. On 18 April they had their first brush with the Israelis. Some Israeli planes approached Sukhna, and the Russian planes scrambled, whereupon the Israelis headed back towards Sinai. The Russians pursued them, all communications between them going out over the intercom in Russian. This was reported to Nasser, who was puzzled. How did this square with all the talk about the need for preserving the utmost secrecy? My own theory was that this was how the game was played between the super-powers: it was a signal to the Americans that the Russians had arrived in Egypt. Whatever the explanation might be, the Israelis themselves got the message. There was no more raiding in depth after 18 April.

The same explanation may be behind the curious story of the arrival in Alexandria, a few days later, of the first shipment of missiles. Again, obedient to the strict injunction about secrecy, we had arranged for the ship to arrive after dark and to be berthed in a remote corner of the harbour. All security pre-cautions were increased. Then the unloading began. When it was completed, the Russians, to our astonishment, chose to drive the consignment to the chosen missile site through the centre of the city, and at noon, the Russians sitting openly on the trucks, waved to the crowds as they passed and shouted '*asdiqa!*' (friends). From which it can be concluded that the Russians had told the Americans in advance of the coming of the missiles, just as the Americans informed the Russians about their sale of arms to Iran.

8. THE ROGERS INITIATIVE

The American Secretary of State launched 'the Rogers Plan' on 9 December. In a speech to a conference on adult education he said that American policy 'is to encourage the Arabs to accept a permanent peace based on a binding agreement, and to urge Israel to withdraw from occupied territory when her territorial integrity is ensured'. He said that 'detailed provisions of peace relating to security safeguards on the ground should be worked out between the parties' under the auspices of Dr Jarring, following the pattern set at Rhodes in 1948. 'In the context of peace and agreement on specific security safeguards, withdrawal of Israel from Egyptian territory would be required.' Such 'security safeguards' should cover Sharm el-Sheikh, demilitarized zones in Sinai, and 'final arrangements in the Gaza Strip.' It cannot be said that either side received the plan with enthusiasm. Officially, Egypt neither accepted nor rejected it; but at *Al Ahram* we at once said that it could not be the basis of anything. On 22 December, on the other hand, the Israeli Cabinet rejected the proposals as 'appeasement of the Arabs'. In a press conference the next day Rogers said he thought 'appeasement' was an unfortunate word to use since it suggested that the Arabs were enemies of the United States, whereas both sides had enjoyed friendly relations for years.

Early in 1970 the Americans announced that they would like to send the Assistant Secretary of State, Joseph Sisco, to Cairo, if Nasser would receive him. Nasser certainly would: he had several reasons for wanting to see the American. In the first place, of course, we wanted to find out the lines along which the Americans were thinking: he also wanted to find out how much they knew about what was going on in Egypt, because work on the missile wall was going ahead at full speed. So Sisco had a quiet reception in Cairo, unlike the stormy scenes which greeted him elsewhere in the Arab world. (In Beirut the American Cultural Centre was burned to the ground and in Amman there were such violent demonstrations that his visit had to be cancelled.) He arrived in Cairo on 10 April 1970 and stayed for four days.

Sisco saw Nasser on 12 April. He told him that the Nixon administration had 'more flexibility' towards the Middle East problem than any other, and that, though he would be a fool if he tried to deny that the United States was committed to support of Israel, what they wanted was a 'balanced policy'. They did not agree with Golda Meir that all that was needed was to get direct negotiations going between Israel and the Arabs. He said that America was the only country which could help to secure Israel's withdrawal from the occupied territories, but that to do this they 'needed a fulcrum'. The Rogers Plan was in his opinion such a fulcrum, and he also gave it as his opinion that it was 'ninety-five per cent in your favour'.

Nasser pointed out that the United States continued to give Israel full support in the Security Council, whatever she did, and never denounced her many illegalities and aggressions. It was American planes which had bombed an Egyptian school four days before, killing fifty children. 'For the first time I feel bitterness,' said Nasser. 'There was no bitterness at the time of Dulles and the Baghdad Pact, but now, with the killing of children and workers and civilians, there is.' The meeting was unproductive.

However, on 1 May Nasser made a Labour Day speech which contained an overture of a sort to President Nixon. He said that he had received Sisco at the President's request; now he wanted to speak to President Nixon directly. 'I want to tell President Nixon,' he said, 'that if the United States wants peace it should order Israel to withdraw from the occupied Arab territories.' The other alternative would be to refrain from arming Israel while she continued there. If she did neither 'we can only assume that she wants Israel to continue the occupation and to force the Arabs to surrender'.

The next day a special letter was sent to President Nixon containing the relevant passages in his Labour Day speech. At a news conference on 25 June 1970 Rogers announced that his government had undertaken a new political initiative to encourage the Arab states and Israel 'to stop shooting and start talking'. The initiative called on all parties to restore the cease-fire for a limited period and to subscribe to certain basic principles relating to peace and security set out in the form of a report from Dr Jarring to U Thant.

The terms of the new Rogers initiative reached Nasser while he and his party, of which I was one, were in Tripoli. Mahmoud Riad studied it and came to the conclusion that it contained nothing new. Another copy of the plan had gone to Cairo,where Anwar Sadat saw it. Like Riad he thought little of it, and made a speech to the Foreign Affairs Committee of the Central Committee expressing his views. But then Nasser himself took a closer look at the plan and decided that it fitted in with his overall strategy. By now the army was ready and the Soviet Union was actively engaged in the defence of our civil population against air attacks. The most important thing in Nasser's view was to finish building the missile wall. When completed this would not only protect our armed forces on the west bank of the Suez Canal, but would give protection over a strip fifteen-twenty kilometres wide on the east bank, and so give cover for our troops crossing the Canal when the time came. I think it was probably from the outset, while he was still in Tripoli, that Nasser decided to accept the Rogers initiative, though nobody knew of his decision until much later.

9. THE SECOND MOSCOW VISIT

On 29 June Nasser paid his second visit of that year to the Soviet Union. I was then Minister of Information and an official member of our delegation. I remember the night we arrived we were greeted with the information that two Israeli Phantoms had been shot down. Next morning we heard that a Skyhawk had been shot down by a missile as well. So when we went into our meeting with the Soviets Nasser greeted Brezhnev: 'We have good news at last today – our boys have accounted for three Israeli aircraft.' Brezhnev looked at Marshal Grechko, who took a piece of paper out of his pocket, looked at it, went to Brezhnev, and talked to him in Russian. Brezhnev then said: 'Tovarish Nasser, I think you are mistaken in your calculations. According to our information your tally of planes yesterday was six.' Grechko had already been on to the chief Russian adviser on air defence in Egypt by the special direct telephone that had been installed to link the Ministry of Defence in Moscow with the office of the head of the Russian Military Mission in Cairo.

Kosygin showed a great deal of interest in Libya. He talked

for more than an hour on the subject, saying that according to his calculations the Libyans had the highest per capita production of oil in the world, each individual Libyan having, so to speak, seventy tons of oil a year. The figures seemed to fascinate him – but then, Kosygin was always fascinated by statistics. He was very interested when Nasser told him of the possibility of a complete union between Libya, Egypt and Syria.

There was one rather odd incident during this meeting in the Kremlin. At one point the door opened and a senior official from the Ministry of Foreign Affairs came into the room and gave a piece of paper to Vladimir Vinogradov, Deputy Minister of Foreign Affairs. Vinogradov gave the paper to Gromyko, the Minister of Foreign Affairs, who read it, got up, and took it to Kosygin. Kosygin read it, and gave it to Brezhnev. Brezhnev, read it, and gave it back to Kosygin. Kosygin then gave it to Podgorny. Podgorny read it, and gave it back to Kosygin, who gave it back to Brezhnev. Then Brezhnev signed it, and gave it to Kosygin, who signed it too. Then Podgorny signed. Then Podgorny gave it to Gromyko, who gave it to Vinogradov, who gave it back to the Foreign Office official. The official then left the room.

The whole transaction took, I suppose, about five minutes. It had begun while Nasser was speaking, but when he noticed that everyone was taken up with something else he stopped. When it was all over Brezhnev saw that the whole Egyptian delegation was staring at him, and presumably felt that he ought to give some sort of explanation. 'This is something that concerns you too,' he said. 'We have received information that there will be an attempt at a coup d'état against General Siad in Somalia tonight. We have accordingly decided to send him a telegram of warning. Now we have seen this telegram and approved it.'

Later, as we were going out of the meeting, Nasser said to me: 'Did you see what happened?' 'Over that bit of paper, you mean?' I asked. 'Yes,' said Nasser. 'It is too bureaucratic. If a telegram to General Siad in Somalia needs the signature of all those three, then we are in trouble. Now I understand why our requests take such a long time to produce results.'

10. ROGERS ACCEPTED

After our talk in the Kremlin Nasser went into Bervikha hospital for two weeks' treatment, and I came back to Cairo. To disguise this stay in hospital, it was put out that Nasser had further talks with the Soviet leadership midway through the period, but in fact these meetings were merely social visits by the leaders to Nasser's bedside. On 16 July, however, the day before Nasser left Moscow, he did have one more meeting with Brezhnev, in which he received a reply to his request for arms. At the earlier meeting he had mentioned to Brezhnev that he was going to accept Rogers's initiative. Brezhnev pushed his spectacles down his nose and stared at Nasser over the top of them. 'Do you mean to tell me you are going to accept a proposal with an American flag on it?' he asked. Nasser said: 'Exactly, I am going to accept it just because it has an American flag. We must have a breathing space so that we can finish our missile sites. We need to give our army a break, and to cut down our civilian casualities. We need a ceasefire, and the only ceasefire the Israelis will accept is one proposed by the Americans. But I don't think the initiative stands any chance of success. I wouldn't rate its chances at more than a half per cent.' Brezhnev was surprised, but I think he understood.

Nasser had decided that his acceptance of Rogers' initiative would be contained in a speech he was to deliver on 23 July, the anniversary of the 1952 revolution. It was a real agony for him to make this speech, the shock waves of which immediately went all round the Arab world. Some people assumed, because he had just been in Moscow, that the speech was a result of Soviet pressure, but as has been seen, the Russian leadership was as surprised by its contents as anyone.

I was at this time acting Minister of Foreign Affairs while Mahmoud Riad was on a visit to the Balkans, and it fell to me to negotiate the details of the ceasefire, which was sprung on us as the immediate consequence of the acceptance of Rogers's initiative. Donald Bergus, who was in charge of American interests in Cairo, informed me that immediately after the ceasefire came into effect the United States would arrange things so that Rabin would be recalled from Israel's Washington embassy to become Prime Minister, after which some real progress could be expected. Rabin had now taken over the role, for which the Americans had cast Dayan at the time of the Rogers Plan, of the de Gaulle who would convince the Israelis of the need to make concessions. We were taken by surprise by the sudden demand for a standstill ceasefire, which was something new for us. We had been thinking in terms of a ceasefire as in 1948 but this time we were told everything must be completed in a matter of hours. Nasser asked me to gain a bit of time for him: he needed six hours so that he could get some dummy missile batteries into position. The Americans would of course photograph from their satellites the exact position of everything at the moment of ceasefire, and Nasser wanted to be able later to replace these dummy missiles with real ones. So, though Donald Bergus was continually on the telephone to me saying that Washington and Tel Aviv were getting impatient, I managed to stall him by saying that we had to make sure the message reached our outlying garrisons in the Red Sea, that we did not want any accidents but a ceasefire that would stick, and so on. Nasser got his six hours, and by some miracle of improvisation the fake missile sites were prepared overnight ready for American photography by dawn the next day. The Americans were extremely annoyed by the moving of the missiles. They accused the Egyptians of cheating and, to punish them, ostentatiously agreed to supply Israel with more arms.

Egypt's acceptance of the ceasefire outraged many Arabs, particularly some of the Palestinians. Naif Hawatmeh and George Habash issued a statement to the effect that those Arabs who had grown tired of the struggle should leave it to the younger generation which was ready to make the necessary sacrifices. Nasser understood their bitterness. He was particularly worried that King Hussein might think his chance had come for a showdown with the Fedayin, on the grounds that their patron, Nasser, had apparently withdrawn his support. So he asked both King Hussein and Yasser Arafat to come to see him. King Hussein came first, on 20 August, and had many complaints to make about guerrillas being a state within a state, etc. Nasser spoke to him very frankly. 'I oppose any action you may be contemplating against the Fedayin,' he said. 'I don't want you to liquidate them or them to liquidate you. No doubt you have the strength to crush them, but to do this you will have to slaughter 20,000 people and your kingdom will be a kingdom of ghosts. I shall be telling the Fedayin that they should not work against you because they can't provide themselves with the things your Government organizes – education, communications, supplies, and so on. Both of you have to co-exist with each other: it's the only way.' King Hussein went away not a very happy man, and then, on 24 August, Yasser Arafat came. The atmosphere was not propitious because, only three weeks before, we had been obliged to close the guerrillas' radio station. This had been attacking Egypt, President Nasser, Rogers's initiative, and everything else in the strongest language. I was Minister of Information then, and was asked to try to get them to tone down their broadcasts. I told Abu Lutf, who was a responsible sort of person, that they could attack the Rogers's Initiative as much as they liked but they could not call those Arabs who had accepted it traitors. Two days later a coded message to the Palestinian radio station was intercepted by Egyptian intelligence. It read: 'Do not yield to pressure from any quarter. Attack anybody you like.' Nasser told the Minister of the Interior to close the station down, and he did so.

Nasser gave Arafat a frank explanation of what he was trying to do. He did not rate the chances of success for Rogers's initiative at more than one half per cent, but even that half per cent chance was worth a trial. He explained about the need to finish the rocket wall and to get the bridging equipment. Continuing the War of Attrition while Israel enjoyed complete air superiority was simply bleeding ourselves to death, he said. Although he could not of course tell this to the Palestinians, it was at about this time that, with the missile wall now becoming effective, Nasser gave General Fawzi orders to prepare for operation Granite 1, which was to provide for crossing the canal and pushing as far as the Sinai passes.

11. THE CAIRO CONFERENCE

By the beginning of September relations between King Hussein and the Fedayin had deteriorated still further. Nasser was on holiday in Mersa Matruh at the time. Doctor Chazov had been sending messages from Moscow that it was absolutely essential he should have at least a month's complete rest: no radio, no interviews, nothing. Nasser agreed to rest for ten days. But the day he arrived in Mersa Matruh, King Hussein started operations against the Fedayin. Some of their leaders who were in Egypt at the time came to see me. They argued that if no word of any sort came from Nasser this would be taken by King Hussein and his entourage as the green light to go ahead. By the evening the situation in Amman was clearly deteriorating and with the greatest reluctance we broke in on Nasser to tell him the news. He decided as a first step to send General Mohammed Ahmed Sadiq, Chief of Staff of the Egyptian Army, to Amman on 17 September to remind King Hussein of his warning against trying to liquidate the Fedayin, and to convince him that civil war in Jordan would simply play into the hands of the Israelis and the Americans. General Sadiq came back with the impression that King Hussein was trying to play for time but that many members of his own family and entourage were urging him towards a final showdown.

From that moment the situation deteriorated rapidly. The Syrians sent some of their tanks across the Jordanian border to Ramtha. The Syrian head of state, Dr Nureddin Atassi, came to Cairo on 21 September and it was clear that the Syrians were anxious to intervene by force in the fighting in Amman. The Americans notified the Russians that they would be unable to tolerate such a development, and the Russians passed this American warning, which was very gravely worded, on to Nasser. The atmosphere was one of an extremely serious international crisis, and it was at this point that Nasser called a meeting of Arab heads of state.

It assembled in Cairo over Tuesday and Wednesday 22–23 September, and from the outset it was apparent that there were two schools of thought among the participants. There were those, like Ghadaffi and Nimeiry, who thought King Hussein should be, as it were, put in the dock, but there were others, including Nasser, who thought it was essential not to lose sight of the main purpose of the conference, which was to stop the massacre. Nasser argued that if we treated King Hussein as an outcast he would have an excuse to break with the other Arab governments and step up his campaign against the Fedayin. Nasser always thought that Hussein had a good side to his somewhat Jekyll and Hyde nature and that the wisest course was to play on this good side.

On 22 September, a delegation was sent to Amman, headed by President Nimeiry and including Bahi Ladgham, Prime Minister of Tunisia and General Sadiq. Their mission was to see King Hussein and try to establish contact with some of the Fedayin leaders, including Yasser Arafat who was thought to be hiding somewhere in Jebel Amman. They came back obviously shaken by what they had seen. Ladgham said it was not what would be described in any civilized country as a 'police action' but rather a huge military operation. General Sadiq thought that an operation of that size must have been prepared a long time in advance. By then Nasser had information that the operation had been planned in co-operation with the CIA and some Jordanians including Wasfi Tel. King Feisal added a word of caution: we had to be certain who exactly was responsible for the fighting – the Fedayin as well as the Jordanian Army had guns. There was a rumour, he added, that Abu Ammar (Yasser Arafat) was in the Egyptian Embassy. Nasser said that he had gone there on one occasion, in order to meet General Sadiq, but he was not, as alleged, hiding there. Perhaps a fragment of the dialogue between the delegates can best give an indication of the atmosphere at this meeting:

King Feisal: 'I agree with Your Excellency [President Nasser] that all this appears to be a plan to liquidate the resistance movement.'

Ghadaffi: 'I don't agree with the efforts you are making. I think we should send armed forces to Amman – armed forces from Iraq and Syria.'

King Feisal: 'You want to send our armies to fight in Jordan? It is not practicable.'

President Nasser: 'I think we should be patient.'

King Feisal (looking at Ghadaffi): 'I think that if we are going to send our armies anywhere we should send them to fight the Jews.'

Ghadaffi: 'What Hussein is doing is worse than the Jews. It's only a difference in the names.'

President Nasser: 'The difficulty is that if we send troops to Jordan this will only result in the liquidation of the rest of the Palestinians. I would like you to hear the contents of a message I received this morning from the Soviet Union. They are asking us to exercise the utmost restraint because the international situation is becoming extremely delicate, and any miscalculation might result in the Arabs losing all the reputation which they have recovered over the past three years.'

Ghadaffi: 'I still object. If we are faced with a madman like Hussein who wants to kill his people we must send someone to seize him, handcuff him, stop him from doing what he's doing, and take him off to an asylum.'

King Feisal: 'I don't think you should call an Arab King a madman who should be taken to an asylum.'

Ghadaffi: 'But all his family are mad. It's a matter of record.'

King Feisal: 'Well, perhaps all of us are mad.'

President Nasser: 'Sometimes when you see what is going on in the Arab world, your Majesty, I think this may be so. I suggest we appoint a doctor to examine us regularly and find out which ones are crazy.'

King Feisal: 'I would like your doctor to start with me, because in view of what I see I doubt whether I shall be able to preserve my reason.'

President Nasser: 'Anyhow, let us get back to the main subject. I suggest a statement be issued immediately, in the name of President Nimeiry, saying that King Hussein gave the delegation a pledge that there would be an end to the fighting.'

Ghadaffi: 'Hussein will not back down unless he feels a dagger at his throat.'

President Nimeiry went back to Amman two days later, on

24 September, and they managed to smuggle Yasser Arafat out with them when they came back next day. King Hussein gave Nimeiry, Hussein el-Shafei, and Saad Abdullah, the Kuwait Minister of Defence, permission to go to Jebel Amman to contact Yasser Arafat. (Shafei was a member of the A.S.U. High Executive Committee in Egypt but, in fact, he was in the delegation simply because the Palestinians had asked that one emissary be 'someone from the Egyptian revolution' and Shafei had been a member of the original Revolutionary Council Command.) Anyway, while the delegation was with the beleagured Palestinians, Saad Abdullah told his secretary to take off his *dishdashah* (the long gown worn in Arabia) and give it to Arafat, who got to the airport in this disguise.

The whole Nile Hilton Hotel had been taken over for the conference, and each head of state was allocated a complete floor to himself, his advisers, guards etc. Nasser was on the eleventh floor. I was talking to him there at about noon one day – it was a fairly slack period in the conference because President Nimeiry was in Amman and there was nothing much we could do till he came back – and said I thought it was rather nice to stay in the hotel from time to time, for a change. Nasser said: 'It doesn't strike me as nice: it's like a barracks.' Then he said he was hungry: 'Heikal, do you think the food at the Hilton is different from the food I get at home?' I said, 'That depends. What are you going to ask for?' He said he wanted some sandwiches, so a waiter was summoned, and came with exactly the same white cheese sandwiches Nasser always had at home – the explanation being that, for security reasons, all the regular kitchen staff of the Hilton had been moved and been replaced by the personal cooks of all the heads of state staying in the hotel. But I told Nasser that this was not the sort of order he ought to give in a hotel like the Hilton. 'What would people order here?' he asked. 'Well,' I said, 'If they wanted something to eat at midday they wouldn't ask for a cheese sandwich. They would probably have a smoked salmon canapé and a dry martini.' I meant to tease him. 'Now you're talking about drink,' said Nasser. 'Aren't they afraid that in after life this will take them to hell?' I said I thought God was probably very tolerant, 'What matters is how a man behaves.' Nasser paused for a minute, and then said: 'Are you a believer?' 'Yes, certainly I am,' I said. 'What happens after this life?' asked Nasser. I said: 'That is a very difficult question. I think that heaven and hell are here on this earth: we can make our lives here a heaven or a hell. But after death I think there is non-existence, nothingness.' 'Nothingness?' said Nasser. 'Do you mean that people who perform good actions on earth do not go to Paradise?' 'I don't know,' I said. 'I think Paradise and Hell are symbolic.' 'That means that after death we finish, and that is all?' he asked. 'That's all,' I said. 'That isn't very reassuring,' said Nasser. Three days later he was dead.

Every conference has its funny side, and this one was no exception. There was, for example, the desertion of Brigadier Mohammed Daoud. King Hussein had made Brigadier Daoud Prime Minister of Jordan when he decided to get rid of Abdul Munim Rifai and substitute a military government for a civilian one, the better to deal with the Fedayin. General Daoud had a daughter living in Beirut and when she heard that her father was attending the summit conference she came to Cairo and appealed to him not to support the King's action against the Fedayin. So, even more vigorously, did Ghadaffi. He told the unfortunate Prime Minister that he was committing treason to the Arab cause and reduced him to tears. 'What can I do?' the General asked. 'Desert!' urged Ghadaffi. 'Stay here and send in your resignation.' The general was persuaded, and Ghadaffi told Nasser, who thought this quite a useful development as it would help to put pressure on King Hussein. But, having won his point, Ghadaffi did not know what to do with his convert. He got in touch with me, and I suggested, as Minister of Information, that the general should give a Press Conference to explain to the world the reasons for his resignation. 'Where's he now?' I asked. 'I can't tell you,' said Ghadaffi mysteriously. 'He is in hiding, but I will take you to him.' So with great secrecy we set out, only to arrive, to my considerable surprise, at Kubba Palace. The renegade's secret hiding place turned out to be Ghadaffi's suite in the Palace. Subsequently Mohammed Daoud went to Libya and was given Libyan nationality.

The meeting ended on 27 September with an agreement signed between King Hussein and Yasser Arafat which provided for an immediate ceasefire and the withdrawal of all army and guerrilla forces from every city in the country on the evening of that day. I was busy with General Sadiq making arrangements for the observation committee, headed by Bahi Ladgham, which was to set off again the next day for Amman. Nasser looked in and I walked with him to the lift, to take any final instructions he might have to give me. 'I want to go home and eat a decent meal,' he said. In spite of his cheese sandwiches there had been too much formal entertainment during the conference for his liking. He said he would go to bed early because the next day he would have to say goodbye to the departing Kings and Presidents. He got into the lift and went down. It was the last time I was to see him, except for a few minutes before his death.

12. THE DEATH OF NASSER

While Nasser was being driven home he heard that Ghadaffi was on his way to the airport: the Libyan leader was leaving without telling anybody because he did not want to disturb his hosts. Nasser told his driver to go to the airport, but found that Ghadaffi had already left and went back home. I spoke to him later that evening on the telephone because the British Ambassador, Sir Richard Beaumont, had come to bring me a message from Sir Alec Douglas-Home thanking the Egyptian Government for its help over the British hostages held by the hijackers in Jordan.

Next morning he was busy seeing off the delegates. He called me up twice – the first time at about 9.30 a.m. – just before setting out for the airport. He said he felt very tired and wanted something to make him sleep for twenty-four hours. 'What I need,' he said, 'is a long, deep, sleep.' His legs were aching. 'What will you do about that?' I asked. He said he would put his legs in hot water and salt – a remedy for aches the village people of Egypt believe in. 'That isn't any good,' I protested.

At one o'clock he called me up again to ask if there was

anything important happening in the world. He also wanted to know the international reaction to the agreement reached in Cairo. Then he said he was going to the airport 'for the last farewell', with the Shaikh of Kuwait, and that after that he would go home and have a long, deep sleep. Somehow, when he said the words 'the last' (*al akhir*) I felt a shudder.

When he was at the airport seeing off the Shaikh he felt unable to stand, so he told his secretary to bring the car to where he was – he could not get back to where it was parked. He got into the car with difficulty and asked his doctor to follow him. By 3.30 he was back home. His wife and children were waiting to have lunch with him, but he said he did not want any; he was too tired. He went to his room and lay down on the bed. Then he felt the diabetic pains which sometimes affected him. He asked his wife to get him a glass of orange-juice. She went and squeezed it for him herself. He had one sip and asked for the doctor to come. Doctor Sawy Habib came and he called other doctors. By four o'clock they had taken an electro-cardiogram reading and found that he had had a heart attack.

I was called on the telephone and told that the President wanted to see me. I noticed something odd about the voice of the secretary who spoke to me, and as I hurried over to his house, I felt a sense of depression. I ran up the stairs to his room, not waiting for the lift (the lift had been put in only after his first heart attack – though he had always managed to keep the fact of his having had an attack secret from his wife). In the bedroom, I found Sami Sharaf and Sharawy Gomaa, the Ministers for Presidential Affairs and the Interior, and Mohamed Ahmed, the President's private secretary. 'What's the matter?' I asked. One of the doctors said: 'Hush: he's very tired.'

The doctors were around him. One began massaging his heart, another put an electric current through his body, and I saw it shivering with the shock. Another jumped on the bed and began working on his chest. There was no response. But nobody realized that the end had really come.

Vice-President Sadat and General Fawzi had been sent for, and soon arrived. All of us stood around in that room for two hours, till seven o'clock, refusing to face the fact that we were in the presence of a dead man. He lay on the bed in his pyjamas; his face looked very calm. I remember General Fawzi saying to the room at large: 'Do something.' Hussein Shafei, another Vice-President, went to a corner of the room and started to pray. It may be that I was one of the first to realize, if only subconsciously, what had happened, because I remember repeating to myself over and over again: 'It can't be true: it can't be true. It can't happen: it can't happen.'

Suddenly one of the doctors collapsed into great groaning sobs. It was then, I think, that the truth which we had all been trying to hide from ourselves came out into the open, for suddenly everyone began to weep. Hearing the noise Nasser's wife came through the door. 'What's happening?' she asked. We saw that we had better leave the room for the family. Sadat went over to the bed, kissed the dead man's face, kissed his hand and pulled up the blanket. Many others of us went up to the bed. I remember, as I was leaving the room, seeing his widow pull the blankets down again and kiss the face and hands of her dead husband as terrible grief overwhelmed her.

13. THE FUNERAL

With the desolate cries of Nasser's wife sounding in our ears we went down to the salon on the ground floor of the President's house. Anwar Sadat was there, and besides him Hussein Shafei, Ali Sabri, a former Vice-President and a leading member of the Arab Socialist Union, Sami Sharaf, head of the Presidential Office, Sharawy Gomaa, Minister of the Interior, General Fawzi, Minister of War, General El-Leithy Nassif, Commander of the Presidential Guard, and myself. What was to happen now? What were we to do?

It was Nasser's custom to open a meeting of the cabinet or his close political advisers by asking me what I thought. He always liked to keep his own point of view to the end. I suspect he felt some of the others might conceal their real thoughts until they knew what his were, whereas I was above all a newspaper man and used to speaking my mind as well as writing it. On this occasion Sadat followed Nasser's example. When we were all gathered he looked at me and said: 'Well, Mohamed, what do you think should be done?'

I have never felt so responsible – perhaps I should say never felt so useful – as I did at this moment. Everyone in that room except for myself had an official career to think of, and though shattered with grief was bound to be wondering what effect the tragedy would have on his own position. But it was only by chance that I was there in an official capacity. I think it must have been as we went down the stairs that I came to the conclusion that my time as a Minister must be brought to an end.

My answer to Sadat was that we ought to call a joint meeting of the cabinet and the High Executive Committee of the ASU, as being the two highest political institutions in the country, and that the official announcement of the President's death should come out of this meeting. I thought we should follow the text of the Constitution, which would mean that he, Sadat, would become acting President until a plebiscite could be arranged to confirm the new President who would be chosen by Parliament on the recommendation of the High Executive Committee of the ASU. Nobody objected to these proposals or put forward any alternative. By this time an ambulance had come to take Nasser's body to the Kubba Palace, where it was to be lodged in the medical department. We all followed in our cars. At the Kubba Palace I drafted a statement announcing the President's death, and then, in my capacity as Minister of Information, I told my office to stop the prepared programmes on radio and television and replace them with Koran readings. The country immediately realized that something was wrong, without knowing what.

Then a preliminary meeting of the cabinet and High Executive Committee of the ASU was held. In it I recommended that the doctors who had attended Nasser should prepare an official report. This they did. Dr Mansur Faiz, the head of the medical team which was responsible for Nasser's treatment, wrote four lines on a prescription form he took from his bag stating that the President had died from a rupture of the aorta. Three other doctors signed.

It was now close to the time for a news bulletin on the radio, and obviously some explanation would have to be given on it for the sudden change of programmes. Sadat wanted me to broadcast the statement I had prepared, but I demurred. 'I don't think,' I told him, 'that I am the right person to do this. I believe, sir, it is essential that at this moment the country should be given a sense of continuity. I remember at the time of President Kennedy's assassination how important it was that the United States should be made to feel that the transfer of power had gone smoothly. I suggest you should yourself go on radio and television and tell the nation of President Nasser's death.'

Sadat agreed, and so we went together to my office in the Ministry of Information, which was on the tenth floor of the same building as houses the broadcasting studios. There Sadat read the prepared statement. In the confusion he had left his spectacles behind, so he had to borrow mine. Then Sadat left, and I went to the offices of *Al Ahram* to write the story.

The next day was one of terrible grief throughout the country. It was decided that the funeral should be on 1 October to give time for the journey for the many representatives from Arab and other countries who would certainly want to attend. Already certain groupings and manoeuvrings for position were taking place among those who were closest to the empty seat of power. I thought much about my own position, and became increasingly determined to leave the government and go back to *Al Ahram*.

Sadat asked us to form a committee to discuss what should be done about renewing the ceasefire, which was due to expire on 9 November. We heard that Kosygin, Chaban-Delmas, Sir Alec Douglas-Home, Elliot Richardson, and many other Asian and African heads of state would be coming to the funeral, and we knew that after their condolences had been paid they would ask us about the ceasefire. So a meeting was held at 6.00 p.m. on 30 September in General Fawzi's office, attended by Mahmoud Riad, Minister for Foreign Affairs, Amin Huwaidi, Minister of State, Hafez Ismail, Director of Intelligence, Sami Sharaf, Sharawy Gomaa, and myself. It was not easy to reach a conclusion. I felt myself that for purely political reasons we would have to agree to an extension of the ceasefire. True, the opera-

107

tional plan for Granite 1 was complete, but who could take the responsibility for ordering its implementation? It was now the end of September; whoever was nominated as the new President would have to be confirmed in office by plebiscite, the campaign for which would take up most of October. Would it be fair to expect him to give orders for a war to start only a few days after he had taken over the reins of office? Would it be fair to the country, still distracted by grief, to plunge it straight into battle? So I came down in favour of extending the ceasefire.

Some spoke up in favour of immediate action. It occurred to me that the best way of settling the matter was to get a professional opinion. General Fawzi had mentioned something about Upper Egypt not yet being covered by missile batteries. I said to him: 'Tell me, from a purely military point of view, are you ready for a resumption of hostilities?' He said: 'I am a soldier. If I am given an order *in writing*, I will do whatever is required of me by the political leadership.' That was significant. Never, while Nasser was alive, had he asked for any written orders. I said: 'That's not exactly an answer to my question. Does it suit you, from a military point of view, to start hostilities immediately, or would you like further time for preparation?' His answer was straightforward enough: 'If I am given two months,' he said, 'I think my position will be better. The missile batteries for Upper Egypt will be in place and I would feel more secure.' I said: 'Gentlemen, I think that gives us our answer. If the commander of the army thinks he could do with two more months, well and good. Two months or three months – there is no great difference. I think we should recommend extending the ceasefire for a further three months.' Some of those present protested that this was an unduly abrupt way to end the discussion, but in fact nobody was prepared any longer to argue in the opposing sense.

As we were leaving the meeting Sharawy Gomaa approached me and said: 'I think we should go somewhere where we can sit down and talk – you, and me, and Sami, and Amin Huwaidi.'

We all four got into his official Ministry of Interior car, a black Mercedes. He sat in the front with the other three of us in the back. My own car followed. Most of the roads were already blocked by the crowds which were pouring into the capital from all directions for the funeral. 'At any rate,' I said, 'in your car we ought to be able to reach the centre of the city.' (Sharawy had realized that there would be no chance next day of reaching his office from his house in Heliopolis, so he and Sami and Amin Huwaidi had decided that they would all three spend the night in the headquarters of the Suez Canal Authority in Garden City. From there they could easily cross to the Revolutionary Council Command building in Gezira, the starting point of the funeral procession. I was going to spend the night in my own flat, just across the river, so we were all going in the same direction.)

But when we got to Abbasiyah Square, four miles from the centre of the city, we found it was already completely blocked. Sharawy told his driver to turn left and try the back road by the citadel. When we reached the Police Training College, he stopped the car and turned round in his seat. 'Those three,' he said to us, 'Anwar Sadat, Hussein el-Shafei and Ali Sabri, are living in Kubba Palace and behaving as if they were a trium-virate, like Kosygin, Podgorny and Brezhnev, while we, the real Nasserites, the people closest to Nasser, have done nothing to decide on any common course of action. This is what makes me think we should discuss the situation together.'

I had always liked Sharawy, who had many good qualities, but I felt that on this occasion his frankness demanded equal frankness from me. 'Let's be clear about each other's positions,' I said. 'I have got a point of order to make and a piece of advice to give. The point of order is: if you want to co-ordinate as Ministers don't do it in front of me. I have made up my mind to quit – to leave the cabinet.' This made Sami Sharaf extremely angry. 'No,' he said. 'Either we all quit or we all stay.'

I urged him to be reasonable. 'I have never been part of the executive, like the rest of you,' I said. 'I have always been a newspaper man. I only accepted the job of Minister of Infor-mation as a result of extreme pressure from Nasser, and only undertook to do it for a year. Now six months have passed and Nasser is dead. I'm going to stick to journalism.'

Sami objected that if I did this it would look as if I was

unwilling to serve under anyone but Nasser, whereas they would give the impression of being willing to serve under anyone. I told Sami he was exaggerating. I had made my decision to leave the cabinet and was going to stick to it. So no 'co-ordination' of Ministers should take place in my presence.

My piece of advice was that it would be wrong for them to try to act together as Nasserites. 'If you do this,' I said, 'you will inevitably provoke a reaction, which will lead to a struggle for power. If there is going to be a clash of ideas I will play my part in it as a newspaper man, but if there is going to be a struggle for power based on personalities I will have nothing to do with it. The whole country will suffer.'

Sami became more and more excited. 'Nasser is not dead,' he cried.

'Come now, Sami,' I said. 'You must face physical facts. The man is dead. From now on everybody is going to be judged solely by what he himself can contribute to the welfare of the country. It's a new page opening for all of you.'

Sami began to weep and to shout that either everybody left or everybody stayed. I lost my temper, got out of Sharawy's car, walked back to my own, which was pulled up just behind, and drove back into Cairo.

Next day, Thursday 1 October, was the day of the funeral. General Fawzi had brought three divisions of the army into the city, but even so he began to doubt whether he would be able to maintain order. I received a telephone call from Anwar Sadat. He wanted to discuss a suggestion that had been put to him that, as the crowds might easily get out of hand and set fire to the city, the procession should be cancelled. I said I thought this would be a catastrophe – everyone would assume that something had gone terribly wrong. To save time the body should be flown by helicopter from Kubba Palace to the Revolutionary Council Command. Sadat put the suggestion to the military and they agreed, but then found that they could not land a helicopter there, so the body was flown to the grounds of the Gezira Sporting Club instead.

Then another problem arose. The doctors were worried that if there was a long funeral in the hot sun the body might begin to deteriorate. Others were worried that the crowds might seize the body from the coffin and suggested that it should be left empty. I said this would be taking an appalling risk. The crowds were certain to want to take turns in carrying the coffin, and if it was discovered that there was nothing in it, not just Cairo but the whole of Egypt would be burnt. The coffin must come, and the body must be in it. So the body was brought by helicopter and the funeral duly started.

I had been assigned to escort Kosygin during the funeral. He was staying in the Soviet Embassy, which is not far from my flat on the west bank of the Nile. When I got to the embassy early in the morning it was clear that we were not going to be able to reach the starting point for the funeral, even on foot, as the bridges had been opened to Nile shipping to stop all traffic across them. We took a boat and crossed from the embassy to the southern tip of Gezira.

Kosygin gave me the impression of being more than usually gloomy. He was never a man to display emotion. In public, indeed, he presented himself as a walking computer – everything he was told he would translate into brisk statistics. Yet in private, as I knew, he was a totally different, very warm man. I recalled an evening on another boat, at Alexandria, when wives had been present and it was gay and everyone had drunk a little. Kosygin had danced with his wife and it was hard to believe, watching him then, that he was the same man who sat so coldly across the negotiating table. But that had been only three or four months before Kosygin's wife had died; and the Russian way of meeting death is not our way. I could see, as we crossed the Nile that morning, that he found the scene strange and even shocking. The crowds were everywhere – on the banks of the river, swarming over the bridges, and packed solid in every street. 'You must try to control things,' he said to me. 'The leadership must get a grip on things. If you allow yourselves to surrender to grief in this way, anything may happen. The whole country could collapse.'

So the funeral took place – an event which has been described by many who were present.

Vladimir Vinogradov, at that time a deputy to the Soviet

111

Foreign Minister, Gromyko, was one of the foreign visitors who called on me. His namesake, Sergei Vinogradov, had recently died from a heart attack, and the Soviet Union was left without an Ambassador in Cairo. Strangely enough, only two or three days before Nasser died we had been talking about this very matter. I had said I hoped the Soviets would send as the new Ambassador 'the younger Vinogradov'. Nasser agreed: 'That was in my mind too,' he said, 'but we can't ask them to appoint a particular person.' So when Vladimir was in my office in *Al Ahram* I said to him: 'Why don't you come and be Soviet Ambassador here?' He said: 'Mohamed, I'm astonished. Have you heard anything?' I asked him what he meant. He said: 'Before I came here there was a meeting of the Politburo and they decided to nominate me for the Cairo Embassy.' I told him this meant that one of Nasser's wishes was going to be fulfilled after his death.

Kosygin asked Sadat if he could arrange for him to see some of those who would be taking over the leadership of Egypt in Nasser's place, so arrangements were made for three meetings. The first, which took place in Kubba Palace on the night of Friday 2 October, was largely concerned with military matters. Beside Sadat on the Egyptian side was Shafei, Ali Sabri, General Fawzi and Sami Sharaf: on the Russian side, Kosygin, Zaharov, Vinogradov and Lashinkov (the former head of the Soviet Military Mission in Egypt who had come back as part of the Soviet delegation to the funeral), and General Katyshkin, Lashinkov's replacement. General Fawzi spoke of the new situation which had arisen following America's massive new arms programme for Israel which included the Shrike missile as well as more Phantoms and Skyhawks. He pointed out how important it was that after Nasser's death the Egyptian forces should have full confidence in the continued flow of Soviet weapons. Zakharov promised to do what he could, though he thought the shopping list for arms which he had been given was too big. He also said – and this struck those who heard him as particularly significant – that he thought we should make every effort to get all Russians in Egypt replaced by Egyptians before the battle started. 'Not that we are in any way afraid for our

A conference in Moscow in June, 1970. The Russian team (from nearest the camera) consisted of Brezhnev, Podgorny, Ponomarev, Gromyko, and Gretchko; the Egyptian of Nasser, Ali Sabri, Mahmoud Riad, Gen. Fawzi and the author.

President Nasser with Colonel Ghadaffi.

The body of President Nasser lying in state at the Kubba Palace.

The funeral of President Nasser. Kosygin found the scene 'strange and even shocking'.

men here,' he said, 'but we think it is much better that you should take over completely.' He stressed the need for alertness at all times, and said that moving around the country he had seen signs of slackness among the sentries on bridges and elsewhere.

There was another meeting next morning, and a third one that afternoon, for some Cabinet Ministers and members of the High Executive Committee of the Socialist Union. Kosygin told us he felt we had got into a state of disequilibrium as a result of Nasser's death. He said he and his colleagues had a great respect for our feelings, just as they had a great respect for the late President, but they wanted to see us regain our equilibrium. Above all they wanted us to preserve our unity. The imperialists were going to attack us now that Nasser was dead: they would try to exploit the vacuum he had left. Our responsibility was very great, because at any moment we might have to face a war. Opposed to us was not only Israel but the United States. We must not let any influences, either from the right or from the ultra-left, distract us. Kosygin reminded us that they had recently had a confrontation with the Americans over Jordan, and that they had then warned America not to interfere. They asked us to exercise restraint, saying that President Nasser had correctly evaluated the situation and reacted to it with responsibility. The Soviets' relations with President Nasser had been very close: they had had their difficult times together, but there had never been any secrets between them. There was never any need for the leaders of our two countries to hide things from each other or lie to each other, because hiding things brought nobody any benefit, and lies would always be unmasked.

Kosygin asked if he could go to the mosque where Nasser had been buried. He was taken to it, and then left for home.

CHAPTER III

Sadat Rides the Storm

1. FIRST DIPLOMATIC CONTACTS

Immediately after the death of Nasser I told the acting President, Anwar Sadat, that I wanted to give up my ministerial post and go back to *Al Ahram*. I knew that if I stayed on as a Minister I would become involved in disputes with some of the leading members of the Socialist Union and the Assembly. In that case I should be nothing but a liability to the new President, whereas from my editorial chair I could give him useful support. He agreed to my request, only asking me to stay on until the conclusion of the plebiscite which should confirm him as President. This I did. A friendly exchange of letters between us was published. After I stepped down I continued to see the President frequently and was happy to maintain with him the informal and confidential relationship which I had enjoyed with his predecessor.

This was a period of intense diplomatic activity. Everybody inside and outside Egypt – and among foreign governments those especially of America and Russia – was eager to find out what post-Nasser Egypt was going to be like. The new President was not well-known outside the Arab world. Was he only going to be a figurehead, under whom stronger individuals or groups exercised the real power? Or a stop-gap, soon to be replaced by someone else? If so, who was going to come out on top? Very various were the answers given to all these questions.

Egypt's relations with the United States immediately after the death of Nasser can best be described as a sort of uneasy truce. Both sides were fundamentally suspicious of each other. The Americans had angrily accused Egypt of moving missiles into the Canal area after the standstill ceasefire had come into force, and to show their displeasure had sanctioned a large new consignment of arms for Israel, which had of course in turn infuriated Egypt. Though the Americans were pleased that Nasser had accepted Rogers's initiative they regarded his successor as a weak man who would probably not be able to stand up to the Russians. Also they tended to regard the most powerful and entrenched rivals to Sadat – the group coalescing around the former Vice-President, Ali Sabri – as purely and simply pro-Russian. They were continually urging that when the ceasefire expired on 7 February it should be indefinitely extended and that there should be some form of 'interim agreement'.

Sadat, on the other hand, did have a chance of moving the Americans towards an understanding of Egypt's position that, to be realistic, Nasser had never had. The mistrust between Nasser and the Americans ran too deep. Sadat was free of that legacy. For rather different reasons, I had been advocating for some time, in articles in *Al Ahram* and in meetings with politicians, the need for Egypt to work towards the neutralization of the United States as a prerequisite of the battle which seemed to me inevitable. I argued that no problem in the Middle East area involving war and peace could be solved without the active participation of the two super-powers, but that there was no need for the Arab-Israel problem to become polarized between the Soviet Union and the United States. While we had to accept that the interests of America and Israel were closely linked we should always strive to ensure that they did not become completely identified with each other. We must work to preserve a gap between the interests and policies of the two countries, and in that gap we should find room to manoeuvre and to bring pressure on Israel. The assets on which we could count for the achievement of these ends included our ability to wage a limited war, our close relations with the Soviet Union (always provided they were kept properly informed of our intentions), the oil weapon, and the solidarity of other Arab countries. I had publicly broached this neutralization argument – concluding that Egypt must be prepared to deal with the United States –

even while Nasser was alive. Nasser disagreed, though he made no move to prevent me airing the argument; but it was clear he was never going to do anything on those lines. Sadat, however, had the chance.

Eventually it was announced that President Sadat was to address the National Assembly on 4 February 1971. It was not until shortly before he was due to speak that the contents of his speech became known to his senior colleagues, and then there was a vigorous reaction. The President was determined that a new initiative must be taken, as the ceasefire was due to expire in a few days. He was proposing to agree to an extension of the ceasefire for a month and was going to propose that work on clearing the Suez Canal should begin, provided Israel was prepared to make a partial withdrawal in Sinai linked with a timetable for a full withdrawal to the international frontiers of Egypt, according to Resolution 242.

The President asked me to point out to the Americans that this initiative was entirely his own and owed nothing to Russian prompting. He saw the American representative Bergus himself and explained that the Israeli withdrawal would have to be a big one, about 100 kilometres, and that Egyptian forces would have to be able to cross into Sinai so that they could protect those who were working on the clearance of the canal.

The Ali Sabri group took strong exception to the President's proposals. There was a stormy scene in the Assembly and the group insisted on the deletion of some parts of the President's speech, though he stuck to his guns and successfully preserved the main points of his proposals.

Four days after the President's speech Dr Jarring asked the Egyptian Government to give him a written commitment to the section of Resolution 242 dealing with the preservation of peace and the Israeli Government to give a similar written commitment to the section dealing with withdrawal. The Egyptian Government agreed to this suggestion but the Israelis refused.

The President had hoped that his proposals would produce some positive response from the Americans, but he was due for a disappointment. A message to him from President Nixon received on 4 March (which showed signs of having been drafted by Rogers) said that if it was thought that setting such an early deadline for the renewal of hostilities was a form of pressure on the US he was mistaken. More time was needed, particularly for the Israeli Government to convince the Israeli people of the need for concessions. Nixon said he did not wish to indulge in resounding proclamations 'either Dostoievskian or Tolstoyan' – that would be easy – but he wanted rather to achieve quick results. He believed there was going to be a lift-off in the Middle East problem, 'but you must give us time'. One of the few positive things to emerge from Nixon's message was that he thought Israel's eventual withdrawal should be all the way back to the international frontiers – abandoning, in other words, all its 1967 gains.

Relations with the Soviet Union had their difficulties too. In mid-January 1971 President Podgorny had come to Egypt, ostensibly to attend the celebrations for the completion of the High Dam but in fact to assess how the new regime was working out. The Russians were afraid that, in order to prove themselves, Nasser's successors might rush into some military adventure, and at a meeting with the Egyptian negotiating team Podgorny sounded so cautious a note that he profoundly shocked his hearers. Warned by the Soviet Ambassador, Vladimir Vinogradov, of the effect of his words he tried, in another meeting the following day, to be more encouraging. He also told General Sadiq that the arms he had asked for would be forthcoming.

After Podgorny had left, Vinogradov asked me for my assessment of President Sadat. My answer was: 'He likes to take time to listen to an argument, but in the end the decision he reaches will be entirely his own. Everyone should give him plenty of time to see and hear things for himself.' (Incidentally Vinogradov, who had stayed on in Aswan after the celebrations there, told me of an amusing incident. He and his wife had started to take photographs of the High Dam when they were stopped by a police officer who said: 'You can't do that, it's secret.')

As with America, Sadat had both advantages and disadvantages compared with Nasser when it came to dealing with the Soviet Union. Inevitably, Nasser had more leverage because

117

his voice was heard over the whole of the Arab world: what Nasser chose to say could affect Soviet relations with, perhaps, Iraq; and this was important, particularly in the perennial arguments over arms supplies. By his influence, Nasser extended the frontiers of Egypt. If you deal with either of the super-powers from the context merely of your own frontiers, well, you are one country much like another; but if you deal with them as the head of a movement, that confers much greater power. It was a power that President Sadat could not hope to possess. Yet, against that, was the fact that Nasser had always believed that there was no choice for Egypt but to deal with the Soviet Union – and, given his relations with the United States, this was correct. So relations had always been patched up; and the Russians had always known, I think, that this would be so. But Sadat was an unknown quantity: he did, for the reasons explained, have a greater freedom to look to the West. The Russians knew this and so they knew that they would have to work to build a new relationship with Nasser's successor, while at the same time harbouring deeper uncertainties about him.

On 1 March, President Sadat went on a secret visit to Moscow. There were three things he wanted to ask the Russians for: the first to arrange a joint military and political strategy; the second for Egypt to be put on an equal footing with Israel as far as arms went – he was not, he told them, asking for superiority in weapons although as Egypt was the defeated and occupied country, he might well have done so. The third item concerned the current flow of arms deliveries. The President found the Soviets disinclined to talk about a joint strategy, though they were prepared to discuss armaments. There was a dispute with them over a missile-launching Ilyushin plane which they had offered Egypt. Ali Sabri, who at that time was respon-sible to the President for problems connected with the Air Force, had agreed to accept the condition laid down by the Russians before delivery of the plane could be made: that it could only be used on orders from Moscow. President Sadat told his hosts he could not accept that. 'Suppose,' he said, 'the Israelis bomb deep inside Egypt again. Am I supposed to wait for permission from Moscow before I retaliate? This would put me in an extraordinarily awkward position. I am the head of an independent country, and I can't surrender any part of my independence of action.' At the end of the meeting Brezhnev tried to reassure him: 'Take it easy; we'll meet you half-way.' When he came back from Moscow, and was telling me what happened there, the President said: 'I had to make an angry scene, but in the end I got what I wanted.'

There was more friction on another occasion later in the same month. On 25 March President Sadat addressed a meeting in the Ministry of War attended by top commanders of the armed forces and senior Soviet experts, including the latest head of the Soviet Military Mission, General Vasily Okunev. (He had commanded the Moscow Air Defence District before coming to Cairo earlier in the year to replace General Katyshkin.) The President reminded his audience that this was the building in which the 1952 revolution had started and which had been Nasser's headquarters during the glorious days of the Suez War in 1956. He said that once again the destiny of Egypt was in their hands, and all should be prepared for action at any time, though there were many problems to be overcome before action could begin. Some of the officers complained about the effectiveness of Soviet arms and about delays in supplying them. General Okunev began to reply to what seemed to him to be criticism of the Soviet Union. The President told him not to be so sensitive. 'They were not attacking the Soviet Union,' he said, 'but in a meeting like this everyone must speak openly.' But trouble was brewing with the Soviets. They were, as has been seen, suspicious of the new regime, while on the Egyptian side mistrust had been generated by the demand for a naval base and by difficulties over arms supplies.

Another incident at about this time created more misunderstanding with the Soviets. Relations with the Saudis were still fairly cool, but in the first half of November 1970, an attempt had been made to improve them. Kamel Adham, brother-in-law of King Feisal, and counsellor to him, with supervisory powers over the Intelligence Service and so one of the most powerful men in the kingdom, came discreetly to Cairo. He talked about the Russian presence in Egypt, saying how much it alarmed the

119

Americans, and pointing out that this was important at a time when the Saudis were trying to get the Americans more actively interested in the Middle East's problems. President Sadat's answer was that Egypt depended on the Soviet Union for so much, whereas the Americans were providing Israel with everything it asked for, to the extent that during the war of attrition they had been able to bomb Egypt for seventeen hours consecutively. The President told Kamel Adham: 'I would not only bring in the Russians – I would bring in the devil himself if he could defend me.' But he added that if the first phase of Israeli withdrawal were completed he could promise that he would get the Russians out. Kamel Adham asked President Sadat if he could pass this on to the Americans and the President said he could. But the President's remarks were leaked by Senator Jackson, presumably with the intention of helping Israel by creating bad blood between Egypt and the Soviet Union.

Another Arab monarch with whom Egypt's relations at that time were difficult was King Hussein. There had been many reports in the international press that the King had had secret meetings with Israeli leaders – the name of Yigal Allon, Deputy Prime Minister, being especially often mentioned. On 19 November the President telephoned me to say that King Hussein was suggesting a visit to Cairo. I was suspicious of this proposal, because if he came it would look as if we were giving our blessing to any clandestine contacts he might have had. I suggested we should send General Sadiq to Amman to ask King Hussein bluntly whether he had seen any Israeli leaders or not. Before he became Chief of Staff, General Sadiq had been Director of Military Intelligence and his duties had included supervision of special operations against Israel and liaison with Fateh. He had retained responsibility for links with the Fedayin since taking up his new appointment. If the King denied the rumours, we could accept his word and let him come to Cairo, but if he confirmed them we could not receive him. So it was agreed, and on 23 November General Sadiq went to Amman. When he came back he told me that he had put the question to the King, who had then talked for an hour about general matters. When he stopped the general said: 'Your Majesty: you haven't answered my question.' To this the King said in a casual way: 'That's because I didn't go to see them.' But General Sadiq got a firm impression that the King *had* seen Allon, and so the proposed visit was delayed.

One Arab leader who did come to Cairo a little later was Yasser Arafat. On 8 March 1971, he and Abu Iyad, Abu Lutf, and Abul Said, came to my house at 6.30 in the evening. Half an hour later we all went round to President Sadat's house in a Japanese car which had been given to the Fateh. Yasser Arafat was driving, but the others, except for Abu Iyad, as a rule refused to use the car because they regarded it as unrevolutionary. President Sadat was keen to know what the resistance could do in the event of a new war, and it was agreed that Arafat should discuss co-ordination with General Sadiq. The President emphasized his view, which was also that of President Nasser, that the resistance should avoid all political or military provocation of King Hussein. He recommended them not to be a party to any international settlement that might be reached: the King could sign but they should not. It was for them to see that the cause of Palestine was not allowed to die. Abu Iyad urged that the King should be allowed to come to Cairo – he thought it would calm him. President Sadat refused. He said he knew that if the King came he would only want to talk about two things: the subsidy to Jordan agreed at the Khartum conference and which Kuwait and Libya had stopped paying after the showdown with the guerrillas in September 1970, and the activities of Yasser Arafat. President Sadat added that Egypt still regarded the Gaza Strip as being its special responsibility: it should not be handed over to Jordan, as some Israelis were hinting it might be.

During April 1971 a variety of problems were coming to a head. On the Arab front the unity of Egypt, Syria, and Libya was agreed to on 17 April. To begin with the Sudan had been named as a fourth partner in this union, but its government had decided that the country was not ready for so far-reaching a step. It was this question of unity that was to have wide repercussions on the internal political situation in Egypt. President

121

Sadat himself was keen on the idea. It represented, after all, the continuation of a policy that had been close to the heart of President Nasser. Moreover, a union of these three countries would involve new political institutions, and this would mean fresh elections which would produce a new parliament and a new Central Committee of the Socialist Union, in both of which bodies there were then majorities on whose loyalty the President could not rely.

2. THE DOWNFALL
OF THE ALI SABRI GROUP

The death of Nasser left the political scene in Egypt uncertain and fluid. Everyone was trying to assess the personality of the new President. Once it had been agreed that the procedure laid down by the constitution was going to be adhered to, with the new President being nominated by the National Assembly on the recommendation of the High Executive Committee of the ASU and approved by plebiscite, the key post in any future government seemed certain to be that of Prime Minister. It was on this post that various individuals and groups began to focus their attention.

Anwar Sadat continued to receive the backing of a number of independents inside the government, including Dr Fawzi and Sayed Marei, the deputy premier with the key domestic offices of irrigation and agriculture. Then there was the group round Ali Sabri which, at the time of Nasser's death, controlled the National Assembly, the Central Committee of the ASU, and the elite Vanguard Movement of the ASU under Sharawy Gomaa, the Intelligence apparatus and the Ministries of Presidential Affairs and Information. Sharawy Gomaa and Sami Sharaf were members of this group, and though they disagreed with Ali Sabri on a number of matters they had a common interest with him in preventing anyone outside their group from having any real say in the decision-making process. They wanted all power in government, party, and army to remain in their hands. They were not personally corrupt, but they were drunk with power, and after Nasser's death the power that they wielded became totally divorced from any social content. They echoed the doctrines and sayings of President Nasser, but in a blind way. They wanted the dead leader to become a fourth pyramid in Egypt and for themselves to be installed as permanent and exclusive high priests ministering to his shrine.

It is impossible to understand the Ali Sabri group without knowing, first, that all the main conspirators came from Intelligence and, second, that none had been a member of the original Free Officers' Movement which brought about the Revolution. They were thus at once conspiratorial by nature, resentful of what they conceived as the Free Officers' continuing influence, and convinced that they were more 'loyal' to the Revolution – had served it better, in some fashion – than these Free Officers had. These attitudes led them, inevitably enough, to that blind worship of Nasser after his death; equally inevitably, they led to plotting.

Ali Sabri, the ringleader, was a strange man. His nature perhaps arose from his background: he came from a rich family – in fact, he was related to Sayed Marei. But whereas Marei came from the rich branch of the rich family, Sabri came from the poor branch. Complexes in that situation are scarcely unknown. Sabri was naturally secretive, and a career in Air Force Intelligence reinforced this. He was ruthless with everyone: his rich relatives, his subordinates, himself; he was a very hard worker, capable of concentrated activity for fourteen hours or so at a stretch. He kept his emotions, like his opinions, under the tightest control.

Sabri had a secretary, a man who had served him for years. One day the secretary's only son died and the secretary took time off to go to the funeral. Sabri, noticing his absence, inquired and was told the reason. When the secretary returned, Sabri summoned him and said just one sentence: 'I'm sorry about what happened.' Then he began to give orders as usual.

As for Sabri's opinions, they varied. He espoused communism at one point, advocating that virtually everything in Egypt except the barbers' shops be nationalized. When that wind changed, so did Sabri. The constant factor was Sabri's search

123

for a power base. First, he tried to use the Youth Movement for that purpose; then he built up support inside the ASU party organization.

Sharawy Gomaa was easier-going, with his plump face and the lisp that he even went to doctors in a vain attempt to cure. Gomaa was, I always thought, basically a good man, an energetic army officer – again from the intelligence side. His downfall began, ironically, when he was promoted to be Governor of Suez just before the 1967 war. It was an important post – Suez, after all, immediately adjoins Sinai – and it gave Gomaa ideas. He decided to become a party ideologue, and he started a 'centre for party indoctrination' in Suez, gathering round him some union activists, a few people who could write and some members of the security forces. Their problem was that none was an intellectual but, as they saw it, intellectualism was the road to respectability; so they borrowed other people's thoughts, taking from all over the place, and served up the resulting *mélange* as their own. I do not even think Gomaa was a genuine socialist: he professed it because it was another way to Nasser's favour, so he thought; but in reality he was concerned with power without a social end. Yet, having said that, I still think that Gomaa was not personally corrupt: his tragedy was that he wanted to be Prime Minister too much and too quickly.

A Lebanese politician came to see me when the affair was over and protested that he could not reconcile himself to Gomaa's arrest; he had known Gomaa, he said, since 1962. 'What was he then?' I asked. 'Just an intelligence officer,' was the reply. 'Well,' I said, 'you must understand that in three short years he has tried to become a politician, an ideologue and a plotter all in one jump. It was too much for him.'

The last of the central trio was Sami Sharaf. The paradox of Sharaf was that although he was given to the most extravagant expressions of loyalty towards President Nasser, he was in fact one of the people who killed him – not deliberately, but through their own failings. As with Gomaa, there were good sides to Sami, but he was unfathomable in other matters. He had, for instance, this crude, primitive way of expressing his loyalty. 'If

President Nasser asked me to throw my four sons and daughters under a train, I would do it without hesitation,' he would say. To prod him, I used to reply: 'I wouldn't do anything of the kind. That's a crazy thing to do . . .' Sami would explode: 'But that's not loyal, that's not loyal . . .' Was he sincere in his protestations? Who knows? I think that of all the plotters, Sami was the most affected by the idea that he had served the Revolution better than some of the Free Officers: his extraordinary outbursts perhaps reflected this.

Yet Sharaf helped to kill Nasser. As Secretary to the President of Information, Sharaf's task was to relieve the burden of paper-work reaching Nasser's desk. He simply failed to do this. Everything that passed across Sharaf's desk landed on Nasser's: for information, for signature, for action. Sharaf was a conduit, not a filter. I was always appalled when I saw Nasser's work-load and I would argue with Sharaf: 'Why should the President be given all this? What should he be bothered with details like that?' Especially in the last year of Nasser's life, when it was clear how ill he was, I pleaded with Sharaf to stem the flood of paper, but to no effect.

Sharaf seemed more interested in electronics than in the core of his job. Like many who discover technology late in life, Sharaf was obsessed with gadgets. He would scour the Western electronics and hi-fi journals and order whatever caught his fancy – some new miniaturized recording device, perhaps – and with the resources of the Presidency, of course, he could have it on his desk in 48 hours from Japan or America or anywhere. It was, in the end, Sharaf's passion for recording things that led to the plotters' downfall.

Ali Sabri himself aspired to the premiership, while Sharawy Gomaa and others put forward the name of Dr Mohammed Labib Shuqair, Speaker of the Assembly, but only as an interim measure since Gomaa, of course, was also aiming at the top position for himself. Hussein el-Shafei was outside the Ali Sabri group, and stood alone.

An unknown factor in the situation was the army. Where its political sympathies lay was not clear. General Fawzi was thought to be a fundamentally apolitical professional soldier,

125

though it turned out that he was to some extent under the influence of the Ali Sabri group, partly because he was a relative of Sami Sharaf.

From the outset the Ali Sabri group had assumed that Sadat was going to be a weak President and that, if he proved recalcitrant, they would have no great difficulty in getting rid of him. 'They want to impose a trusteeship on me,' he said, 'but I'm not going to stand for it.' He was quickly to show that he meant what he said for on 21 October 1970, much to the annoyance of the Ali Sabri group, the announcement was made that Dr Mahmoud Fawzi was to be Prime Minister.

Soon after the plebiscite had confirmed him in office on 15 October, President Sadat had asked me who I thought would be the best choice for Prime Minister. I had recommended Dr Fawzi. My reasons for doing so were two – first, I thought it important from the international point of view that the new Prime Minister should be someone known abroad. It was essential to show the Third World, as well as the super-powers and Europe, that the death of Nasser did not mean that Egypt was going to sink into obscurity. President Sadat was not himself yet well known abroad, but Dr Fawzi was. They would make a strong team. My second reason for suggesting Dr Fawzi was that the people wanted someone in charge whom they knew and trusted – a sort of father figure. They were afraid that a struggle for power among Nasser's heirs was about to break out and the appointment of Dr Fawzi would reassure them.

President Sadat told me he was thinking along the same lines, but there was one snag. Dr Fawzi had resigned from the High Executive Committee of the ASU on 3 October – the same day as I had, as a matter of fact, though there had been no co-operation between us. The President asked me if I could persuade Dr Fawzi to accept the post and I undertook to do so. I went to his house in Badreshein and for seven hours we talked over the problem. Dr Fawzi was at first very reluctant. He did not feel ready for the task and feared there was inevitably going to be a struggle for power ahead. He was not sure how much real power he would have as Prime Minister. But eventually he was convinced, and we called up the President with the good news.

126

President Sadat was due to go that day, 18 October, to the National Assembly to take the oath as President, and he suggested that Dr Fawzi should come to Tahra Palace after the ceremony was over. We drove round in Dr Fawzi's car, but found Labib Shuqair there. He had come, as protocol demanded, to thank the President on behalf of the Assembly for having attended its session. So it was not until the following day that the Ali Sabri group knew of Dr Fawzi's appointment. It made them extremely angry, and part of their anger was directed against me because they knew of my friendship with Dr Fawzi. They began to have the feeling that the President listened to the independents.

On 6 March there was another meeting of the High Executive Committee of the ASU and the War Council to discuss the next steps to be taken about the ceasefire. The President had agreed in his speech of 4 February to extend it for one more month: that month had now elapsed and a decision on the next step had to be taken one way or another. The Ali Sabri group practically forced the President to agree to give an order for the opening of hostilities and did their best to pin him down to a precise date in the near future – 26 April. And the pressure on the President was such that he had to give his consent – or, at any rate, it is in the minutes of the meeting that he gave his consent, though in fact I do not think he had any intention of actually going to war so soon. I was opposed to the decision, and spoke against it as frankly as I could in *Al Ahram*, because those advocating war had not properly weighed the obstacles in Egypt's path, and it seemed to me utterly wrong that a decision regarding so vital an issue as peace and war should be determined by considerations of purely internal politics. The Sabri group, outraged by my articles, wanted me to be arrested for treason.

On 21 April there was a stormy meeting of the High Executive Committee of the ASU. After it was over the President called me on the telephone – 'The situation has exploded,' he said. The meeting had been debating the proposal for a union with Libya and Syria, something which the group had always opposed, ostensibly on the grounds that the unfortunate experience of the 1958 union with Syria should not be repeated.

127

The Baath Party in Syria, they said, was not to be trusted, and as for the Libyans, who were they? Ali Sabri once described them at a meeting of the Central Committee as 'a bunch of boy scouts'. Ghadaffi, he said, was mad, and it would be wrong to tie the destinies of Egypt to such people. In fact the group's real reason for opposing the union was a well justified fear that it might break their monopoly of power. There would have to be new institutions and new elections. It was, of course, partly for this very reason that the President was anxious for the union.

At this meeting Ali Sabri, the Secretary General of the ASU, Abdul Muhsin, Abul Nur, Diaeddin Daoud, Sharawy Gomaa, and Labib Shuqair had all spoken strongly against the union. Only the President and Dr Fawzi had spoken in favour of it. The President told me that there had been hard words on both sides, and it had finally been agreed that the Central Committee should meet to discuss the apparent breakdown in the political leadership of the Party. It was understandably not long before news of the row leaked out, and some elements inside the Central Committee began to mobilize their forces against the President. Sharawy Gomaa, who was responsible for political organization inside the Socialist Union, became the focal point for the dispute. He tried desperately to avoid taking sides openly, so, when President Sadat asked him what he thought about unity, he protested that he was not a member of the High Executive Committee. But when the President pressed him he was obliged to concede that he was against unity.

On 22 April President Sadat called the Soviet Ambassador to see him. After they had been talking for a time on other matters the Ambassador said: 'We hear a lot these days about disputes inside the High Executive Committee. Is this true?' President Sadat confirmed that it was, and added, 'Now I have some news for you. I am going to get rid of Ali Sabri.' The Ambassador's jaw dropped. 'Why are you telling me this?' he asked. The President said: 'Because people will try to capitalize on it. They will make a war of nerves out of it. They will tell you that the Soviet Union's number one man in Egypt has been liquidated. The Western papers will dance in front of you with *galgalas* [castanets] trying to provoke you. But, I assure you, there is

128

King Hussein with President Sadat during a visit to Cairo.

President Sadat and President Podgorny visiting the High Dam at Aswan in January, 1971.

Yasser Arafat paying his first call on President Sadat.

Presidents Sadat, Ghadaffi and Asad at a tripartite conference.

nothing directed against the Soviet Union in this. It is a purely internal dispute. If anyone suggests to you that what I am going to do is directed against the Soviet presence in Egypt you can tell them that I would be delighted if you would intensify your presence.'

There was an extraordinarily tense and emotional atmosphere inside Egypt all this time. I remember Sami Sharaf telephoning to me on the 23rd saying that he had put a photograph of President Nasser in front of him and had been talking to it and sobbing. Sami Sharaf told me that after seeing President Sadat at his house by the Barrage below Cairo he had been so unhappy he had thought of jumping into the Nile. More serious, as was later to be revealed, were the seances which General Fawzi, Sharawy Gomaa and others used to hold with a medium who was supposed to speak in the voice of President Nasser. He had been introduced to them by a professor at Ain Shams University who was interested in spiritualism. They put all sorts of fundamental questions to the supposed spirit of the late President – Should they or should they not attack Israel? Was Sharawy Gomaa going to be made Prime Minister? and so on. So determined were they not to lose a single word of the voice from beyond the grave that all the seances were recorded on tape. It was a humiliating moment in Egyptian history when its senior soldiers and politicians could behave in this way; but the fact is that they had become so used to taking orders from Nasser that they were incapable of thinking on their own.

Meanwhile President Sadat made efforts to drum up support in Parliament, especially among deputies from Upper Egypt, while the dissident group tried to organize its forces inside the Central Committee. It was not absolutely certain of its own strength, and was seeking a postponement of the promised meeting of the committee, preferring to keep its supposed majority there as an indirect form of pressure rather than a weapon which, if actually used, might backfire. As part of this strategy, I recall, Sharawy Gomaa telephoned me, very cross because the President had called him up and told him that he saw no solution except for the Central Committee to meet and vote for the creation of a union. Sharawy had said he did not see how the Central Committee could agree to this. President Sadat had asked him if he had read H. C. Armstrong's biography of Ataturk, *Grey Wolf*: 'Ataturk got fed up with his Parliament and one day he went there and told the deputies – "Gentlemen, you are not of a high enough standard to be my collaborators, so I suggest you go home. You are all dismissed!" ' The implications of the story were not lost on Sharawy.

When the Central Committee met on 25 April, there was a violent quarrel between the rival factions. President Sadat was heckled when he tried to address the committee. Ali Sabri complained that President Sadat was interrupting him: 'Nobody can stop me from speaking,' he shouted. The atmosphere was exceedingly tense. A recess was called and the High Executive Committee of the Socialist Union began a meeting on the upper floor of the building. I was not a member of the High Executive Committee, though I was of the Central Committee, but I found myself walking upstairs in company with Sharawy Gomaa. When we got to the door of the room where the meeting was to be held I was going to leave, but President Sadat saw me and called on me to come in.

I had gone to the Central Committee meeting intending to speak and had brought with me the minutes of the Benghazi meeting at which the idea of a union between Egypt, Libya and Syria had first been agreed. I had been a member of the Egyptian delegation at this meeting, sitting beside President Nasser, and had taken the minutes. When we got back to Cairo the minutes had been typed out and one copy returned to me with some handwritten comments by Nasser on it. It had been my intention to ask what we were quarrelling about, since here was documentary proof that the union was something President Nasser had agreed on. President Sadat was doing no more than completing Nasser's work. But the atmosphere in the Central Committee after the flare-up between the President and Ali Sabri became so tense that it was impossible for anybody else to speak.

However, I now asked permission to speak in the High Executive Committee. I said my piece, adding that General Fawzi and Mahmoud Riad had been present at the meeting in

Moscow at which Nasser had told the Soviet leaders about the union which he was proposing, so if anyone had any doubts about the truth of what I was saying they could ask these two for corroboration. I did not have a chance to finish. Abul Nur interrupted to complain that, instead of healing the rift between the two factions, I was widening it. Since he was still anxious for the resolution to be passed, and as a way of gaining time, the President then suggested that the subject was much too important to be decided at a single meeting; instead a sub-committee should be appointed to go into the whole question and try to get some modifications agreed by Libya and Syria. This proposal was accepted, though the dissenters, being in a majority were able to insist that the sub-committee be chaired by one of them, Abul Nur.

After the meeting had broken up I went to the President's house. He was in a rather depressed mood and mentioned the *Grey Wolf* story more than once. Perhaps the dissidents knew, however, that the President was seriously considering the dissolution of the Central Committee; or perhaps they wanted to lie low while they gained strength. Whatever the reason, Abul Nur's sub-committee made merely minimal amendments and the Central Committee had to meet on 29 April for only fifteen minutes to pass them. Everyone knew that the real confrontation would come somewhere else.

But a few days later the opposition's continuing determination to force the issue was shown when the President visited the industrial town of Helwan on 1 May. The Socialist Union laid on a hostile demonstration intended to frighten him. It failed to do this, and he made a speech in which he spoke openly of his determination to liquidate all 'centres of power'. The next day President Sadat went over to the offensive. A statement was issued which said simply: 'President Sadat has decided to relieve Ali Sabri from his post as Vice-President, with effect from today.' Immediately Sami Sharaf and Sharawy Gomaa tried to contact the President and get him to change the word 'relieve' to let it look as if Ali Sabri had resigned. The President refused to do this: he wanted to make it quite clear where the real authority in the Government lay.

The internal struggle for power was complicated by the fact that Rogers was due to arrive in Egypt on 4 May. He had for some time been pressing for Dr Fawzi or some senior minister to come to Washington, but this had not proved possible, so he was coming to Cairo instead, bringing with him Joseph Sisco, the Assistant Secretary of State. When he arrived it was clear that he brought no new proposals. He was still harping on the old 'partial solution' theme – an indefinite prolongation of the ceasefire, the re-opening of the Suez Canal and a limited Israeli withdrawal. We told him that this was unacceptable and explained the Egyptian point of view: Israel should be persuaded to give a positive response to the Jarring questionnaire and should agree to withdrawal in two stages. The first stage would be to a line between Al Arish and Ras Mohamed, whereupon we would start work on clearing the Canal and Egyptian forces could cross to the eastern bank. The second stage would include Israel's withdrawal from the rest of Sinai and the Gaza Strip. UN Forces should supervise the withdrawal and would stay in the Gaza Strip and Sharm el-Sheikh. When these two stages were complete we could agree about demilitarized zones and a six month prolongation of the ceasefire. If Israel failed to withdraw completely we reserved the right to liberate occupied Egyptian territory by force.

Rogers expressed the view that the extent of Israeli withdrawal would be exactly balanced by the strength of the guarantees for peace and security we were prepared to give. Mahmoud Riad returned to the question of Dr Jarring's latest proposals for a written commitment by Egypt for peace and by Israel for withdrawal, based on Resolution 242. Egypt had accepted, but Israel had refused; yet the United States went on supplying Israel with arms. Rogers said his government wanted peace but they were unable to put pressure on Israel. At this Mahmoud Riad exploded. 'Is there no difference,' he asked, 'between the US and Upper Volta or Gabon? Here is Israel giving you a flat challenge. You say you were trying to put pressure on her, but she rejects your pressure. How do you explain this?' He suggested, not for the first time, that the only effective form of pressure on Israel would be an American embargo on arms.

After Rogers had returned to Washington, Sisco went on to Israel. He came back with some extraordinary information. Apparently the Israelis were now talking about a withdrawal (on their terms) of 5–10 kilometres along the eastern bank of the Canal. This would involve the Bar-Lev Line but they made a condition that this fortification should not only be left intact, but also be manned with Israeli civilians under UN supervision, so that if anything went wrong it could be returned to them. They used the analogy of the base staffed by civilians which Britain was allowed to keep on the Canal under the terms of the agreement with Egypt in 1954.

Early in the morning of 10 May the President's daughter came round to my flat at Giza and gave me a message that her father wanted to see me urgently. It astonished me that he had not called me on the telephone or sent one of his secretaries. I went at once, and found him sitting in an armchair, dressed in pyjamas and a dressing-gown, and with a tape-recorder in front of him. He had a most extraordinary story to tell.

At 2.00 a.m. that morning a police officer had rung the bell of his house. He had told the guards that it was essential he should see the President personally, as he had evidence of a conspiracy against him. The President's secretary was brought to talk to him and tried to urge the impossibility of waking up the President at that hour of the night. The police officer was very insistent and finally said, 'All right, I will go away if you will sign a written statement that I have done all I can to see the President, but have not been allowed in. I don't want to be blamed subsequently for anything that may happen to the President.' This impressed the secretary. Further questioning showed that the policeman was one of the officers in the Security Department responsible for the custody of the tapes and taped conversations. He had brought with him two tapes, which he wanted the President to hear. The President was woken up, and the young officer played the tapes to him. He was horrified at what he heard, and sat with the tape-machine in front of him till dawn, when he sent his daughter round to me, not trusting any longer to use the telephone.

After hearing the tapes myself I said I thought the two key

133

figures in the situation were General El-Leithy Nassif, Commander of the Presidential Guard and the Chief of Staff of the army, General Sadiq. The President had had a talk with General Nassif in March, when he first began to feel that active opposition to him was building up. General Nassif had then said that, as a professional soldier, he would obey any orders given to him by the proper constitutional authorities. At this time Sami Sharaf, one of the leading members of the Ali Sabri group, was Minister for Presidential Affairs, and as such was in fairly constant communication with the Commander of the Presidential Guards. General Nassif was a friend of Sami Sharaf, and trusted him, but, as events were to prove, his loyalty to the legitimate authority in the state came first. On 12 May the President, still concealing his knowledge of the tapes while he prepared his counter-strike, went to address the troops at a military base near Suez in the company of General Fawzi and General Sadiq. The latter obviously knew what was in the wind and took the opportunity to say privately to the President, 'We understand your position.' It was enough.

It was after this that the President knew he could move. On 13 May he issued an order dismissing Sharawy Gomaa and appointing Mamduh Salem, the Governor of Alexandria, Minister of the Interior. By a curious coincidence Mamduh Salem was a leading member of the semi-secret Vanguard movement, which was supposed to be an inner cadre of the ASU, and his particular function in this was to keep an eye on the police. His superior in the Vanguard was Sharawy Gomaa. Now Sharawy's right-hand Vanguard man was to be responsible for giving him the coup de grâce, which shows what an edifice of straw the Vanguard had become. Sami Sharaf tried to persuade the President not to proceed with the order dismissing Sharawy. Three hours later he rang up to say that he was going to resign if Sharawy was dismissed.

The group's mania for wire-tapping was quite extraordinary, and one of the causes of their undoing. There are three telephone systems in Egypt – the ordinary one; a system for government officials, ministers and so on; and a small circuit confined to about twenty-five individuals – the President, Prime Minister, some members of the High Executive Committee, the commanders of the armed forces, the Director of Intelligence and a few more, including at that time myself, as I had been connected to it when President Nasser made me Minister of Information. This limited circuit had been put under surveillance by Ahmed Kamil, Director of Intelligence, from the end of April. Every conversation made on it was recorded, including a large number between various members of the group. At about the same time Sharawy, as Minister of Interior, had instituted security taps on the telephones of all the President's friends, which was tantamount to putting a tap on the President himself.

In the early evening of 13 May the President told the new Minister of Interior to seize all the tapes housed in the Security Section of the Ministry, and to take a detachment of the Presidential Guards if he needed any help. This he did, taking two officers from the Guards with him.

The group then played what they thought would be their trump card: they resigned en masse, calculating that, without the ministers responsible for the armed forces, the intelligence, and information, and without most of the leading members of the ASU, the government of the country would be crippled. They also expected a massive reaction from the rank and file of the ASU, demanding their reinstatement, but there was never any sign of this.

I had been with the President until about 10.30 that evening and then went home, meeting on the way the Commander of the Presidential Guards. Everything seemed to be quiet. I had just begun to eat a quick supper when I turned on the radio and heard the news of the resignations. It was clear to me that this amounted to a virtual coup d'état, and I was on the point of calling up the President when the telephone rang. It was the President calling me; he too had heard the news on the radio and wanted me to come back to his house at once. I found him in good spirits; his nerves were holding out well. He had accepted all the resignations. Several times during the night he saw General Nassif, whose guards were standing by in case of any rash move by the group. He got telephone reports on the situation in the army from General Sadiq. It appeared that a meeting of senior commanders had been called, at which General Sadiq and General Fawzi were both present. General Fawzi had harangued them, saying that there was going to be a sell-out to the Americans and that he was resigning. General Sadiq intervened to say: 'Mr Minister, since you have resigned I suggest you should go home and have a rest. We must try to keep the army out of politics.' Then he got a call from the President asking him to come round to the President's house. He did so, and the President immediately made him take the oath as Minister of War in place of General Fawzi. He also promoted him full general. General Ahmed Ismail was called out of retirement and made Director of Intelligence. With the Presidential Guard and the army secure there was no longer room for any anxiety. It is strange to see how completely the group miscalculated. They never realized how unpopular they were in the country. I have described how almost all of them – notably Ali Sabri, Sharawy Gomaa, and Sami Sharaf – had had some connection with the intelligence network under Nasser. Now, Nasser's regime had two aspects: it had great achievements to its credit but also it had a repressive side. I do not myself believe that the achievements – the realization of independence, nationalization of the Suez Canal, the role played by Egypt in the non-aligned world and against imperialist influences in the Middle East area such as the Baghdad Pact, improvements in the conditions of labour, free education for all, land reform, and the whole social transformation involving the building up of a welfare state in spite of continuous attacks by imperialist powers and Israel – could have been carried out without some degree of enforcement. But after the 1967 defeat the positive achievements came to an end, because all resources were geared to the coming battle, while repression became more obvious. When Nasser died the executants of repression took it on themselves to be the ideologues of the new regime as well. They held almost all the key posts in the country. The people resented this and came to hate what they saw as their oppressors. Also, I am sure the Ali Sabri group underestimated the strength of legality in a country like Egypt which has throughout its history depended on the discipline of irrigation, and so needs a central authority to distribute the water as much as it needs the water itself. The Egyptians have always been very conscious where legal authority lies. They knew that Anwar Sadat was their legally elected President. This was a great source of strength to him.

For two days we all lived in a sort of limbo, while the last details of the affair were tidied up and its implications sank home. The conspirators were at their homes and policemen were with them, though they were not technically under house arrest. But on 16 May, the President at last ordered their formal arrest. It was then that the Soviet Ambassador came to see the President. He seemed rather embarrassed. President Sadat pointed out that he had given him a warning of what was going to happen and assured him once again that it was in no way directed against the Soviet Union. The Ambassador said it was a matter for regret that many of those arrested were people who had taken part in confidential negotiations in Moscow.

I heard a story about Sami Sharaf, who had headed the Egyptian delegation to the Congress of the Soviet Communist Party in Moscow in early April, which Vinogradov later confirmed. Sami Sharaf had asked afterwards for a private meeting with Brezhnev, in the course of which he had told the Soviet leader that Nasser on his death-bed had made him responsible for preserving bonds of friendship between Egypt and the Soviet Union. Brezhnev had looked at him and said: 'All right. Now let me spank you.' Sami Sharaf was astonished. 'Why do you want to spank me, Mr Secretary General?' he asked. Brezhnev launched into one of his characteristic anecdotes: 'Don't you know the story of the Russian farmer who on his death-bed made his son promise to keep safe an ancestral family vase which was an emblem of good luck for the family? He asked his son if he would accept responsibility if the vase should get broken. The son said he would. Whereupon the farmer said, "Then I will spank you," and did so. The son asked him why he did it: "I have not broken it." "I spank you now," said his father, "so that you will always remember it. What would be the use of spanking you after the vase was broken?"' But I doubt whether Sami Sharaf understood all the implications of the story.

While in Moscow, Sami Sharaf had been authorized to discuss two subjects with the Soviet authorities: the drawing up of a treaty which should put on a formal basis all our relations with the Soviet Union and the creation of a naval 'academy' in Mersa Matruh. The latter was something on which the Soviets still set great store. It was agreed that a high Soviet official should come to Cairo to continue discussions on both subjects, and on 25 May President Podgorny arrived. (After the stormy meeting in the High Executive Committee, Sami Sharaf had tried to persuade Vladimir Vinogradov not to have any more direct dealings with President Sadat, but to wait for the arrival of the Soviet emissary. Vinogradov gave a non-committal answer. Sami Sharaf recorded all that conversation on tape too.)

On 26 May the President gave me an account of Podgorny's visit. He said he had got the impression the Soviets felt that everything in Egypt was topsy-turvy as far as they were concerned. In spite of his warnings they had clearly been a good deal affected by what had been written in the Western Press about the fall of the Ali Sabri group. Podgorny had brought with him a treaty ready for signature, and the President said he was going to sign it. He would have preferred to wait, but apparently the Soviets were in a hurry. From his own point of view the most important clauses in the treaty were one which said that the two signatories would co-operate with each other in the event of any threat to the peace, and one by which the Soviet Union pledged itself to supply Egypt with the equipment needed to undo the results of the aggression against her. While not in the least objecting to making closer our relations with the Soviet Union I had some reservations, which I expressed on television, about the whole idea of treaties between big nations and small ones, in particular feeling that in Egypt the 1936 Anglo-Egyptian Treaty had given such arrangements a bad name. It seemed to me especially unfortunate that the new Soviet-Egyptian Treaty, like the Anglo-Egyptian, was to last for twenty years (and in fact its duration was changed to fifteen years.) President Sadat said he had taken Podgorny in an open car through Heliopolis where they had had an enthusiastic reception. This had obviously surprised Podgorny who had believed popular sympathies were with the Ali Sabri group.

The Americans were naturally happy to see the fall of the group, but they were puzzled at the treaty with the Soviets coming so soon afterwards. Bergus, who left Cairo for the States in early June, saw President Sadat before he left to give him another message from President Nixon. This said that Nixon was looking forward to more contacts with President Sadat 'through quiet diplomatic channels', and assured him that every message he sent to Washington would get the closest attention.

3. PALESTINIANS AND SUDANESE

Once the downfall of the Ali Sabri group proved to the world that, far from being a weak or stopgap President, Anwar Sadat was very much a person to be reckoned with, the super-powers began to make more positive approaches to him, while leaders of the Arab world paid him increasing attention.

In the middle of June King Feisal, who had been in Washington at the invitation of President Nixon, stopped off at Cairo on his way home. The Americans had questioned him closely about his interpretation of recent events in Egypt, including the treaty with the Soviet Union, and he had informed Nixon he was sure Egypt would never become communist. The meeting shifted from Cairo to the cooler breezes of Alexandria, and while he was there King Feisal told me of a dinner party Nixon had given in his honour at which he had expounded to the President his pet theory that Bolshevism was the offspring of Zionism. The President, he said, had shown great interest and had asked him to repeat his remarks to Vice-President Spiro Agnew and to the Director of the CIA, Richard Helms, which he did. The King was obviously pleased at having, as he felt, convinced these powerful figures of a profound and neglected political truth.

Three leaders of the Palestine Resistance, Yasser Arafat, Khalid el-Hassan and Farouk Qadumi, were in Egypt at that time and were anxious to see both President Sadat and King Feisal. I was able to arrange this for them, though the only time available for a meeting with the King and the President was in the train taking them from Alexandria to Cairo. President Sadat told them that the key to King Hussein lay through King Feisal who, though he might not be able to help in a positive way, could help to prevent further action against them. The outcome of this talk with the King was an agreement that the governments of Egypt, Saudi Arabia, Kuwait and Syria should make another effort at mediation between King Hussein and the Fedayin. But later King Feisal decided he did not want the Kuwaitis in, and President Asad of Syria declined to take part, so eventually only Egypt and Saudi Arabia were left with this thankless task.

Nixon's message about 'quiet diplomatic channels' was followed on 4 July by one from Rogers in which he said that they had completed their study of the situation and had ideas that they would like to present to the interested parties. (Contact with the Americans was exceedingly confused throughout this period, mainly because they insisted upon using two quite separate means of communicating with Egypt. Rogers's messages to Riad came by the usual diplomatic channels; but other messages – most of those from Nixon to President Sadat, for example – came through contacts between the CIA and Egyptian Intelligence. What made this more confusing was that the messages were not always reconcilable: Donald Bergus on occasion told the President things which had not been transmitted to Riad. Why the Americans insisted upon this dual approach baffled us at first; then we assumed it arose from battles in Washington between the State Department and President Nixon's powerful National Security Adviser, Henry Kissinger.)

But, in his July message, Rogers asked if Donald Bergus and Michael Sterner could bring the new ideas to Cairo for discussion. Sterner, a State Department official dealing with the Middle East – particularly Israeli affairs – had been attached to President Sadat when, as President of the Assembly, he had paid an official visit to Washington in 1966, and since then Sterner had most recently visited Cairo that April, to prepare for Rogers's May trip. He and Bergus duly came, and I was present at a meeting they had with President Sadat on 6 July, all of us sitting under the huge old ficus tree, planted at the time of Mohamed Ali, which grows outside the President's house at the Barrage. The purpose of the visitors was to state their belief that the whole situation was beginning to move, that when it did it would move quickly. They also wanted to ask whether the signature of the Soviet-Egyptian Treaty, which had occurred since Rogers's visit, meant that Egypt's intentions towards a peace settlement had changed. President Sadat's answer was a clear No. 'Give me a piece of paper with reasonable terms on it,' he said, 'and I'm ready to sign it here and now, under this tree.' The optimism of his American visitors infected the President, who thought things might be beginning to move towards a negotiated settlement. But in fact nothing happened. Sisco was sent to Israel for talks with Dayan, on whom the Americans were pinning great hopes at that time, but was unable to get anything out of him. First Sterner and then Bergus went back to Washington, and nothing more was heard from the American side for several months. This was a great disappointment to the President and from this time his feeling grew that nothing was to be achieved through the State Department: if there were going to be any results they would only come via the 'other channel', Henry Kissinger.

On 19 July there was a coup d'état in the Sudan which was to create further misunderstandings between the Soviet Union and Egypt. Three left-wing members of the original 1969 Revolutionary Council, Major Hashem el-Ata, Colonel Babakr el-Nur, and Major Farouk Osman Hamadullah, called for the overthrow of the Government of President Nimeiry. Both the Egyptian and Libyan Governments were active in rallying support for Nimeiry, and when Babakr el-Nur and Osman Hamadullah, who had been in London when the coup started, tried to fly back to Khartum their BOAC plane was forced to land in Libya. They were then handed over to President Nimeiry, who had been imprisoned in the presidential palace but managed, on 22 July, to stage a successful counter-coup. With several others they were executed a day or two later.

One of those arrested for his part in the original coup was the head of the Labour Association, Shafie Ahmed el-Sheikh – a person of whom I myself had an extremely high opinion and who, I thought, had no part in the conspiracy which led up to the coup. On 23 July I was with President Sadat on the barge *Estar* which is always moored off the presidential rest-house at the Barrage, when a telephone call came to say that Boris Ponomarev, a member of the Politburo and the Secretary General of the Soviet Central Committee, who was in Cairo to attend the 23 July celebrations, wanted to see the President urgently on a most important matter. Ponomarev, we knew, was the ideologue of the Soviet party and, though not responsible for Russia's relations with the 'Third World', he took a keen interest in its problems. Indeed, he and his assistant, Olinovsky, had developed a well-known theory of 'the non-capitalist way of development in the Third World'. We both of us thought it might be that he now wanted the President to intervene on behalf of Abdul Khaliq Mahjoub, the Sudanese Communist leader, who was reported to have been sentenced to death. Half an hour later Ponomarev and the Soviet Ambassador, Vinogradov, arrived. I left them alone with the President. The interview lasted about forty minutes. After it was over President Sadat said: 'Guess who they were concerned with? – not Mahjoub but Shafie. Apparently he shared the Lenin Prize for Peace this year with Khalid Mohieddin, and they think it would be a terrible affront to the whole Socialist Camp if anything happened to him.' He said he reminded them that he had often told the Soviet leaders that there was no country in the Arab world that was likely to accept a Marxist regime, and he warned them that they must expect Nimeiry to be out for vengeance because some of his close associates had been killed and he himself humiliated.

President Sadat immediately tried to get Nimeiry on the telephone. The line was very bad but eventually he made contact and repeated Ponomarev's plea for clemency for Shafie. Nimeiry's answer was: 'It's too late; he's just been

142

hanged.' President Sadat then asked what was the fate of Mahjoub, whom he thought a much more dangerous person, and was told that he had been hanged too. So all he could do was to report back to Ponomarev, who was naturally most upset – as too was Moscow. Later I learned that the whole telephone conversation between Sadat and Nimeiry had been monitored by the Soviets – who thought that Sadat had not put enough pressure on Nimeiry. And some reports afterwards said that, in fact, Mahjoub was not hanged until two days later.

4. DINNER AT THE SOVIET EMBASSY

The next day, 27 July, Vinogradov asked me if I would dine with him at the Soviet Embassy. In answer to my enquiry he said that the only others there would be Ponomarev and an interpreter. I was interested in talking to this senior Soviet official because I knew that the Soviet leadership misunderstood many of the things I said and wrote. More than once they had insinuated to President Nasser that he would be wise to dismiss me, and when Podgorny came to Egypt in January 1971 he had said to President Sadat: 'Now is the time to get rid of Heikal.' I had a chance to talk about all this with President Sadat before going to the dinner, and asked him how he thought I should tackle the subject. He said he thought the direct approach was the best – 'Tell them about Podgorny.'

At dinner Ponomarev, despite his interest in the region, showed an imperfect knowledge of the Arab world. He could not make out why there had been no revolution in Jordan against King Hussein, and when I tried to explain to him about the Hashemites and their history, and about the special nature of the Jordanian army and the obstacles in the way of change in that country, he countered: 'Then how do you account for the assassination of King Abdullah and for the pressure that was brought on Tallal to abdicate?' I pointed out that assassination was not the same as revolution and that Tallal had been removed by the Hashemite family itself. After which Ponomarev started

143

to talk about China, which seemed to interest him more than anything in the Arab world.

Eventually he got round to the recent events in the Sudan, and this gave me my cue. I told him that I knew that he had asked President Sadat to intervene in the Sudan. 'How do you know that?' he asked. 'When I talked to the President there was no one else there except the interpreter.' I said the President himself had told me. He looked astonished.

I told Ponomarev that I needed no certificate from anyone for my nationalism or for my socialist convictions, nor was I going to claim, as some others had done, that Nasser had bequeathed to me special responsibility for fostering Egyptian-Soviet relations. But I could not understand why some Soviet leaders were so ready to attack me. Vinogradov interposed to say that no Soviet leader had ever attacked me – on the contrary they all knew how highly Nasser had valued my contribution to the Egyptian revolution. 'But,' I said, 'Brezhnev once asked Sami Sharaf to arrange for my removal – at least that is what Sami reported.' Vinogradov said that this could never have happened. 'Well,' I said, 'at any rate Podgorny made the same request to President Sadat.' Ponomarev interjected: 'You mustn't listen to rumours.' I told him it was not a rumour and that the President had told me the story himself and had given me leave to mention it at this dinner. 'I want to bring all this out into the open.'

Ponomarev went quite white. Vinogradov said: 'If this conversation did take place it must have been outside the regular meetings between the two Presidents, because I attended all of them.' Recovering himself, Ponomarev said: 'The only time I ever criticized you was to Sharawy Gomaa. I had seen a cutting from an English newspaper, *The People*, in which you were reported as having made some offensive remarks about the Soviet Union to Edward Heath. I told Sharawy Gomaa that if this report was true the Egyptian Government ought to issue an official repudiation of you.' 'Why do you believe what you read in *The People*?' I asked. 'Why should the Egyptian Government repudiate something I am supposed to have said? For the

A summit conference: from left to right, Presidents Boumedienne, Asad and Sadat and King Feisal.

Gen. Ahmed Ismail, Minister of War.

Gen. Gamasy, Director of Operations.

Gen. Fahmy, O.C. Air Defence.

Gen. Shazli, Chief of Staff.

matter of that, why should I deny lies attributed to me? My attitude has always been to ignore such lies.'

Ponomarev said that if I knew, as I said, that some of the Soviet leadership had reservations about my attitude, I ought to have done something about this report. I said it was impossible that I should attack the Soviet Union to Heath. 'Let me give you my reasons. First, such an attack would only weaken the position of Egypt. Second, my views about the Soviet Union have been made perfectly clear in what I have written in *Al Ahram*, and if I wanted to say something different I would not do it secretly. I have always had the courage of my convictions. Third, my meeting with Heath was also attended by our Ambassador in London, Ahmed Hassan el-Fikki, who made minutes of the meeting, and when Sharawy told me the Soviets were suspicious of what went on at this meeting I suggested the Ambassador should give him a copy of these minutes.'

Later on in our conversation, which lasted for four and a half hours, we came back to the same subject. Ponomarev asked me what I would think if the Soviet Union tried to put pressure on Israel. I said I thought this would be most welcome, provided it was not done through Victor Louis (the Soviet journalist who was always going on well publicized 'semi-official' missions and who a few days before had been reported on a visit to Israel). At this point Ponomarev and Vinogradov began talking to each other in Russian, apparently about Victor Louis, but I interrupted them: 'Everyone can see,' I said, 'that Israel is trying to sow mistrust between our two countries, not just by making great play with Victor Louis's visit to Israel but also by spreading rumours that when Golda Meir was in Finland recently she met some members of the Soviet Politburo.' Ponomarev asked: 'Who is she supposed to have met?' I said, 'Your own name has been mentioned in some newspapers. And in view of what you were saying not so long ago I think we should ask you to issue an official denial.' Vinogradov laughed: 'That's a blow below the belt,' he said.

Ponomarev showed a good deal of interest in the mission of Bergus and Sterner to Cairo, particularly in the curious business of what became known as the 'phantom memorandum'. This still unexplained incident arose out of a visit Bergus had paid to the Egyptian Ministry of Foreign Affairs one day in late April, just after Sterner's April mission to Cairo and a week or so before Rogers arrived. Bergus met the Under-Secretary, Mohammed Riad. He told Mohammed Riad that it seemed to him Egypt had always failed to get its case clearly understood through 'failures in presentation', and that if it was he who had to present the Egyptian case he would do it in this way – whereupon he took a sheet of paper and wrote some headings on a piece of paper, which he took home with him and expanded into what amounted to a draft proposal by the Egyptian Government for a settlement. This he sent (without a title or a signature) to Mohammed Riad the next day. The aftermath of this strange initiative trailed on for some time, but it was doomed by Egypt's suspicions. Bergus tried to convince Mohammed Riad that this was a personal move, inspired by his regard for Egypt, and that he would be ruined if his authorship of the memorandum were revealed. But nobody in Cairo would credit that this could really have been a personal or spontaneous gesture, and it was generally interpreted as representing an initiative that the American Government wished to take though they wanted it to appear as originating from the Egyptian side. So the affair leaked (though now I tend to believe that Bergus was right after all).

But, as I recounted the affair to Ponomarev that evening, he had no doubt that the 'phantom memorandum' must represent the official American attitude and asked me what I thought America's real objectives were. I said that, to speak quite frankly, I thought America genuinely wanted a solution of the Middle Eastern problem – provided that it was an American solution. This would mean it would have to fulfil three conditions – that it should result in the expulsion of Soviet influence from the whole area; that it should leave Egypt weakened and unable to exert any influence in the Arab world; and that the Egyptian revolutionary experiment should be shown to have been a failure. Ponomarev agreed with this analysis and asked what I thought could be done. I said that the main task facing the Egyptian people was the coming battle for the recovery of lost Egyptian and Arab land, which meant that the greatest need was to build up Egypt's military capacity at least to equality with that of Israel.

This led Ponomarev to talk about the Ali Sabri group – apparently the two subjects were connected in his mind. He said the Soviets had never had any special relations with them. They only knew them because they had been from time to time sent as emissaries by President Nasser or President Sadat. 'All I am asking for them,' he said, 'is a fair trial.' He began quoting some of the things that had been written about them, particularly the revelations of how some members of the group had sought guidance from the spirit world through mediums. I told him that this was in no way aimed at prejudicing the trial of the group, but simply at showing the mental state of people who had been aiming at taking over control of the country. This was something the Egyptian people had a right to know about. 'It is my belief,' I told him, 'that the Egyptian people twice escaped by their own spontaneous act from situations that would have dragged them down – the first time was on 9 and 10 June 1967, when they forced Gamal Abdel Nasser to withdraw his resignation, and the second time two months ago when they rejected the attempt by a small group to set up a dictatorship.' Ponomarev repeated that he was only asking that the Ali Sabri group should be granted all the safeguards the law allowed them. I think he must have seen me smile, because he went on: 'Very well, I admit that we made mistakes against legality ourselves, but that was in the thirties, before the Twentieth Congress of the Soviet Communist Party. We only want you to avoid the sort of mistakes which we made.' After that the conversation turned to Cuba.

5. THE RANDOPOLO AFFAIR

Egypt's relations with the United States were aggravated by the 'phantom memorandum', by the complete silence that prevailed on their side after the Sterner mission, and then by a serious clash over what can be called 'the Randopolo affair'.

A few miles south-west of Alexandria at a place called Janaklis a large estate, almost exclusively devoted to the cultivation of grapes and the production of wine, had been built up by an enterprising Greek family called Pirakos. Tanashi Randopolo, whose parents had immigrated from Greece and become Egyptian citizens, was a senior employee on the estate and, when it was nationalized according to the socialization laws of July 1961, was kept on as manager. He was a man aged about sixty, of considerable charm and ability, who was twice elected to Parliament as deputy for the district, which was virtually a domain of the company. Most of the time he lived in the pleasant company rest-house built on the estate and showed himself an adept at public relations by the judicious distribution of wine, brandy, and fruit in the right quarters. Then, in 1970, he acquired new neighbours. Just beyond the boundary of the estate was an airfield, and it became one from which Soviet planes operated in defence of their Mediterranean fleet and of Egyptian positions in depth.

My own involvement in the affair began one day in September 1971 when I was in Alexandria and received an extremely agitated telephone call from Donald Bergus saying that the home of an American citizen in Cairo had been attacked by police using machine-guns and pistols. 'This is a very grave matter,' he said. I asked what this was supposed to have to do with me, and suggested that he should get in touch with the Ministry of Foreign Affairs. His manner abruptly changed, and in a chastened voice he said, 'Yes, Sir,' and rang off.

He later, apparently, got through to Mahmoud Riad on the telephone, and though it was by then the middle of the night woke him up to say that an American's house had been attacked and an American citizen arrested. 'If this sort of thing is going to happen,' he stormed, 'I'm going to advise all Americans in Egypt, including those working in the oilfields, to quit because it won't be safe for them to go on living there.' A somewhat irritated Mahmoud Riad told him he knew nothing of the matter and recommended him to get in touch in the morning with Ahmed Osman, the legal adviser to the Ministry.

What in fact had happened was this: the CIA had got hold

of Tanashi Randopolo and asked him to report to them on Soviet activities at the airbase. They were able to persuade him to act as a spy because he had a son who had emigrated to the States whom he was desperately anxious to help. Contact between him and the CIA was maintained through a girl called Miss Swain, who was nominally a secretary in the visa section of the American Consulate. Several months earlier the intelligence people had become suspicious of Tanashi Randopolo and had begun to shadow him. Three letters written in invisible ink containing information about the base were intercepted, and he was arrested at Agami. An American who was with him at the time produced evidence of his diplomatic status and was therefore allowed to go.

Miss Swain was less fortunate. After Randopolo had been arrested her superiors decided it was time for her to disappear. She had called at a friend's flat to say goodbye, and on her return home, after leaving her car in the garage, she was approached by two plain clothes intelligence officers. She tried to escape, but was caught, arrested, and taken to intelligence headquarters. Her flat was searched. Contrary to what Bergus had claimed, no arms of any description had been involved in either arrest or search. General Ahmed Ismail, Director of Intelligence at that time, had been careful to have the whole process of her arrest filmed, so that there should be no argument about what actually took place.

When Bergus had an interview with Ahmed Osman the next morning he still maintained that force had been used against Miss Swain. Ahmed Osman denied it. A full report, he said, had already been sent to the President showing that everything had gone smoothly. Miss Swain was in custody, and Tanashi Randopolo had made a full confession. Bergus then made the mistake of saying that General Ismail must have given the President false information.

When General Ismail heard this he immediately sent for the head of the CIA in Egypt, whose identity was of course known to him, a certain Eugene Trone, who had diplomatic cover as a member of the mission looking after American interests. Trone urged that the business should be cleared up with the minimum of fuss and pleaded for the girl's immediate release. When he got back to his office he wrote a letter to General Ismail of quite extraordinary frankness. 'I want to assure you,' he said, 'that any information we obtained through the girl did not go to Israel. It was only for the benefit of the United States. As a matter of fact, this was to the benefit of Egypt too, because it enabled the American Government, when Israel asked for more arms on the ground of the arms being sent by the Soviet Union to Egypt, to tell them that they were exaggerating. I want you,' he went on, 'to understand that Egypt is not the target in this espionage affair. As you know the United States and the Soviet Union are involved in a global confrontation. Here was a base from which the Soviets were operating, and we were naturally interested in what they were doing. We were spying on them and not on you.'

On his side, Ahmed Ismail was anxious not to let the affair get out of hand. Trone brought Bergus to see him, and Bergus made a complete apology. Poor man, all he had tried to do in Egypt appeared now to be in ruins, and during the interview he more or less collapsed. Miss Swain proved of tougher fibre. She refused to admit anything. The Americans used all their blandishments to secure her release, but President Sadat refused to sanction it until some months later. Tanashi Randopolo had from the moment of his arrest been in a state of almost complete collapse, and I was told later that he had died from a heart attack.

There was considerable fallout from the affair on the Russian side too. It seems that the Soviet base staff had at one time asked for all the surroundings of the runways to be planted with fruit trees to improve concealment, and Tanashi Randopolo had said that before he could arrange for this he must have a look at what was involved. They had flown him over the airfield in a helicopter, and a full report of his jaunt was contained in one of the letters found on him when he was arrested. He had also struck up a close friendship with three commanders of nearby Soviet missile batteries, who used to visit his home, and to whom he sent presents of wine and fruit. General Shazli was instructed to ask his counterpart, General Shwartzkopf, the Russian Adviser to the Chief of Staff, to withdraw the three missile commanders and to give orders that all Russian experts in Egypt should be forbidden to discuss with any Egyptians any subject unconnected with training matters.

On 15 September Vinogradov and I were having lunch together. He said there was a matter he would like to raise in a purely personal and confidential way. If Egypt asked three senior Air Force experts to leave the country, he said, it would have an immediate prejudicial effect on the work of all the other experts. None of them would believe for a moment that any of them could betray the mission with which they had been entrusted. They had come voluntarily to Egypt, and were prepared to die for Egypt. Marshal Grechko and the whole Soviet army would take it very much amiss, particularly since no official investigation was apparently to be asked for. As for the proposed order limiting conversations between Soviet experts and Egyptians to training matters, it had to be remembered that the experts were human beings. It was perfectly legitimate to put a ban on any discussion of internal Egyptian politics, but to confine their talk wholly to training was too much.

However, at about the same time President Sadat told me he heard that some Russian experts had been putting highly political questions to the Egyptian officers they were working with: what did they think of the trial of the Ali Sabri group? What did they think of Sadat as President, and of General Sadiq? That, the President thought, was intolerable. When I told him about my talk with Vinogradov, however, he got in touch with General Sadiq and instructed him to cancel the order for the immediate expulsion of the three offending experts. Instead, when our investigation into the affair had been completed, the report was to be sent to the chief Soviet expert and it should be left to him to decide what action should be taken. When I reported this change of plan to Vinogradov he was a very happy man.

6. THE LAST MEETING WITH ROGERS

In one respect the Randopolo affair was particularly significant: it showed the working of that 'other channel' of communication between Egypt and the United States, which was to become increasingly important – the channel from President Sadat to our Intelligence, then to the CIA, and from them to the American National Security Council and Kissinger. It was to keep this channel open that President Sadat finally agreed to the release of Miss Swain.

Of course, this underground link effectively cut out the State Department, and the last days of September 1971 saw a final attempt by Secretary of State, William Rogers, to achieve agreement on the cherished American proposal for an interim settlement, and at the same time to drive a wedge between the Egyptian Presidency and Ministry of Foreign Affairs. In neither respect was it successful. The scene was a working lunch in the State Department. Present on the American side were, beside the Secretary of State, Sisco, Patterson, McCloskey, the State Department spokesman, Atherton, liaison between the State Department and the National Security Council, and Sterner; and on the Egyptian side, Mahmoud Riad, Dr Zayyat, and Ashraf Ghorbal. Rogers started off by saying he was really puzzled about the attitude of the Egyptian Ministry of Foreign Affairs towards an interim agreement. From all the exchanges he had had with President Sadat over the last six months he had come to the conclusion that the Egyptian Government wanted an interim agreement 'as a practical way of starting the process towards peace'. Yet in an interview Mahmoud Riad had given on television the day before he had said: 'I don't understand what is meant by an interim agreement.'

Mahmoud Riad explained that he was genuinely not clear what the US really meant. It seemed to him that the United States was distorting President Sadat's proposal of the previous February (for opening the Suez Canal). What President Sadat had been suggesting then was a first phase in a process towards a final peace settlement according to Resolution 242. What the Israelis wanted, on the other hand, was a prolonged truce which would leave them in permanent possession of at least ninety per cent of the territory they had occupied in 1967. If the Americans thought that the opening of the Suez Canal should be the signal for Jarring to draw up a timetable for the complete withdrawal, within a period of six months, of Israel from all Arab territories, then Egypt agreed one hundred per cent. Rogers countered by saying that the United States simply did not think a final plan could be drawn up at this stage, and that was why they had been talking about an interim agreement. If Egypt insisted that Israel should acknowledge an obligation to withdraw completely from all the conquered territories then he had to state in all frankness that the United States had no means of convincing the Israelis of the need to do this or of imposing such an obligation on them.

The discussion continued along the same lines for some time. Mahmoud Riad tried to get some more precise information as to what the interim agreement was supposed to cover. Who would sign it? What would the UN's role in it be? How long would it last? In answer to this second question Rogers said it should contain a clause calling for revision after eighteen months. Would this mean, Mahmoud Riad asked, that after eighteen months, if nothing had been achieved, Egypt would have the right to cross the Canal and liberate the occupied territory by force? Rogers said that if there had been no progress Egypt would obviously then have the same right it had now – to do whatever it thought necessary for its own security.

The Americans kept going back to the advantage they saw in an interim agreement – that it would set a precedent for an Israeli withdrawal, that it would be a practical movement towards the end they all had in view. Mahmoud Riad pointed out that the Israelis had been made to withdraw from the whole of Sinai in 1957, so this would not be a precedent and he stressed the danger of allowing Israel once again to convert what was meant to be a temporary arrangement into a permanent one. Finally, Rogers said that the discussion had left him extremely depressed. He felt that Mahmoud Riad was saying he could not accept ninety-nine per cent of what he wanted and would hold out for one hundred per cent – no problem in the world could be settled on that basis. Sisco echoed Rogers by saying that if Egypt insisted on all or nothing it would end with nothing.

Some points of interest emerged from this otherwise unproductive meeting. One was that the Americans were still convinced Egypt was incapable of making any serious initiative on its own. At one point Rogers said: 'I can imagine you, my dear friend, Mr Riad, coming to the General Assembly at the age of seventy-five preparing the same speech that you have prepared this year and with the Egyptian position exactly as it is this year.' Another was that the State Department thought there was a divergence of view between the Presidency and the Ministry of Foreign Affairs in Egypt. This was probably based on a misunderstanding of something President Sadat had told Rogers when he visited Cairo. Talking of his 4 February speech and the proposal to open the Suez Canal he had said: 'Everybody was against it at the time, even Mahmoud Riad.' He was trying to convince the Secretary of State of the importance of the concession he had made, but of course once the speech had been made its contents had become official policy and were loyally supported by everyone in the Government.

It must have been because he thought this divergence was a real one, and capable of being exploited, that Rogers shortly after sent a direct message to President Sadat which was aimed at discrediting Mahmoud Riad. In this he said that Mahmoud Riad had been jumping to conclusions about the interim agreement. He had accused the United States of wanting to make the interim agreement an end in itself, and seemed unable to understand that it was really the beginning of a practical effort towards a final settlement. Mahmoud Riad, he said, had wasted a lot of time discussing semantics, but the Americans were going on using the expression 'interim agreement' because it was one used by all the other nations and to them it seemed quite precise. It meant, he thought, exactly what the Egyptians had in mind too – practical arrangements of a temporary nature that could lead to other stages of progress towards a final settlement. But Rogers showed his continuing misunderstanding of the Egyptian position when he referred to President Sadat's 4 February speech as containing 'a proposal for an interim agreement which we consider an imaginative and constructive step', whereas of course President Sadat had been talking about the first step in a planned programme for final settlement, each stage of which was to be agreed within a specified period. At any rate, after this lunch meeting Rogers and Mahmoud Riad ceased to have any active part in negotiations over a Middle East settlement, which were conducted thenceforward between Kissinger and Hafez Ismail, Assistant to the President for National Security Affairs, or between Kissinger and President Sadat himself.

7. INTO 1972

Nineteen seventy-one was to have been the 'year of decision' and now it was drawing to a close without any decision. I had always had my doubts about this phrase – or at least thought that 1971 should be the year for taking a decision and not the year for implementing it. It was better to avoid fixing a definite period within which action was to be expected. The Soviets had been very much against the idea too, and several times asked exactly what it meant.

Egypt's relations with them on the military side were strained because there were still hesitations over which of several possible operational plans should be adopted. There were various modifications to the plan to seize a bridgehead across the Canal – Liberation 1, 2 or 3 – and then, after the missile wall had been erected in 1970, there was the plan Nasser had ordered for going as far as the passes in Sinai, which was code-named Granite One after the hard rock of Aswan from which so many of Egypt's monuments have been made. When General Sadiq took over, he thought Granite One did not go far enough, so he developed Granite Two, which involved a canal crossing, storming of the passes, and a sweep towards the international frontiers of Egypt. Granite Two was still further expanded into Granite Three, which envisaged our moving into the Gaza Strip, whose liberation we considered a responsibility Egypt

155

could not renounce. The military planning staff went on working all the time, adjusting according to the changing internal and international circumstances. The trouble was that all these operations required different arms and equipment. The Russians would never discuss operational plans with the Egyptian authorities; nor would they take part in the basic studies behind these plans: they were willing to help with material, but regarded the method by which the occupied territory was liberated as being entirely up to Egypt. Whether they realized that changing demands for arms were dictated by changes of plan I do not know, but they sometimes used to say that Egypt seemed to be mainly interested in accumulating arms in warehouses. Whenever President Nasser or President Sadat went to Moscow, meetings would start off with General Grechko reading out a list of arms – 'You have got this, you have got that' – all aimed at showing that Egypt had acquired as much as the Israelis. But the Russians concentrated on quantity rather than quality.

One sidelight on Egyptian-Soviet relations at this time; on 9 November 1971, after an inconclusive visit to Moscow, President Sadat called General Okunev, the chief Soviet adviser, to his office. The President was wearing the uniform of Supreme Commander of the Egyptian Armed Forces, and after welcoming Okunev he asked him: 'Who are you talking to now, General?' Okunev looked astonished and said: 'Mr President, I'm talking to you.' 'And who am I?' asked Sadat. 'President Sadat,' said Okunev. 'No,' said the President, 'I am Stalin. For your information I am Stalin, not Kalinin. You made use of Kalinin as Head of State to review the troops in World War Two, but he knew nothing of what was going on. It was Stalin who was the leader responsible for the conduct of the battle and the management of the whole war. So now, General, in my capacity as Stalin and not as Kalinin, I want you to sit down and tell me exactly how things stand. Give me your real appreciation of our position. If Stalin had summoned you and asked you that question would you have given him a frank answer?' 'I most certainly would,' said Okunev. 'Very well,' said the President. 'If you don't carry out this order of mine now I'll treat you exactly as Stalin would have treated you.' Okunev laughed, and the discussion moved on to problems of training, the supply of arms, Egypt's military potential, and so on.

At the end of 1971 we submitted the whole Middle East problem to the General Assembly of the United Nations and started a concerted drive to focus world public opinion on it. But suddenly the attention of everyone was diverted by the war in the Indian sub-continent. This provided us with an excuse for not doing anything positive about the year of decision, but that was all.

Nineteen seventy-two was to prove a difficult year. It started badly with disturbances among the students, frustrated by the lack of action, and by the Cabinet changes. Dr Fawzi was asked to resign and Dr Aziz Sidqi took over as Prime Minister. Although Dr Sidqi was an able manager and the architect of Egypt's industrialization programme, the reasons for the change were not understood.

President Sadat, too, had a sense of frustration after the anti-climax of the year of decision. He knew that his personal popularity had suffered and he felt that this was at least in part because he was shouldering the blame which should more properly have attached to the Soviets. He decided to go to Moscow once more to try to clear the air, but before setting out he went in January to Aswan to inspect the defences of the High Dam. In talks with young officers he found that they were profoundly dissatisfied with the TU-16 long-range bombers with long-range missile launchers with which they were equipped. It was estimated that if used operationally no more than twenty per cent of the planes would return from their first mission.

President Sadat left for Moscow on 2 February and stayed for two days, returning to Cairo via Yugoslavia, Syria and Libya. I saw him at the Barrage just after his return, and he started his account of his Moscow talks by saying: 'Who would have thought that the turning-point would have been King Feisal?' What had happened was that a few hours before he was due to go to Moscow he had received a message from King Feisal offering to make him a present of twenty Lightning fighter-bombers which had been bought from Great Britain some years before. 'I hope,' the King had said in his message, 'that this will persuade some others to accelerate their aid.' President Sadat had wanted to show his gratitude to King Feisal so he had got General Sadiq to send a message to Prince Sultan, Saudi Arabian Minister of Defence, to the effect that should an emergency arise while he was in Moscow the Egyptian army command was to take orders from King Feisal. Prince Sultan made the contents of the message known to senior officers and it created a deep impression in Saudi Arabia. It has to be admitted that the end of the story was not quite so happy. The twenty Lightnings never arrived; instead some of our pilots were sent to Saudi Arabia to train on them. At the same time other pilots were training on new machines in Kuwait and Libya, so that a large part of our air force was in effect scattered through the Arab world.

However, King Feisal's gesture may have helped to influence the Russians, because they agreed to supply Egypt with TU-22s, whereas in the past they had always resisted this demand. In fact, Brezhnev had more than once said to President Sadat that he was sick and tired of being asked for new aircraft and refused to discuss it any more. On this occasion he fought one more rearguard action. 'Why are you so afraid of bombing from the air?' he asked. 'We were continuously bombed in World War Two and won.' President Sadat answered: 'I'm not afraid of bombing, but I want to be able to bomb the people who bomb me. Let me remind you that there are two thousand vital targets in Egypt. If Israel bombed one of our stratetic barrages it might mean the flooding of 250,000 *feddans*.' The Soviets also agreed to let us have the T-62 tank, which was a great advance.

President Sadat told me that Brezhnev had taxed him with stories that in Cairo the Russians were being blamed for holding Egypt back from fighting a war for the liberation of the lost territories. 'I told Brezhnev,' said the President, 'that as a matter of fact there were many people who thought that, and did so because I had been promised so many things by you that never came. "In October you promised me equipment that hasn't arrived; more was promised by Podgorny in May, and it hasn't arrived; more was promised by Ponomarev in July, and that has not arrived either. Why the delay?" Brezhnev looked at me and said: "As a matter of fact it was I who took that decision, and nobody else." ' President Sadat added that in order to smooth things over he had told Brezhnev that if the decision came from him, of course he would accept it. Then he laughed, and said to me: 'You know, they are orientals like ourselves.'

During this period relations with Libya had not been easy, which was why President Sadat made Benghazi a stopping point on his return journey. Ghadaffi disapproved of several lines of Egyptian policy. He disliked our acceptance of Resolution 242 and our close association with the Soviet Union. He doubted the value of the new equipment with which the Russians had agreed to supply us, though President Sadat explained to him the superiority of the TU-22 and the T-62 tank and tried to convince him of the Soviet Union's good intentions. He was also critical of King Feisal and had recently made a speech in which he called Feisal 'king of the reactionary forces in the Arab World'. President Sadat asked him if he would please stop attacking Feisal – 'that king of reaction gave us the Lightnings.' Ghadaffi's answer was to suggest they should go ahead and start implementing the idea of unity. 'All right,' he said, 'why don't we, Libya, abolish our Ministry of Foreign Affairs? As it is we have our own seat in the United Nations and are obliged to express our own revolutionary point of view, and attack Resolution 242 and reaction and the Soviet Union because it's collaborating with the other super-power in a détente, whereas if we scrapped our Ministry of Foreign Affairs and gave up our seat at the UN we should save you – and us – the embarrassment of Egypt and Libya speaking with two voices. We could air our differences in private instead of in public. I don't care about national sovereignty; I care about unity.' President Sadat was not enthusiastic. He thought the proposal premature.

However, one outcome of this discussion was the decision to send Major Jalloud to Moscow in February on an arms-buying mission on behalf of both Libya and Egypt. He was to offer to pay the full price in cash – in hard currency – and see if it would help to speed up deliveries. He took with him Mustafa Kharubi, the Libyan deputy Chief of Staff, as well as a member of the Revolutionary Command Council and a devout Muslim. During

159

one of the negotiating sessions Kharubi looked at his watch and announced that it was time for the midday prayer. Standing up, he enquired which was the direction of Mecca and, having received the information, began to pray. All conversation stopped. Kosygin and Podgorny looked astonished. But Kharubi had made his gesture, and the prayers of a Muslim believer had been heard in the citadel of atheism.

Another subject on which President Sadat and Ghadaffi failed to see eye to eye was King Hussein's proposal for a United Arab Kingdom – a federation of Jordan and the West Bank – which he announced in March. Ghadaffi was boiling with indignation over it. Both President Sadat and President Asad tried to get him to calm down. President Sadat's point of view was that King Hussein was completely isolated, knew this, and was trying to escape from his isolation. He thought the scheme must have been prepared in advance with the Americans, and that America, with the assistance of Israel and the connivance of King Hussein, was preparing to draw new permanent frontiers in the Middle East. Part of the plot, he thought, involved Gaza, which, under King Hussein's plan would become Jordan's corridor to the sea and so isolate Egypt from Palestine (and of course it was at Rafah that Dayan was busy making preparations for the big new Israeli port of Yamit). President Sadat suggested a special meeting of the PLO should be called and that whatever attitude they decided towards King Hussein's proposal should receive the backing of Egypt and Libya.

8. MORE TROUBLE WITH THE SOVIETS

It was in the course of another of President Sadat's visits to Libya, in May, that a fresh crisis blew up with the Soviet Union. General Sadiq had found out that Russian experts in Egypt, going home either permanently or on leave, were in the habit of taking large quantities of gold with them. Some estimates gave the amount taken out between the time when they first arrived in 1970 and the beginning of 1972 as high as several hundred

President Sadat and Gen. Ismail inspect SAM 3 missile sites.

Gen. Ismail crossing the Suez Canal by pontoon bridge.

Mr Kissinger shaking hands with President Sadat.

kilos. At first they only took small gold ornaments with them, but later they grew more confident and took out a great deal of jewellery – bracelets and brooches for their wives, rings for themselves and so on – and some even took out gold blocks. General Sadiq arranged that the customs people should start asking them to declare their gold. The first time this happened some produced the gold they had but others objected, and refused to be searched. The head of the Military Mission and the Russian Ambassador were called to the airport; the plane taking the Russians home was delayed for eleven hours. Attempts were made to get General Sadiq on the telephone and even to contact President Sadat in Libya. There was a great deal of excitement and tension but eventually President Sadat was reached. He said it was unnecessary to make too much of the incident: a written report of what had happened should be prepared, and meanwhile the Russians should be allowed to go with what they had got.

There was another clash with the Soviets at the same time on a different matter. Part of the 1970 agreement, by which the Soviet Union undertook responsibilities for the air defence of the Egyptian interior, had been that some Egyptians would go there for training on SAM-3 missiles, so that when properly qualified they could come back and take over from the Russian technicians. By now eighteen teams were so qualified and General Sadiq considered it was time for them to make the changeover. Dr Sidqi thought it would be a mistake to ask for all eighteen Soviet crews to leave at once – it would look too much like a mass exodus, and the President agreed. General Sadiq talked to the President again and it was decided that, as a compromise, Egypt should take over twelve batteries, keeping six trained crews in reserve. The President asked General Sadiq to write to the chief Soviet expert telling him that on a certain date the substitution was to take effect. After all, as he said, the Egyptian crews had already been back in the country for six months, they had had actual combat training, and the services of the Soviet experts had to be paid for in hard currency.

But the Soviets were upset by the suggestion. Marshal Grechko came to Egypt within a few days. He said it would create bad feeling among the Soviet missile crews, and would be taken as an indication that they were not wanted here. Moreover, coming just before President Nixon was due to visit Moscow, this would appear to be giving America a propaganda victory on a silver platter.

Another problem which tied up with this concerned payment for Russian aircraft. The last time he had been in Moscow President Sadat had been promised some of the latest Soviet fighters, the MiG-23, when they came on to the production line in sufficient quantity, and had undertaken to pay hard currency for them – which was being provided by Ghadaffi. But when a delegation headed by General Abdel Qader Hassan, Deputy Minister for War, arrived without publicity in Moscow around this time, he found that they were not ready to give us MiG-23s but offered a modified version of the MiG-21 instead. They wanted us to pay hard currency for these planes, but President Sadat refused, saying they properly belonged to an earlier contract, which was not a hard currency deal.

There was a curious story attaching to this modified MiG-21. On 30 July 1970, soon after the Soviet crews had arrived in Egypt with their original version of the MiG-21, some Israeli Phantoms crossed over into the Sukhna area. The Soviet pilots scrambled from Minya airfield but flew into an Israeli trap, and within seconds four MiGs had been destroyed and another badly damaged, the pilot baling out. I remember talking to President Nasser the same day and his saying to me: 'Something very odd happened today. The Israelis have shot down five Russian planes. In a way I'm sorry this happened and in a way I'm not sorry. The Russians have always been accusing our pilots of not being able to learn from experience, of going on making the same mistakes, and of not being up to the standard of Israeli pilots. Naturally this annoys our boys who blame many of the things that go wrong on the planes they have to fly. Now the Air Force feels itself justified, because they know that the Russians at last have proof that the MiGs are no match for Phantoms.' No mention of the Russian losses was made in Egypt at the time, and the Israelis were cunning over them too. Of course they informed the Americans, but they did not release the news publicly in order to avoid public embarrassment for the Soviets which might have led them to escalate the fighting. The Russians learned their lesson too, and introduced modifications to the MiG-21s.

Anyway, these questions of the battery crews and payment for the aircraft were the occasion for much negotiation involving both President Sadat and Brezhnev. At one point President Sadat asked Murad Ghaleb, who was then Minister of Foreign Affairs, and Hafez Ismail, Security Adviser to the President, to write a memorandum for Brezhnev outlining the position between us and the Soviet Union. He told the Soviet Ambassador to expect this, but later in the evening Vinogradov went to see the President and gave him a message: 'Comrade Brezhnev is grateful for the explanation you have sent him. He sees no need for a written analysis of the differences between us which, he feels, would be of no benefit to anyone.' So the crisis was temporarily patched over.

But there was one rather curious footnote – it came during that May visit of Marshal Grechko. Four reconnaissance versions of the MiG – the X-500, the Russians called them, but they are now known as the MiG-25 – had been delivered and President Sadat was invited to Cairo West airport to see them in action. Marshal Grechko suggested that a statement should be issued to the Press to the effect that Egyptian pilots had now had experience of flying planes at three times the speed of sound and that President Sadat had witnessed them doing so. This would have given the impression that Egypt had received MiG-25s, and, though not true – it was not even true that the aircraft had Egyptian pilots – President Sadat was prepared to agree to it because he thought it would commit the Soviet Union to supply us with them. As soon as he had said he agreed Vinogradov took a draft statement out of his pocket, issued in the name of the Central Committee of the Soviet Union. I was not happy about the statement because I thought it would put the air force in an awkward position. The rest of the Arab world would conclude that Egypt had these most up-to-date aircraft and would wonder why it showed no sign of making any use of them.

Admiral Gorshikov, the Soviet naval commander, had come

to Egypt with Marshal Grechko and had revived the idea of our giving the Soviet Navy 'facilities' at Mersa Matruh and Bernis in the Red Sea. The army and navy were strongly opposed to the idea, but Admiral Gorshikov was very insistent, claiming that only with these facilities would the Soviet Navy be able to operate properly, and that it would enable them to give Egypt much better reconnaissance information and so on. I disliked the proposal myself, and told President Sadat I thought it would commit Egypt too deeply to the naval strategy of the Soviet Union. It was at this time I started writing a series of articles in *Al Ahram* called: 'No Peace: No War,' in which I argued that the Soviet Union might have a vested interest in preserving such a situation.

I had always felt that Soviet policy had two aspects. As a super-power the Soviet Union had to think in global terms, and these sometimes came into conflict with its role as helper and protector of countries like Egypt which were going through their own revolutionary experience. I had the greatest admiration for what the Soviet Union had done for Egypt, which had proved it Egypt's most reliable friend. No other country could have given Egypt anything approaching what the Soviet Union gave during the years while the Egyptian social system and economy were being transformed. Egypt had benefited enormously in many fields – from the Soviet political example, trade, industrialization, arms supply, and so on. The Egyptian social system was far closer to the Russian than to the American. But the fact remained that the Soviet Union was deeply concerned with the détente and with the development of its naval strategy. No doubt they wanted a solution of the Middle East problem which would satisfy Arab aspirations, but they did not want a war.

At about this time an exercise was carried out in Cairo with a computer to assess the degree to which the various countries benefited from the existing 'No Peace: No War' situation. All the relevant considerations were fed into the computer, and the result awarded Israel 420 points, the United States 380 points, and the Soviet Union 110 points.

9. THE BREAK

It can now be seen how the situation was building up to the climax which was to come on 6 July when President Sadat gave the order for Soviet technicians to be withdrawn from Egypt. But before describing this event in detail it is necessary to look back a bit.

After the 1967 defeat Nasser's attitude towards the Soviet Union was a complex one. He saw that the two super-powers were edging towards a détente and he could sense that the Johnson administration was unsympathetic towards the Arabs in general and towards him in particular. He was therefore determined to get the Soviet Union as deeply involved in the Middle East problem as he could. He wanted them to feel that his defeat had been their defeat, and to make them take the lead in diplomatic efforts to overcome the disastrous legacy. When-ever Egypt had a proposal to make he would not let Mahmoud Riad or any other representative of Egypt put it forward: he preferred to pass it to the Russians and let them present it to Jarring or Washington. He felt that if, with Soviet help, a satisfactory political settlement could be reached, that would be fine; but if, as was much more likely, no such settlement was found, then the Soviet Union would be obliged to give him the material help of which he was in need. His whole aim was to lift the Middle East dispute from the local to the international level; at the local level Israel had proved its superiority – at the international we might be more evenly balanced.

I used to write articles at this time on the theme that in the Middle East there were two local powers which could not make peace and two super-powers which could not make war. Of course, there were obvious dangers in this: in the manoeuvres of the two super-powers the rights and wrongs of the Middle East conflict might be completely overlooked. The seriousness of the Middle East crisis might hasten the détente; and Nasser was always determined to make use of the détente in Egypt's interests and not to let the détente use him. But to do this he needed mobility and flexibility.

165

So it was that he kept his options open, particularly with America. The first gesture was to send his congratulations to Nixon on his election in 1968. Then he agreed to receive William Scranton, the special envoy Nixon sent to the Middle East even before he was inside the White House. Dr Mahmoud Fawzi, Assistant to the President for Foreign Affairs, was sent to Washington at the beginning of 1969 to attend Eisenhower's funeral, which gave him the chance to talk to Nixon, Rogers, and others. Later came Nasser's acceptance of the Rogers's Initiative, his talks with Sisco, and so on. He was also ready to cultivate better relations with Western Europe, especially with France, Britain, and West Germany, and with the non-aligned countries. But he was never under any illusion how America regarded him.

Even so, Nasser was careful to draw a line in his dealings with the Soviets which would keep them involved but not allow them to dominate. Thus, when Podgorny explained how important it was that the Soviet Fifth Fleet in the Mediterranean should have somewhere where they could draw fresh water (instead of getting it from Odessa) and where the crews could enjoy shore leave he was quite prepared to give them these facilities in Alexandria, Port Said, and Mersa Matruh. But when they went on to demand quarters for naval families in Mersa Matruh and Bernis, to be guarded by Soviet marines, and to claim the right for any unit of the fleet to enter any Egyptian port without prior notice, he dug his heels in, and said No. The same with the Soviet Air Force: they wanted permanent staging and overflying rights and the right to use Egyptian airfields at only a few hours' notice. Nasser refused, and insisted that in every case full notification must be given well in advance. It was a difficult tightrope to walk, but he managed it.

President Sadat continued the Nasser policy. He took a firm stand against those who even then were maintaining that the Soviets had achieved too dominant a position in the life of the country – in fact in some respects he perhaps went too far in that direction. For example, it was after he became President that the Russians virtually took over control of Cairo West Airport, to the extent that there was not even a representative of the

Egyptian customs there. Soviet planes landed and took off just as they pleased. This was far from being to everybody's liking. Some people feared that if friction developed with the Soviets they might repeat their Czechoslovak tactics: after all, they had their technicians and their own airport and could bring as many of their troops into Egypt as they wanted. There were plenty of stories of huge crates being unloaded from Soviet planes at Cairo West and these were rumoured to be full of arms destined for unknown but nefarious ends.

On the Soviet side doubts about President Sadat's intentions were multiplying. There was the President's comment to Kemal Adham, already mentioned (p. 120), which Senator Jackson leaked. Somebody reported to them a discussion in the Central Committee of the Socialist Union in 1971 when the President in answer to questions about Soviet experts, said: 'Do you think I want to keep them? We need them to give us protection in depth, but they are a burden on us because we have to pay for them in hard currency.' Brezhnev was extremely annoyed when he heard this and sent a message to President Sadat asking if he thought the Soviet experts were mercenaries.

Above all there were the arguments about arms supply which were the main theme of all four visits the President paid to Moscow between the time he took over and the end of April 1972. I think both sides were at fault. Egyptian demands were always changing as the assault plan under review changed, and were sometimes excessive. Like many under-developed countries Egypt had an exaggerated idea of the productive capacity of the super-powers, and assumed that even the most sophisticated weapons were permanently available, to be handed over for the asking. But, even supposing the Soviet Union's annual production of tanks was double that of the United States (say about 720 a year), there was a tendency to forget that it had to supply not only all her Warsaw Pact allies but also eight or nine other countries in the Arab world besides Egypt, not to mention what it was supplying to India and North Vietnam. As far as aircraft went, Egypt was so obsessed with Israel's successful pre-emptive strike of 5 June 1967 that to begin with all thoughts were concentrated on how to achieve the degree of air superiority that would enable Egypt in its turn to neutralize Israeli bases. Egyptian planning was complicated by a mixture of frustration and hope, as the projected attack was put off while the planning for it ground on. We were impatient. It was a long time before Egypt became ready to accept the idea of a limited attack aimed primarily at opening up political possibilities.

On the other hand the Soviets were sometimes extremely tactless. They would give a flat yes or no to requests, without adding any reasons, and some of the delays in arms deliveries in 1971 were difficult to explain, particularly to the military. Towards the end of the year India had first call on Soviet supplies, because of the war with Pakistan, and permission was sought to send these via Egypt. But one of the Egyptian commanders was in the habit of repeating at this time the Arabic proverb – 'water does not pass by the thirsty man.' There was also a fear on the Soviet side that Egypt might rush into some foolish military adventure in an effort to justify the 'year of decision' slogan. A further pinprick: when President Sadat was in Moscow in April 1972 Marshal Grechko gave him a lecture on the three prerequisites for fighting a successful war – arms, training, and the will to fight. 'The first two you have,' he said, 'but as for the third you will have to consult your own consciences.' The President naturally found this somewhat presumptuous.

Another implied reproach from the Soviet side concerned conditions in Egypt. It was Marshal Grechko, again, on that visit to Egypt in May 1972, who quoted one of the Soviet technicians from a SAM site near Alexandria, who had compared the disciplined austerity of his operational station with the bright lights and apparently carefree normality of Alexandria where he went occasionally on leave. He felt the Egyptian people should be permanently on a war footing. Our view was that to try to keep up a war-time atmosphere while no actual fighting was going on would only lead to an explosion. More than once President Sadat told the Soviet leaders: 'You don't understand our people. You worry about our mobilization – but I can assure you that when the first shot is fired that will mobilize everybody as nothing else could.'

Another element in the mounting tension was the approach of the fifth anniversary of the 1967 war. The knowledge that after 5 June we should be beginning a sixth year without a start being made on undoing the legacy of defeat and with the enemy every day consolidating his hold over the lands he had stolen from the Arabs had a profound effect on the people. This was enhanced by the knowledge that Nixon was due to visit Moscow in May and that thereafter, as the American election campaign got under way, Israel would, as usual, be able to extract whatever promises it wanted from the candidates, while diplomatically the whole Middle East problem was likely to go into cold storage until the new administration took over.

On 12 April President Sadat sent a letter to Brezhnev, the purpose of which was to put in writing his appreciation of the situation before his own visit to Moscow which was due on the 27th. In it he gave warnings of what might be expected from Nixon's forthcoming visit to Moscow: 'Any new American policy will certainly be against our interests.' He accused the Soviets of not having been as active in support of their friends as America had been in support of Israel, and for the first time brought up the question of the flow of Soviet immigrants to Israel: 'Some of them are young men, intellectuals and scientists, who are going to be of great material assistance to Israel.' Finally he reminded Brezhnev that within seven weeks they would be celebrating the twentieth anniversary of the Egyptian revolution, and that 'the coming dangerous period will not weaken our determination to regain our rights or our refusal to negotiate with Israel.'

When Grechko came to Cairo in May it had been agreed that General Mohammed Ahmed Sadiq, the Minister of War, should pay a visit to Moscow. The Soviets were particularly anxious to receive him because they felt that he was largely responsible for the anti-Soviet line (as they saw it) which had been taken by the armed forces over the gold-smuggling affair and the refusal of bases at Mersa Matruh and Bernis. They believed he was winning popularity among the armed forces by his reputation for standing up to the Soviets. So when he arrived in Moscow on 8 June he got the reception due to a Head of State and not to a Minister of War. President Sadat had sent a letter of introduction to Brezhnev with him (dated 7 June) in which he thanked Brezhnev for defending the Egyptian position in his recent talks with President Nixon. 'But,' the letter went on, 'we have noted public statements by leading Americans since those talks which expressed points of view contrary to the principles expressed in the joint communiqué issued after the Moscow talks.' The President repeated his conviction that 'no political solution is possible unless continued pressure is exerted on the United States and Israel and unless Israel is made to understand that the balance of military strength is not in its favour,' and again emphasized the need for the speedy implementation of the agreed programmes for the supply of arms and for training.

General Sadiq submitted a report on his Moscow talks to the President on 15 June. What went on in the President's mind between that date and 6 July, when the order for the withdrawal of the Soviet experts was given, will never be known for certain, unless President Sadat chooses to give his own version. Talking to me a few days after the event he said that for a month before he had been unhappy, with a feeling that something was brewing at the back of his mind and yet being unable to decide exactly what it was. But even after studying all the documents in the case and talking to all the people most closely involved I am still unable to decide exactly what it was that triggered off the President's decision.

The first person to know about it was Dr Mahmoud Fawzi; this was on Thursday 6 July. President Sadat had gone to the Vice-President's farm at Badrashein to offer condolences on the death of one of his relatives, and told him in an almost casual way that he was thinking of asking the Soviet Union to withdraw its military personnel from Egypt because they had become a burden to us. 'Afterwards,' he said, 'we can start fresh negotiations under the terms of our treaty with them.'

The next person to be told was General Sadiq. That was on Friday 7 July. The General was at his home, preparing to go to the Friday prayers and then to a lunch which had been arranged with Prince Sultan, the Saudi Minister of Defence, when a call came from the President: 'Come and pray with me. I am at the

Barrage.' General Sadiq apologized to Prince Sultan for breaking his appointment and went to the Barrage. On their way back from the mosque the President said to him: 'I'm going to tell you something that will make you smile all over your face. I have decided to ask the Russians to get out.' General Sadiq was understandably surprised and tried to argue the case, but he found the President adamant.

The third person to be told was the Soviet Ambassador, Vladimir Vinogradov. Some days before President Sadat had asked him to give him a fuller account of exactly what happened at the Moscow summit talks with President Nixon. In the evening of Saturday 8 July, Vinogradov came round to the presidential palace to hand over a letter from Brezhnev. The only other person present was Hafez Ismail, the President's Counsellor for National Security Affairs, and according to President Sadat, when Hafez Ismail heard the President's decision his lower jaw dropped and remained hanging down for the rest of the interview. Brezhnev's letter said, among other things, that they had done all they could to present Egypt's point of view to President Nixon but that they were worried by reports of lies against the Soviet Union being spread by 'certain elements in Egypt'. While the Soviet Union would continue its military support to Egypt it was important that the political morale of the armed forces should be raised 'to fill them with courage, determination and vigilance, and to educate them in the struggle against imperialism and Zionism'.

President Sadat then gave Vinogradov his reply to Brezhnev's letter. He said he found himself once again obliged to complain about the non-delivery of arms. A time-table for deliveries had been agreed with Marshal Grechko, but had not been kept. 'It seems,' he said, 'that the Soviet Union has no confidence in the Egyptian leadership and fails to appreciate the dangers of the situation. While Egypt is anxious to maintain the friendship of the Soviet Union she is unable to submit to a position of trusteeship to anyone, including the Soviet Union.' The President had therefore, he told the Ambassador, taken certain decisions: (1) He thanked the Soviet Union for all the help it had given Egypt through its technicians, but now wished the services of these technicians to be terminated with effect from 17 July. (2) Soviet arms which were in Egypt should either be sold to Egypt and Egyptians be trained to use them or should be withdrawn. (This was a reference to those four latest reconnaissance aircraft.) (3) Any remaining Soviet forces should be placed under Egyptian command or be withdrawn. (4) Under the terms of the Soviet-Egyptian Treaty of Friendship immediate high-level consultations should be initiated. (5) Any technicians who were in Egypt for training purposes and who came before the main body of experts arrived should stay.

Vinogradov's reply to this message covered four points: (1) He said that Brezhnev's letter to the President should be regarded as only an interim one. (2) The Soviet Union had full confidence in the Egyptian leadership. (3) He admitted that there had been problems connected with the delivery of arms, but these arose from transport difficulties. (4) The decision of which the President had now informed him implied that Egypt believed the allegations spread by the Americans that the Soviet Union had changed its policy towards Egypt.

I did not myself see the President until Tuesday 11 July, when the orders for withdrawal were still a well-kept secret. I was in Alexandria at the time and the President had rung me up asking me to come and have dinner with him at the Barrage on Sunday. Then the President of Syria, Hafez Asad, came through Cairo on his way home from Moscow and took my appointment, and no meeting could be arranged for Monday. When we did meet I began by saying I feared I must be causing him a lot of embarrassment by my 'No Peace: No War' articles. 'It seems you don't know what's going on,' he said. 'We have broken with the Soviets.' I was stunned. I may have felt that some such decision was possible, but the timing of it was surprising.

In some ways the fullest account of what led up to the President's decision is to be found in a confidential briefing which he gave to a small group of Cairo editors rather later and which I attended. He said then that it was in December 1971 that he decided there would have to be what he called a 'halt' in our relations with the Soviets. He would wait until after President Nixon's projected visit to Moscow in May but 'after that we must be firm, because otherwise things could continue as they are now for twenty years'. The President went over the whole course of his dealings with the Soviets since he came to office – describing how 'the seeds for doubt were sown in January 1971 when the "conspirators", the Ali Sabri group, went to the Soviet Ambassador and told him that Anwar Sadat was an American and was going to kick him out at any moment'; his first meeting with the Soviet leaders in February 1971 ('I felt they were evasive; they wanted to gain time'); his talks with Rogers ('the Soviet Union bewilders me: they tell me to find a peaceful solution; Rogers comes and we talk about a peaceful solution; they say Sadat has sold out his country'); and so on. But the main theme of his analysis was the evasion and delay over the delivery of arms to which, he claimed, he had been continuously subjected. He went into a great deal of detail over dates and quantities, and gave a graphic description of the events that led up to the showdown. He said that before Nixon's visit to Moscow he had explained the importance he attached to the period between that visit and the Presidential election in November – 'five months, and we shouldn't waste any of them.' He had told Marshal Grechko: 'You want Nixon to be re-elected, so do I, because a Democrat would be worse for me as well as for you. He is the lesser of two evils. But the important thing is that after the elections I should have some strength backing me; unless I can show that I have got force behind me the situation will never change.' Grechko said he would pass the message on and the Nixon-Brezhnev meeting took place. No word of what had happened then came: 'I was sitting in Egypt, counting hours, counting days, because of its importance to us.' After fifteen days the Soviet account of the meeting arrived. It was only two pages long. The first page was full of vague words and phrases – 'maybe, if . . .'. The second page said that there had been no change in the position of the imperialists and Zionists but that they had persuaded the Americans to include a reference to Resolution 242 in the communiqué.

President Sadat said he had sent an answer to this message and waited for a further communication from Moscow: 'One, two, three weeks passed. I knew from working with President Nasser that from the end of July all communication with the Soviet leadership is broken off because they all go on holiday for the whole of August. But at last, on Thursday 6 July, the Soviet Ambassador asked to see me.'

Then he gave us his version of the fateful interview. 'I felt so tense that I didn't want to see the Ambassador. I said "let him come on the Saturday". I went to the Barrage. I could guess what the contents of the letter were going to be, and I planned the attitude I should take up to put them in their place. I felt they needed an electric shock. For four years first Nasser and then I had been suffering at their hands. It was clear to me that in Moscow the two super-powers had agreed that there was to be no war in the Middle East area. There was to be nothing for us but surrender. "Still," I said, "Perhaps there will be something in the Ambassador's message. Perhaps there will be something to offer, though I doubt it. Anyway, let the Ambassador come at eight o'clock." The message was two and a half pages long with an Arabic translation attached to it. I was sitting on a sofa listening to it being read, leaning with my head on my stick. The first page explained how the Soviet Union had persuaded Nixon to include a sentence in the joint communiqué about Resolution 242 and the Jarring mission. I said, "I may be crazy but surely Nixon didn't need any persuading over this: after all, they took part in the drafting of the resolution and I remember Goldberg saying that America would put all its weight behind it." It was bad luck for the Soviets that the day before the Ambassador came the Americans had sent me a message saying, "you can relax, and do whatever you like, but remember that the key to a solution is here." The second page of the message was a complaint over what Heikal had been writing about the "No Peace: No War" situation. The third page was still going on about "saboteurs like Heikal". I was sitting listening, not looking. In the last ten lines they got on to the question of the battle. They said: "We are used to battles. Wars need much preparation, including psychological preparation and the building up of morale." They killed Nasser with that sort of talk. Whenever we get on to a subject that is awkward for them they start talking about morale. I told the Ambassador everything that had happened since my first meetings with the Soviet leadership in February 1971. I said: "Brezhnev lied to me in March 1971; Podgorny lied to me in May 1971; Brezhnev lied to me in October 1971. Do you think I don't know your game? You have agreed with the Americans that there is to be no war. Let me tell you that you have no tutelage over us." I told the Ambassador: "All this is not aimed at you but at the Soviet leaders." Then I looked at my watch, and asked Hafez Ismail: "What is the date? I can't see without my glasses." He said: "It's the eighth." I said: "All right, then, I'm giving you ten days, till the seventeenth. After that the old way of doing business between Egypt and the Soviet Union is at an end." '

I think the Soviets were shocked by the President's decision but not surprised. They were deeply annoyed and hurt, but had prepared themselves in advance for something of the sort. Their reaction was very restrained. After his interview with the President, Vinogradov was of course in immediate touch with Moscow. He saw General Okunev, who contacted Marshal Grechko, and by dawn on the Monday he had received instructions that he was to comply with the Egyptian demands. That same day Okunev saw General Sadiq and within a few hours was able to present him with a plan for the evacuation of the experts, whose numbers had by that time risen to 21,000. They were to be taken home by air, and each day he presented the Egyptian Minister of War with a programme for the day's withdrawal. At one point he did make a suggestion that an office should be retained in the Egyptian Ministry of Defence for the chief Soviet expert only, with a staff of about eighty, to supervise questions of co-operation and training. General Sadiq advised the President against granting this concession because he felt it would amount to their keeping a military mission in another guise. The President refused the request and the Russians acquiesced. They were probably less insistent on this because neither the facilities in our ports for their fleet nor the Egyptian-Soviet Treaty of Friendship were being cancelled, as they had obviously feared might be the case.

On 13 July Dr Aziz Sidqi was sent to Moscow. He was instructed to apply balm to the Soviet wounds and to try to arrange for the purchase of some of the Soviet equipment left behind in Egypt, notably the four reconnaissance planes (X-500s) and the Quadrat missiles – I use the Soviet name for them – defending the High Dam. As part of the balm he suggested to Brezhnev that there might be a joint communiqué to the effect that the work done by the Soviet experts in Egypt had been completed. This would be an answer to the charges made in the Western press that they had been expelled. Brezhnev refused. He said: 'You asked for the experts. If you want them to leave that is your decision, and we will comply with it. But we are never going to be party to a cover-up story and will not take the responsibility before history of suggesting that they are being withdrawn at our request.' He refused to sell us any of the equipment we had asked for. Kosygin handed Aziz Sidqi a letter confirming the refusal to sell arms. President Sadat's view was that 'the Soviets were idiots to refuse our offer of a communiqué'.

By the beginning of August the Soviets had got over their initial shock and Brezhnev sent President Sadat a message which reached him in Libya. Some people, particularly the Prime Minister, thought there were some constructive points in it, but there was one paragraph that President Sadat did not like at all. This read: 'We cannot be indifferent to the direction which the Arab Republic of Egypt is taking, because this is something which concerns the mutual interests of the Soviet and Arab peoples. You may remember, Mr President, that the leaders of our two countries were agreed on the need to strengthen and consolidate your own forward march and that of all progressive forces in the Middle East. We feel we have the right to remind you of this because you yourself have several times spoken to us about the increasing activities of the reactionary forces inside Egypt and of the efforts being made by rightist elements directly or indirectly allied with imperialism to halt Egypt's march along the progressive road and turn it back. Where is Egypt going? Where is it being driven by forces inside and outside its borders? What is the relationship between us to be in the future? These are the questions which are causing anxiety to your friends and giving encouragement to your enemies. We look forward to receiving an answer to these questions and hope that it will be made in all frankness.'

The President thought this insulting and amounted to interference in the internal affairs of Egypt, so he himself drafted a stiff answer. He also dictated an item which he wanted published in *Al Ahram*: 'We have heard from well-informed sources that the message from Brezhnev is of no significance and is not expected to lead to any new contacts between Egypt and the Soviet Union in the near future.' After some discussion he agreed that this should not appear, but he told me he wanted the importance of the message to be played down. Another news item published at his orders was that the Egyptian Ambassador in Moscow had been recalled home on leave.

Why had the Soviet military presence become so unpopular in Egypt? Why was the decision to dispense with their services so well received, in spite of all the arms and the assistance they had given us? Why had General Sadiq become such a popular figure in the armed forces because of the resistance he was supposed to have put up to Soviet influence?

To answer these questions we have to go back to 1955 and President Nasser's first arms deal with the Soviet Union. This was extremely popular in Egypt because it broke the West's arms monopoly in the area and enabled us to get weapons with which to defend ourselves at a time when America was denying them to Egypt, and when Israel by such action as the Gaza raid which killed thirty-nine people was showing itself at its most aggressive. But in practice the arms deal created difficulties. The officer corps found itself getting arms it was unaccustomed to; the instructors were Russian, the instruction manuals were written in Russian. The whole army was obliged to switch from a Western to an Eastern outlook. When the Sinai war came on us a year later we won a great political victory, but the new Soviet armament did not show up well – though, to be fair, it did not get a proper trial.

That was the first phase of Egypt's association with the Soviet Union. The second phase covered the seven years between Suez and the June War of 1967. President Nasser decided that the armed forces would have to be remodelled and that to do this missions would have to be sent to the Soviet Union to learn on the spot about Russian military thinking as well as about Russian weaponry. The first to be sent were generals because obviously those who were to command the new army must be in a position to give the necessary leadership. So it was that men like General Abdel Munim Riad, General Ahmed Ismail, General Fawzi, General Mortagi, General Sadiq, General Abdel Qader Hassan, were enrolled at the Moscow War Academy. Most of these men were already graduates of West European or American military institutions. They naturally found the atmosphere of Moscow very different from that of Sandhurst or West Point. It was irksome for them to find themselves back in the classroom, often being taught by instructors younger and lower in rank than themselves, and receiving their instruction through the medium of interpreters – and it must be admitted that at that time the standard of Arabic interpretation in the Soviet Union was very low indeed. Moreover, because of the language barrier the Egyptian generals did not share instruction with their Soviet colleagues; they were given special – and, they inevitably felt, inferior – tuition. Even when some of them had acquired sufficient knowledge of Russian to dispense with interpreters they were still conscious of an element of discrimination because they were excluded from some lectures on the more advanced and confidential aspects of Soviet military science. Nor could they supplement their studies, as they had been able to in the West, by reading technical magazines and reports: none such existed for the public eye in the Soviet Union. Finally, of course, they found living conditions and the whole class structure of the Soviet Union completely different from what they were accustomed to at home.

Then came the disaster of 1967, and a period of bitter recrimination all round. Egyptian officers blamed their Soviet equipment – for example the tanks were designed for arctic conditions and so wholly unventilated, either to cool the crews or the engines, for fighting in the desert in the summer. On the other side Party publications in the Soviet Union accused the

Egyptian officers of belonging to a bourgeois society which lacked the social background necessary for a successful arms struggle. In fact, I have always insisted that the Egyptian army was never given the chance to fight in 1967. Field-Marshal Amer's catastrophic order to withdraw from Sinai across the canal meant that eighty per cent of the army was never in contact with the enemy at all. No doubt Egypt had a few of its own 'chocolate soldiers' who ran away, but the great mass of all ranks of the army were willing and able to stand and die.

Anyway, President Nasser took the decision to rebuild the army from top to bottom, and with this end in view the decision was taken to accept the services of Soviet experts down to battalion level. This decision inevitably created a lot of dissatisfaction. Was the advice given by the experts indeed only advice, or had it to be acted upon? When a ruling was given that the advice was, in fact, binding on them, many officers felt humiliated. They did not consider that Egypt's defeat was due to any deficiencies on their part that foreign experts, again with their inevitable (Soviet) interpreters, were likely to be able to put right. After all, they had combat experience and their advisers had not. They had commanded tanks and flown MiGs against the enemy, which the Russians had not. They knew local conditions in a way that their advisers never could. Russian military thought was still conditioned by memories of World War Two's 2,000 mile front, whereas the Egyptian army was never likely to operate on a front of more than 100 miles (the length of the Suez Canal). The Russians sometimes gave the impression that they were wooing the other ranks and cold-shouldering the officers, because this was a 'class army' and so on. Moreover, the quality of the experts varied considerably. Some, like General Lashinkov, who came with Marshal Zakharov in 1967 and stayed on as head of the Soviet mission, commanded universal respect, but others were less admirable and, as the proverb says, sickness is contagious but health is not. In the Air Force in particular the quality seemed to drop rather rapidly, arousing suspicions that the Soviets were using Egypt largely as an ideal all-weather training ground for young pilots. The number of crashes – in 1971 and 1972 no fewer than 68

179

planes with Egyptian or Russian pilots were lost in training flights – gave some support to this, and of course the losses had to be paid for by Egypt. On top of all this were incidents already mentioned like the gold-smuggling affair, or the occasion when Admiral Gorshikov arrived in Alexandria and flew straight to Cairo for consultation without first paying his respects, as courtesy demanded that he should, to the Egyptian Naval Commander in Alexandria. Rear Admiral Mahmoud Abdul Rahman Fahmy, a highly punctilious naval officer, was extremely mortified and refused to come to Cairo to meet the Russian admiral.

It must be appreciated that all this time, the period of the 'War of Attrition', was a great stimulus to Egyptian nationalism. It kept the Egyptian people in a state of psychological mobilization; it consolidated the home front, since civilians were as much under fire as soldiers; it inoculated the army with a feeling of continuing battle. All this encouraged resentment of what was seen as alien tutelage and restraint.

It was General Sadiq, the Commander-in-Chief of the Army, who, as we have seen, became the focus of those who resented the position the Soviets had acquired in Egypt. But it was not long after their withdrawal that the General's own downfall was accomplished. President Sadat and General Sadiq had long failed to see eye to eye on many matters. They had fundamentally different views of how the battle should be fought. General Sadiq, still wedded to the 'Granite' plans, was not convinced of the possibilities of the limited war which the President believed capable of paying such large political dividends. This meant that General Sadiq inevitably made demands for equipment and so on which the President thought excessive. The President also thought him too extreme in his attitude towards the Soviets, and felt that he tended to get himself too involved in politics – he was, for example, strongly opposed to the Prime Minister, Dr Sidqi, whom he accused of being pro-Russian – and expressed his opposition in front of other senior officers.

In the meanwhile Dr Sidqi had been sent in October on another mission to Moscow aimed at patching things up, and the Russians certainly seemed to have recovered themselves sufficiently to adopt new tactics. They seemed anxious to recover lost ground by speeding up the flow of arms, to such an extent that I remember President Sadat saying to me one day: 'They are drowning me in new arms.' Between December 1972 and June 1973 we received more arms from them than in the whole of the two preceding years. President Sadat felt that after the American elections would be the time for Egypt to take an initiative in the military field as the only way of breaking the apparent fossilization of the Middle East situation.

On the evening of 24 October a meeting of the Supreme Council of the Armed Forces was called at the President's house in Giza. Fifteen generals and Admiral Fahmy were present, and discussions, heated at times, went on from nine till after midnight. The President argued strongly in favour of a limited war, making his favourite point that if he could win only ten millimetres of ground on the east bank of the Suez Canal this would immeasurably strengthen his position in subsequent political and diplomatic negotiations. Some of the generals were sceptical. General Sadiq thought we lacked the arms and equipment for the sort of war he had in mind, and his deputy, General Hassan, got into such an energetic argument with the President that he was obliged to threaten to dismiss him. Then the President temporarily left the room. Both General Sadiq and General Hassan went out and apologized to him. But the meeting ended miserably and inconclusively.

Two days later the President's mind was made up. At 4.00 p.m. he sent for General Shazli, the Chief of Staff, and told him: 'Consider yourself Commander-in-Chief of the Army till further orders. I am about to dismiss General Sadiq.' Then he sent for General Ahmed Ismail and ordered him to take the oath as Minister of War. At 4.45 he sent his secretary to the house of General Sadiq with the message: 'The President has accepted your resignation' (which in fact had not been offered). The next day the Deputy Minister of War, the Commander of the Navy, the General Commanding the Central Military Area, and the Director of Intelligence were all dismissed.

It was plain to see why President Sadat appointed Ismail and Shazli. Ismail was the classic officer, the soldier *par excellence* –

an infantryman, professional, honest, wholly above politics. He compensated for any lack of intellectual brilliance by dogged hard work; in Moscow he was the most studious of all our generals – while many of his colleagues considered it beneath their dignity to take notes like students once more, Ismail was always writing, always sketching. He had not been part of the Free Officers' Movement: he was even then considered so unpolitical that the movement's leaders did not dare to tell him of the plot. But it was, apart from any considerations of expertise, largely because of Ismail's lack of politics that the President appointed him – that, plus the fact that he and the President came from the same class: they shared many attitudes. And Ahmed Ismail was a good choice. His strictness, even his tendency towards a certain narrow-mindedness not uncommon among military men, were valuable qualities for the task ahead.

Shazli was quite a different character: his stocky, handsome figure contrasted with Ismail's bulk. Shazli was dashing; he could socialize, talk well, impress people – after tours as a military attaché in London and then at the United Nations, Shazli was *mondain* in a way that few Arab generals are. He was a paratrooper – one of the first generals from that branch in the Egyptian Army – and he jumped until very recently, which of course added to his allure.

In all prima donnas there must be something of the actor and Shazli was no exception. But he knew what he was doing in using his glamour to achieve his military ends, above all the raising of the army's morale for the task it faced. Beneath his charm and his daring, Shazli was a calculating and meticulous officer. He was not a military genius, but he did have that precise grasp of logistics and attention to detail which is essential to the paratroop officer. Shazli's planning of the crossing, and the studies behind it which he personally supervised, were to be so brilliantly successful at least in part because Shazli concerned himself with the individual movements of virtually every boat in the operation; and the order 'Operation for the Crossing of a Division' which, under his signature, was finally given to the army as the Order of the Day, is a classic military study.

The drawback to the partnership between Ismail and Shazli was that they did not like each other. The origins of their dislike lay in the Congo in 1960, when Shazli had commanded a force seconded by Egypt to the United Nations. Ismail had been sent from Cairo to inspect these, and Shazli had resented this. Of course, promoted by the President to positions of such critical importance for the future of their country, the two endeavoured to get on. But the inevitable differences in attitude and some-times opinion gave added importance to the work of the man who, in any recounting of the operation, should properly be named with the pair, the Director of Operations under Shazli, General Abdul Ghani el-Gamasy.

Intellectually, Gamasy was perhaps Egypt's best equipped general; he read a good deal and he pondered what he read. He would take articles of mine from *Al Ahram*, annotate them with a stream of comments and send them back to me. At meetings, however, he was very quiet, though his advice, when given, was listened to with respect because of its shrewdness. Gamasy, too, was non-political – indeed, Arab politics shocked him to his bones. I once advised President Nasser to take some generals with him to the summit conference in Tripoli and he decided to take General Hassan el-Bedri and Gamasy. As we sat round the negotiating table, they were in the usual advisers' seats behind; and as he surveyed the quarrelling factions, I heard Gamasy mutter to himself: 'My God, *this* is the united Arab front we are to fight with?'

There is just one footnote to the story of the break with the Russians. In the briefing which he gave to the Cairo editors the President spoke of a message he had got from Washington 'under the table' to the effect that he should remember that the key to the situation was there. It happened that Prince Sultan, the Saudi Arabian Minister of Defence, had been in Washington just before the President's demand to the Soviets was made. Kemal Adham was also in Cairo. Whether there was any connection between these facts, and whether King Feisal was informed of the measures the President was going to take, I do not know, and none of us are likely to know unless President Sadat chooses to tell us. One person who apparently was not

183

informed in advance was Henry Kissinger. A few days after the withdrawal had become public knowledge he said to one of his assistants: 'I don't understand President Sadat. If he had come to me before this happened and told me about it I should have felt obliged to give him something in exchange. But now I've got it all for nothing.'

My own belief is that whether the Americans knew before the event or not, afterwards King Feisal tried to press the Americans very hard that now was the time for them to make some move. There is plenty of evidence from Saudi Arabian sources of the extent to which the King emphasised to President Nixon what an awkward position he personally would find himself in if the Americans did nothing. He complained that whenever the Americans did anything that affected the Middle East the Arabs blamed him, and he did not understand why he should be regarded as America's representative in the Middle East. He must have pointed out forcibly to Washington that now the Russians were gone from Egypt the main American excuse for inaction had disappeared, since they had always asserted that it was the presence of Russian troops in Egypt that gave the Middle East situation the chance of a global confrontation. If they simply went on helping Israel they could no longer claim that this was a strategy directed against Russia – it would be purely and simply helping the Arabs' principal enemy for its own sake.

10. LIBYA

President Ghadaffi of Libya was one of those who for a different reason welcomed the order for the Russians to be withdrawn. But he feared it placed President Sadat and his Government in peril – he thought the Soviets might try to take their revenge – and he wanted to be of assistance. The method he chose was to propose a complete merger between the two countries, Egypt and Libya.

The idea of unity had always been dear to Ghadaffi. I have already told how, on only the second day of the Libyan revolution, when we met in the Egyptian consulate in Benghazi, he brought up the question of a union. He told me it was because he was such a fervent believer in Arab unity that he had called his movement the United Free Officers (*Dubbat al Wahdawiyin al Ahrar*). 'Go back to Cairo,' he said to me, 'and tell President Nasser that we do not want to rule Libya. All we have done is our duty as Arab nationalists. Now it is for President Nasser to take over himself and guide Libya from the reactionary camp, where it was, to the progressive camp, where it should be.'

On several occasions after that Ghadaffi proposed a union with Egypt, and the reply he always got was that it should be done in the proper way, with careful preparation. We must, he was told, learn from the lessons of our ill-fated attempt at union with Syria. But before tracing the chequered history of relations between Egypt and Libya we must take a look at the personality of the man who so largely dictated the course of events – Muammar Ghadaffi.

Two people and two backgrounds combined to make Ghadaffi the man he was. The people were the Prophet Mohammed and Gamal Abdel Nasser. His thinking was an amalgam of the ideas of Islam at the time of Mohammed and the revolutionary doctrines of Nasser, particularly as expounded during the formative period of Ghadaffi's life when, as a schoolboy and a young soldier, he first became aware of what was going on in the world around him – in the period, that is, between the Suez War in 1956 and the June War in 1967. His two backgrounds were the army and the desert. It was in the army that he first really found himself, but it was to the desert that he would return for solace. He responded eagerly to the army with its orders and discipline, but his instincts remained those of a free *bedu* from the desert. If, for example, he heard that one of his colleagues on the Revolutionary Council had acquired a flat in town he would order him back into camp or oblige him to have his head shaved. Ghadaffi's difficulty was that he lacked the resources and the experience to enable him to digest all the conflicting influences that operated on him. But the result of this conflict was a personality of fascinating complexity.

Here is a small but characteristic incident. On one occasion

185

when he was in Cairo, and had been invited by Nasser to dine with him, the first course was shrimps. It was the first time Ghadaffi had seen shrimps, and he looked at his plate with horror. 'What are these?' he said. 'Locusts? Do you eat locusts in Egypt?' Nasser laughed and said, 'No, those aren't locusts, they're shrimps.' 'What are shrimps?' asked Ghadaffi. Nasser explained that they were a sort of fish. But Ghadaffi refused to eat them. 'I can't eat fish,' he said, 'because it is not killed according to correct Muslim ritual with someone saying *allahu akbar* at the moment of slaughter. These have just been allowed to die: I couldn't possibly eat them.' Of course we all laughed – yet this same man showed that he perfectly well understood how to use broadcasting to extend his influence outside Libya. Sometimes his propaganda was effective, sometimes not, but there can be no doubt that he built up an extremely efficient broadcasting network.

Another contradiction – when Ghadaffi, as a young officer, was sent on a course to Britain he refused to go near London because he regarded the city as an evil place. He went straight from the airport to the training camp, stayed inside the camp for the whole of the course, and when the course was finished went straight back to the airport and so home. Yet this was the man who, immediately after the Revolution, managed to grapple successfully with the most formidable problems. In the first six months of his rule he had got the British and Americans out of the country, recovering the bases at Al Adem and Wheelus Base, and had negotiated new and favourable agreements with the oil companies.

Ghadaffi could at times display a terrifying innocence of how things worked in the modern world. He was capable of gross oversimplification. Many of his friends, for example, were annoyed at the way Ghadaffi interfered in countries like Ireland. I myself at one time explained to him that the I.R.A. was not a liberation movement in the sense that we understood the term – but in vain. Many times I tried to convince him that the Bangladesh problem was one of self-determination and that the new state therefore deserved recognition from Libya. But he could not see this. To him Pakistan was the biggest Muslim country in the world and Bangladesh a disruptive, separatist movement – an Israel in embryo.

Like a *bedu*, Ghadaffi could change in a moment from one position to a completely opposite one. Yet he was fascinated by the game of power. Again, though fundamentally a patient man, he could show the greatest impatience. When he started to industrialize his country he wanted everything to be done at once. He had no time for feasibility studies, surveys, tenders, the negotiation of contracts, and all the rest. He had the money, and if he wanted something done the only thing that interested him was how quickly it could be done. Yet he had started his revolutionary movement while he was still only in secondary school, and all those years, from the age of fifteen or sixteen until he reached the age of twenty-seven and felt the time had come to strike, he held together an underground nucleus of conspirators, keeping them loyal, silent, and patient.

The strength of his religious feelings is well known. For some years he refused to deal with the Soviet Union because he regarded it as the land of atheists. When Kosygin came to Egypt and some derogatory remarks were made there about Kissinger, Ghadaffi's comment was: 'I don't make any difference between Kissinger and Kosygin: They are both enemies.' Nasser tried to alter his outlook. 'Muammar,' he said, during the first visit he paid to Libya, 'we can't put the Soviet Union and the United States on the same footing. Although the Soviet Union is an atheist state it is with us, and although the United States is a Christian state it is against us.' But Ghadaffi went on lashing out at imperialism and atheism and the Soviet Union indiscriminately, until Nasser warned him that if he insisted on doing this he would refuse to appear on the same platform with him. Ghadaffi said: 'All right; I will keep silent.' 'No, I don't want you to do that,' said Nasser, 'I just want you to be able to distinguish between friend and foe.'

Ghadaffi remained unconvinced. He refused to admit that marxism was a doctrine with any relevance to his problems. In many talks I had with him I tried to persuade him that, however out of date marxism might be in some respects, it was an essential ingredient in the political thought of our time. But Ghadaffi

187

refused to see this. Whenever he was in Cairo he would always come along to *Al Ahram* where I arranged for some of the best brains in the country to meet him and argue with him on every conceivable topic. I think he enjoyed these meetings, though many of the things which he heard in them must have horrified him. Often when the discussion became particularly interesting he would ask for a notebook and start making notes. I remember one occasion when he filled three complete notebooks. Sometimes he would take almost everything down verbatim. I offered to get a transcript made for him, but he preferred to take it all down himself.

Ghadaffi's outlook was inevitably influenced by the state of the Arab world when he came to power. The autumn of 1969 was not a happy time for the Arabs. Egypt was still in the 'No Peace: No War' aftermath of the 1967 defeat when it was difficult for anyone to see a clear road ahead. There was plenty of money coming in from oil, but most of it belonged to conservative regimes. Everybody tried to get a foothold in Libya, tempted by its oil wealth and its strategic position – the Algerians, Egyptians, the rival Baathist sects in Syria and Iraq, not to mention the Americans, the French and the British. Even King Feisal tried to woo him. One day he said: 'What could I have possibly imagined better than this young man who is now preaching the pure doctrines of Islam?' But all the Arabs were, not uncharacteristically I am afraid, prepared to speak ill of each other. The Sudan claimed a special relationship with Libya because it had had a revolution just a short time before, on 25 May – 'sister revolutions', the Sudanese called them. There was one occasion when President Nimeiry of the Sudan wanted to tell Ghadaffi about his 'revolutionary experiences'. This annoyed Ghadaffi: 'What do you think you have to teach us?' he asked. Three months seniority, he felt, did not give anyone the right to lecture.

Fairly soon Ghadaffi and his colleagues were so flooded with conflicting opinions and advice that they did not know which way to turn. The only conclusion they came to was that nobody was really to be trusted. They still had confidence in Nasser personally, and as a legendary figure, but they saw little of him. I remember one day in 1970 when I was with Nasser in Tripoli and we were staying in the palace of the former Crown Prince which had been turned into a residence for state guests, when Ghadaffi (who was himself still living in barracks) took me aside and said: 'You must know all about the Sudanese revolution, don't you?' I said I thought I knew a bit. 'Well,' said Ghadaffi, 'they tell me that Nimeiry is a Neguib, not a Nasser. Is this true? Is he a figurehead or the real leader?' I laughed, but this was typical of the sort of information which was all the time being fed to Ghadaffi and which made it so difficult for him to know what was what. At first he believed everything he was told; later, when he found how often he had been deceived, he became more cynical.

Ghadaffi was a simple puritan caught up in a complicated world full of intrigue and manoeuvre. Towards the end of the Rabat summit conference, which was Ghadaffi's first appearance on the international stage, he came up to me and said: 'What are you going to write about this conference? As far as I can see it's a failure.' I said: 'If I write anything it will probably be about you.' He looked astonished: 'About me? What is there to say about me?' 'I shall write an article,' I said, 'and call it "Tarzan in New York".'

Ghadaffi was very upset by the death of Nasser. It was not just that he admired Nasser more than any other living man but he had always believed in the central role of Egypt in the Arab world. True, many things about Egypt shocked him – the cabarets, the idea of men and women going to restaurants and dances together, the free discussion of religious ideas, and so on – but he never wavered in his belief that Egypt was the key. When Nasser died he felt that there was a vacuum in the Arab world which was too big for any one man to fill, and he thought that there should be a collective leadership by Egypt, Syria and Libya.

For my part I have always been a believer in a union between Egypt and Libya. I still believe in it. I thought then that both countries had a unique and historic opportunity to pool their resources, to combine their lands, peoples and economies into one country which in ten years or so would become a single strong country, a major power placed at the strategic centre of North Africa and on the bridge between Africa and Asia. This state could have become the real nucleus round which the old dream of a united Arab nation crystallized. I never thought that the realization of this great design should be subordinated to personality. Of course personality is important, but once the desirability of the goal had been admitted everything else could have fitted into place. I have never believed that there are such things as revolutionary people but only revolutionary situations, and in 1971 and 1972, at a time of crisis and near-despair in the Arab world, here was such a situation. Had we seized the opportunity we could have made a great step forward towards a better order in the world.

Looking at relations between Egypt and Libya in this period it is possible to see them falling into three phases. The first is from the Libyan revolution to the death of Nasser (September 1969–September 1970), during which the Libyans considered themselves the children, so to speak, of the Egyptian Revolution. The second is from the death of Nasser to the expulsion of Soviet experts (September 1970–July 1972), during which Ghadaffi was puzzled by what was going on in Egypt – by the struggle for power and by our relations with the Soviet Union; the third was from July 1972 to the October War of 1973, during which the proposal for a complete union was made by Libya, accepted by Egypt, discussed, and finally abandoned. Ghadaffi was prompted to this by his fear that the Soviets might exercise some sort of pressure on Egypt in retaliation for the withdrawal of the experts – pressure that might be military, political or economic – and that in consequence Egypt might find itself obliged to accept some partial and unsatisfactory settlement.

Ghadaffi had been talking of union, as I say, from the day he took power; but his ideas – as presented to President Sadat in February 1972 when the President called in on Libya on his way home from Moscow, for instance – gradually hardened. Finally, on 26 July, Ghadaffi sent President Sadat his first concrete proposals. The President thought these serious enough to be worth discussing at last, and flew to Benghazi for talks with Ghadaffi starting on 1 August. It was decided to have just over a year of preparation, from the beginning of August 1972 to 1 September 1973. Joint committees were set up to examine every aspect of the new state – the drafting of a new constitution, the creation of a new Parliament, the co-ordination of legal, economic and educational systems, and so on. One thing which was quickly agreed was the name of the new state – it was to be the United Arab Republic again (though Ghadaffi, knowing the affection Egyptians have for the name of their country, thought that the Cairo province should continue to be called *Misr* (the Arabic name for Egypt) – whereas after the union with Syria the whole of Egypt was just called 'the southern region'.

Fairly soon it became plain to me that things were not going well. As usual in such cases, many of those nominated to serve on the committees were people whose services could most easily be dispensed with by the two Governments concerned. They made difficulties. They stressed the contrasts between the two countries and minimized the similarities. These bureaucratic obstacles were aggravated by personal differences between the two Presidents. President Ghadaffi thought President Sadat not revolutionary enough; President Sadat thought President Ghadaffi unbalanced and immature. There came a time when President Ghadaffi accused President Sadat of not in his heart wanting unity, and when President Sadat suspected that what President Ghadaffi was after was not so much union as a wider field for his ambitions. President Ghadaffi said he was prepared to resign once the union had been effected: President Sadat did not believe him, but told him that he represented the coming generation of revolutionaries, and that if he was prepared to wait his time would come. They were not helped by some of the intermediaries who seemed only to worsen relations between the two men.

By the beginning of 1973 hopes of achieving anything were beginning to fade. Then came a very serious incident which nearly precipitated a crisis well outside the confines of purely Egyptian-Libyan relations. A Libyan Airlines plane en route to Cairo lost its way over Sinai on 21 February and was shot down by Israeli fighters with the loss of one hundred and eight lives including that of a former Libyan Foreign Minister, Saleh Bou

191

Yasir. Ghadaffi was, as might be expected, beside himself with anger. His instinct was to inflict some immediate and appropriate revenge on the perpetrators of the outrage. He was determined that Libya should not become one of those Arab states which meekly submitted to acts of Israeli aggression. President Sadat tried to calm him down, telling him that we were preparing for a battle with Israel, which would be suitable revenge for the Libyan plane as well as for many other Arab humiliations. He pointed out that if Libyan planes bombed Haifa (which was one of the proposals made by Ghadaffi) the most probable consequence would be that the Israelis would bomb Libyan airfields, an outcome which could not possibly help the Arab cause.

The situation was complicated by the rumours circulating that Egyptian Air Force planes could have gone to the rescue of the Libyan plane and guided it to safety if they had wanted to. The air force said the weather at the time was unsuitable for a scrambled rescue, to which Ghadaffi's natural retort was, if the weather was all right for the Israeli planes why was it not all right for ours? The day when the Libyan victims of the disaster were buried in Tripoli saw anti-Egyptian demonstrations there. The son of Saleh bou Yasir had leaflets printed accusing the Egyptians of cowardice, but Ghadaffi put him in jail. He still loved Egypt, though he was bitterly disappointed in her.

Now comes a very strange story. Israel was due to celebrate the twenty-fifth anniversary of the founding of the state on 15 May, and a group of wealthy Jews from the United States and Europe had chartered the Queen Elizabeth II to take them from Southampton to the Israeli port of Ashdod. Naturally the strictest security precautions were taken for the whole of the voyage because it was realized that here was a splendid target for one or other of the Palestinian commando groups to attack. But there was one possible source of danger that seems to have been overlooked.

The Queen Elizabeth II left Southampton on 15 April. On 17 April the commander of an Egyptian submarine which was stationed in Tripoli received a message asking him to come and see President Ghadaffi. The young officer, wondering what on earth it could all be about, duly presented himself, and found Ghadaffi with a map of the Mediterranean spread out in front of him. The Libyan leader was extremely affable. 'I speak to you', he said, 'as an Arab nationalist and as Commander-in-Chief of the Armed Forces of Libya. You are now working here with us. Can you identify the Queen Elizabeth II in the Mediterranean? Would it be easy?' The officer said he thought it would be easy. Ghadaffi's next question was: 'In that case, could you aim two torpedoes at it and sink it?' The officer said that in theory it would be possible, but that it would be a very considerable undertaking, and he would have to have a direct order before he could carry it out. 'All right,' said Ghadaffi, 'I'm giving you the order: and if you want it in writing I'll give it to you in writing.' Which he did.

The submarine commander went back to his ship and ordered the crew to stand to for an immediate secret operational move. Ghadaffi had insisted that as soon as the submarine left Tripoli harbour it should dive, because he said it was certain to be watched. This it did, but when night fell the submarine commander surfaced and sent a coded message to his home base at Alexandria, reporting what his orders were. The naval commander in Alexandria was appalled and got in touch with the Commander-in-Chief of the Egyptian Armed Forces, Ahmed Ismail, who in turn got in touch with President Sadat, who gave instructions that the submarine should be ordered back to Alexandria. I remember the President called me up that day and said: 'It seems that Ghadaffi wants to put us on the spot. He is trying to sink the Queen Elizabeth II.' He shuddered to think of the international complications which would have arisen from attacking without provocation a British ship in the middle of the Mediterranean with such a cargo of passengers. The President said he was not going to tell Ghadaffi what he was doing, but when the liner had reached Ashdod he would tell Ghadaffi that the submarine commander had failed to spot the Queen Elizabeth II and so had been unable to carry out his mission. Ghadaffi was not deceived. He could not understand why Israel should be allowed to shoot down a civilian plane on innocent passage and he should be forbidden to reply in kind.

He was terribly disappointed. The Queen Elizabeth II may have been saved, but Egyptian-Libyan relations were not.

As weeks went by Ghadaffi's sense of frustration mounted. His pet scheme for unity was bogged down in detail: he had been forbidden to take the revenge he felt his due: in every way the Arabs seemed to be impotent. So he resigned, but his colleagues on the Revolutionary Command Council – presumably used to his ways – simply refused to accept his resignation. On 12 June, therefore, Ghadaffi took the extraordinary step of printing leaflets announcing his resignation which he then took into the streets of Tripoli and tried to distribute to the passers-by. If his colleagues on the Revolutionary Command Council would not let him resign he would take his decision direct to the people. But his colleagues stopped that too. There was then a great deal of discussion in the council at the end of which he decided that he would no longer stay in Libya but would go to Egypt. He collected his mother, his wife, his newly born child, all his books and personal belongings, boarded a plane, and flew to Cairo on 22 June. By choosing this city as his destination he hoped to demonstrate that his dissatisfaction was not directed against Egypt.

Ghadaffi, installed in the Tahra Palace in self-imposed exile, was not an easy guest for President Sadat, who came to the conclusion that the best plan would be for him to go round the country, expounding his ideas on unity to the Egyptian people and listening to their comments and criticisms. I think this was an unfortunate project because there were so many elements in Egypt which had their own axes to grind and complaints to make, none of them really relevant to the main debate. Things like women's liberation or the strict Islamic punishment for theft were not the real issue. They could have been settled later, once the basic principles of unity had been agreed and acted upon. But these were the sort of subjects Ghadaffi found himself having to discuss as he went around, and the volume of opposition he encountered shocked him. He said to himself, 'If Egypt doesn't want me, I'll go back to Libya.' And he did, on 9 July. He then proceeded to write a letter to his colleagues on the Revolutionary Command Council saying that he had now been

194

to Egypt and seen that there was no hope of unity, so he was still resigning – and now, he said, it was definite. He sat at home and refused to come into the office. Only when crowds of Libyans trooped out to plead with him to return would he consent to take up his duties once more.

This strange episode led to another, the 'Libyan march on Cairo'. One of the arguments most often brought up against unity was that it was purely Ghadaffi's own scheme and not one supported by the mass of the Libyan people. Now, from February until he disappeared to Cairo, Ghadaffi had been deeply involved in what he called his 'cultural revolution'. When he got back from Cairo, a frustrated and disappointed man, he insisted that his resignation still stood and that 'the people' should take over and save him from the agony of ruling. At this point somebody – I do not myself think it was Ghadaffi, who was, so to speak, in *purdah*, but more likely one of his colleagues – got the idea of sending 40,000 Libyans on a march to Cairo. There they would join thousands of Egyptians and all together go to the Abdin Palace, where, in the name of the combined masses of Libya and Egypt, they would demand from President Sadat the complete and immediate amalgamation of their two countries.

I was in Europe when I heard of preparations for this march, and I must confess I thought it a healthy sign. It looked like a real demonstration of political consciousness; to get 40,000 Libyans, out of a population of little more than 1,500,000, marching 1,500 miles to ask for unity would be a considerable achievement. Once in Cairo ten times their number of Egyptians could have joined them, and the impact of this mass movement clamouring for unity would have been irresistible. It would have cut through the bureaucratic delays and squabbles that were strangling the proposal.

But many people in Egypt took fright at the idea. It was said that some of the Libyans would be armed, and that they planned, once they had arrived in Cairo, to smash the cabarets and restaurants on the Pyramids Road in an orgy of puritan violence. The march was treated not as a political happening but purely as a problem of security. The road from Mersa Matruh

195

to Alamein was blocked by laying a railway carriage across it. Further on a part of the road was mined. In their panic some officials even argued that it would be impossible to object to Israeli occupation of Sinai if we allowed ourselves to be 'invaded' from Libya. President Sadat sent an angry telegram to Ghadaffi, who replied that as he had resigned he was not responsible for the march. Sadat sent another, angrier message, as a result of which it was decided there should be a meeting in Mersa Matruh between representatives of Egypt's Socialist Union and Libya's Cultural Revolution. They met and agreed that a delegation of thirty to forty should go and see President Sadat. They saw him, and seemed far less formidable people than rumour had painted them. As the President talked of his hopes for unity many of them wept.

The union of the two countries was due to take effect on 1 September, and as the date approached everyone was asking what was going to happen. By 25 August Ghadaffi had become so restless at the indecision and waiting that he ordered his plane to be got ready and landed unannounced at Cairo airport. There was no car waiting for him, so he took a taxi into town and booked in at a second-class hotel. President Sadat was out of the country at the time, visiting Saudi Arabia, Syria, and Qatar, but as soon as he got back he arranged for a meeting with Ghadaffi in his own village of Mit Abul Qom. That was on 27 August. It was not a success. Many attempts were made to find a compromise formula which would save people's faces, and eventually a document was prepared for signature by the two Presidents which proclaimed the principle of unity on 1 September and announced a plebiscite on the question to be held in both countries three months later. I was at this meeting and I had a strong foreboding that nothing was going to come out of it. I could see how frustrations were mounting on both sides. Ghadaffi was under the impression that we were never going to fight a battle, though in fact preparations for Operation Badr were accelerating all the time and the countdown was shortly to begin. But President Sadat felt unable to reveal this to Ghadaffi because he knew that Ghadaffi disapproved of the concept of the operation, and there was always the danger that information about it might leak out. It must in fairness be pointed out, however, that Libya contributed no less than $1,000m. towards preparations for the battle.

A few days before the battle actually started there was another example of the sort of misunderstanding which seemed to dog relations between the two Presidents. The Libyan students at Alexandria University had asked Ghadaffi to address them on 28 September, the third anniversary of the death of Nasser. Ghadaffi asked President Sadat for permission to do this but Sadat pointed out that he would himself be addressing the Central Committee of the Socialist Union in Cairo that day and it would look odd, he thought, if they both spoke simultaneously in different places. Would it not be better if they both appeared in Cairo on the same platform on the 28th, and then Ghadaffi could go the next day for his meeting in Alexandria? Ghadaffi agreed. He arrived at Cairo airport in the afternoon of the 28th, went to the mosque where Nasser was buried, and then went to call on Nasser's widow. It was Ramadan and he stayed with her for the *iftar* meal (the breaking of the fast), and then went on to Tahra Palace, where he was as usual to stay, expecting President Sadat to pick him up there. But by then President Sadat was due at the Central Committee so he had left a message asking Ghadaffi to come along independently and join him. Ghadaffi felt insulted and decided not to go to the Central Committee. On his way back from the Central Committee President Sadat called at Tahra Palace to see what had happened to Ghadaffi. He was told he had gone to the Saidna el-Hussein mosque in the centre of the old city. Next morning Ghadaffi, still nursing a grievance, flew back to Libya without seeing President Sadat.

Unfortunately, when the battle did come, Ghadaffi, though he gave the news of it an enthusiastic reception, and scoured Libya for arms and aid of every description, stripping shops of food and hospitals of medicines and piling them into lorries for despatch to Egypt, made the great mistake of saying in public that he had always had reservations about the plan, though adding that once the operation had started everyone should do everything they could to ensure its success. This was not under-

197

stood at a time when so many people in Egypt were fighting and dying, and cost him much goodwill. In the early days of the battle Ghadaffi sent two members of the Revolutionary Council, first Abdel Munim el-Houny and then after a week Omar el-Meheishy, to observe its progress. After the ceasefire he came to Cairo himself and thought he was being kept out of the operations room while some Saudi princes were being allowed in. He did not believe President Sadat when he said that at that time there was nothing operational happening.

When the Israelis managed to cross over to the west bank of the canal Ghadaffi felt his misgivings about the plan were justified. He objected to the ceasefire, and tried to speak to President Sadat on the telephone to explain his objections – which annoyed President Sadat who felt, with reason, that he knew a good deal more about the true facts of the situation than Ghadaffi did. President Sadat was very conscious of Ghadaffi's suspicions of him, and I remember one day soon after the battle started his saying to me: 'Now that I have pulled it off I hope that people like Ghadaffi, who thought I was only interested in expedients for gaining time, will realize they were wrong.'

11. RELATIONS WITH THE USA

As soon as Nixon was elected President in 1968 Nasser sent him a telegram of congratulations. They had met at the beginning of 1963 when Nixon, then out of office, had visited Cairo, bringing with him a letter of introduction from President Kennedy. Nasser gave instructions that he should receive the best possible treatment. 'We must all remember,' he said, 'that he was Eisenhower's vice-president in 1956 at the time of Suez.' He was flown to Aswan in a special plane to see the High Dam and when he came back he expressed the opinion that America's withdrawal from the financing of the dam was the gravest mistake of the Eisenhower era; he put the blame on Dulles.

After the Nixon telegram came the Scranton visit to Cairo, Dr Fawzi's journey to Washington in 1969 as Nasser's special envoy for Eisenhower's funeral, Sisco's visit in April 1970, the

Rogers' initiative, Elliot Richardson's visit to Cairo for Nasser's funeral – all these in addition to the normal diplomatic contacts which continued in spite of the fact that officially diplomatic relations between the two countries had been broken since the June war in 1967.

But by the beginning of 1972 there was a growing conviction in Cairo that in the Nixon regime the State Department was only used for routine diplomatic business, and that the really big issues of foreign policy were dealt with by Henry Kissinger in the White House. It was he who had engineered the Vietnam settlement, negotiated the détente with the USSR and knocked on the door of China. If Egypt's own problems were ever going to get proper attention in Washington they would have to be hot enough for Kissinger to handle.

All through 1972 two channels of communication between Egypt and the United States were being employed. There was the normal Foreign Office to Foreign Office channel, and there was the undercover link through our own intelligence and the CIA (always particularly active in the Middle East). In addition all sorts of attempts were made to create new contacts, in at least one of which I found myself involved. In 1972 the chairman of the Pepsi-Cola company, Donald Kendall, came to Cairo. He was a personal friend of Nixon, who had acted as lawyer for the company, and got in touch with me through one of the most distinguished Egyptian lawyers, Dr Zaki Hashim, who later became Minister of Tourism. His proposal was that Kissinger and I should meet, and he offered his house in Connecticut for a long weekend of private discussions. When he got back to the States he pursued the idea with Ambassador Ashraf Ghorbal, who was looking after our interests there at the time, and with Dr Mohammed Hassan Zayyat, our permanent representative at the UN. A date for the meeting was suggested. Dr Zayyat sent a report about it all to the Prime Minister, Dr Fawzi, who sent it on to President Sadat, who then discussed it with me. I was not enthusiastic about the idea. I thought we should strengthen our internal and external positions before we got into serious talks with anyone, even if they were only called 'exploratory', and I did not feel we were clear enough in our

own minds about what we wanted. So I sent a telegram to
Donald Kendall calling the meeting off and apologizing. But
this incident helped to whet appetites in Cairo for a top level
meeting.

Such a meeting did finally take place on Friday 24 February
1973. The preliminaries had a touch of theatricality about them.
At first it was suggested that it should take place (secretly of
course) at an American base near Barcelona, but there was no
enthusiasm for the idea of an American base as their venue.
Then, when Washington had been agreed as the place and Hafez
Ismail, National Security Adviser to President Sadat (and so
Kissinger's opposite number) had been chosen as Egypt's
special representative, it was decided to obscure the real purpose
of his visit, which was a meeting with Nixon and Kissinger, by
sending him to Washington via Bonn and London, where he
had talks with Brandt and Heath. Before the secret meeting,
Hafez Ismail made his public visit to the White House on 23
February, where he did for a few minutes meet Kissinger, who
explained that he himself would only appear very briefly at the
meeting with the President because the impression must not be
given that he was taking over the Middle East problem from the
State Department. He did not want any mention, in the papers
or anywhere else, of this private meeting between them in the
White House; they would, however, meet again next day,
ecretly, in Donald Kendall's house in Connecticut.

Hafez Ismail was received by Nixon in the Oval Office. With
Hafez Ismail was Dr Mohammed Hafiz Ghanem, Counsellor to
the Presidency. Nixon, apart from the brief appearance by
Kissinger, had with him only one of Kissinger's assistants,
General Scocroft, who took the minutes. The opening part of
the meeting was, as usual, open to the Press and the television
cameras. Nixon gave a cordial welcome to the special envoy of
President Sadat. Then the media withdrew and the meeting
got down to business.

Nixon began by saying how glad he was that Egypt had
agreed to go ahead with the meeting. (This was because the
shooting down by the Israelis of the Libyan plane had taken
place only two days before and there had been widespread de-

mands in the Arab world for the meeting to be cancelled.) He said he could not accept the excuses Israel had made for the incident, nor could he believe Mrs Meir's statement that she and her Government knew nothing about it until after it had happened. 'I don't buy this,' was the exact expression he used.

Nixon then went on to say how much he had enjoyed his visit to Egypt in 1963 and what respect he felt for the late President Nasser. He said he wanted to play his part in the building of a permanent peace in the Middle East, though he could not say in advance what shape a final settlement should take. He did not wish to impose his ideas on anyone. We had to remember, he said, that while Egypt wanted to keep its sovereignty, Israel wanted to keep its security. (This theme, reducing the whole problem to a simple equation between sovereignty and security, probably owed its origin to Kissinger, and was one which we were to hear with increasing frequency.) He asked Hafez Ismail to give a frank expression of Egypt's point of view and added: 'In spite of all my faults, not keeping my promises is not one of them.'

Hafez Ismail then launched into his analysis of the situation – the extreme danger of the present state of affairs; Egypt's historic role in the area; her determination to keep out of spheres of influence, as exemplified by the withdrawal of Russian experts. He said that the only reason for differences between the United States and Egypt was the total military and political backing which the United States gave to Israel, and he warned the President that one day Israel would challenge America's position in the Middle East just as it had challenged Britain's. He said that the main reason for the crisis in the Middle East was the clash between two societies, the Jewish and the Palestinian, and that it was essential Israel should try to settle directly with the Palestinians. If Israel wanted peace, it would have to behave as a Middle Eastern State and not continue to rely on support from the outside world. It would have to put an end to immigration, cut its links with world Zionism and abandon the claims of its citizens to dual nationality.

Nixon said he thought that, as with China and a Vietnam

settlement, future discussions with Egypt should be conducted at two levels; one through the State Department, where everything would be in the open, and the other through secret channels supervised by Dr Kissinger and without the knowledge of the State Department: that would be the channel for a real settlement. Secrecy would have to be guaranteed so that Israel should not know what was going on, at any rate for the time being. (He asked General Scocroft not to record this passage in the minutes, though we must now assume that the tapes were running all the time.) Contacts with Kissinger should be continuous, and we should talk to him frankly, just as if we were talking to the President. Nixon ended by saying he would like to tell a personal story. Two days previously he had been having dinner with his daughter and asked her which of all the countries she had seen she would most like to visit again. She had said Egypt. The impression which Hafez Ismail got from his seventy minutes meeting with the President was that he was extremely relaxed and that his expression of goodwill towards Egypt was genuine. Nixon, he felt, was eager to play a personal role in solving the Middle East problem.

The three secret meetings which Hafez Ismail then had with Kissinger in Donald Kendall's house on 24–25 February were not very productive, though they throw some light on the way in which Kissinger operates. He laid down three principles that should guide their dealings – mutual confidence, 'no cheating', and complete secrecy. He said that America could not 'impose' anything on Israel though there were ways of bringing pressure on Israel which Israel could not ignore and which his Government was prepared to use if a 'moral basis' for their use existed and could be shown to exist to American public opinion. He said that America had no objection to Egypt's friendship with the Soviet Union, but that if Egypt thought it could throw a spanner into the relationship between America and the Soviet Union it would find itself mistaken. The United States was ready for a general discussion on Middle East questions with the Soviet Union, but when it came down to details it preferred to deal only with the parties directly concerned. Then he went on to his favourite sovereignty – security equation. He argued that any withdrawal by Israel would mean the abandonment of a concrete and material basis for security. Israel would have to be convinced that material security was not everything. The Egyptians would have to make up their minds what they were prepared to offer in exchange for some Israeli withdrawal. It was clear that Egypt, the country under occupation, was the one which was being asked to make concessions. Verbal guarantees, Hafez Ismail was told, were not enough. The concessions expected from Egypt were political and territorial.

Unfortunately, any good effects these contacts might have produced were largely nullified by the visit of Golda Meir to Washington a few days later. At the end of her visit it was announced that Israel was to receive a massive new consignment of Phantoms and Skyhawks. It was clear from the size of the deal that the United States was once again underwriting Israel's offensive strike capacity. There was great disillusionment on the Egyptian side.

Looking back at this period it is possible to see six guidelines influencing American policy in the Middle East. 1. They wanted to keep the Russians out of the area and out of active participation in its affairs. This was partly because they objected to a Russian presence there as such and partly because of the risk of a collision between the super-powers which it involved. 2. They wanted to keep the various strands of negotiation separate – to negotiate a settlement between Israel and Egypt, between Israel and Syria, between Israel and the Palestinians (if that ever became possible), and so on, but all separately and not as part of an overall settlement. 3. Each separate settlement should be negotiated stage by stage. 4. Accepting the Israeli thesis, the Americans were convinced there could be no return to the 1967 borders. 5. The Palestine problem was to be looked at purely as a refugee problem. 6. The end result should be a *Pax Americana* guaranteeing American interests in the area.

12. PRESSURES TOWARDS WAR

Before going on to describe the course of the battle which was to be the culmination of those three years, we should take a brief look at the pressures from within and without which were driving the President inexorably towards war.

By 1973 the economy of Egypt was under an almost intolerable strain. Industrial development, the High Dam, and the burden of war in the Yemen had made the early and middle sixties a period of extreme difficulty. Then had come the 1967 defeat and the need for an almost complete rebuilding and re-equipping of the army. In five years between 1968–1973 Egypt spent $8–9,000m. on the war effort. For the Egyptian people it had been a decade of sacrifice and austerity, such as no people could be expected to put up with indefinitely.

Since 1967 the credibility of the whole regime had been at stake. It was De Gaulle who said that any regime which fails to protect the frontiers of the nation automatically loses its legitimacy. That failure was applicable to Egypt. Even in Nasser's lifetime there were some symptoms of revolt, in spite of the enormous prestige which he continued to enjoy. Then came his death, and a period of shock and bewilderment. But after the anti-climactic 'year of decision', the youth exploded. The explosion was contained, but rumblings continued below the surface.

Ever since 1967 the army had been in a state of almost complete mobilization. Year after year it had been in the desert, training and manoeuvring. Officers and men, in the graphic phrase of President Sadat, had been 'eating sand'. Yet no end seemed in sight. There were signs of strain at every level. There was the occasion when a young lieutenant led a convoy of seven armoured cars into the middle of Cairo, went into a mosque and started denouncing the Government. Then there was the row which led to the dismissal of General Sadiq. Some of the conscripts, many of whom were university graduates, had been under arms for five or six years and felt that their education had been wasted and that their chances of a useful civilian career were jeopardized. The army was eager to prove itself – and rightly so. One of the most remarkable things about 6 October was the exemplary way in which all ranks behaved. Discipline could not have been better nor morale higher.

By 1973 Egypt had almost become the laughing stock of the Arab world. We claimed to be the leader and protector of the Arabs, but gave no lead to our own people and showed ourselves unable to protect our own territory. We asked others to use their oil weapon but showed no sign of using our own weapons. Each day that passed was a day of humiliation for Egypt.

A point had been reached where our friends abroad – in Africa, Asia, even in London and Paris – were in a state of near despair. They had given us all the political backing we had asked them for but nothing happened. A typical reaction was that of the French Foreign Minister, M. Jobert. One day our Ambassador in Paris was expounding to him the gravity of the Middle East situation and saying that if nothing was done it would explode. 'And why not?' said M. Jobert. 'Let it.'

One of the most potent forces acting on President Sadat was the attitude of Israel. The almost incredible arrogance of Israeli politicians in public reached its peak as the general election, due on 31 October 1973, came near. During the spring and summer parties and candidates were outbidding each other in their plans for what to do with conquered Arab territory. The Labour Alignment, under pressure from General Dayan, changed its position over annexation. Creeping annexation, or 'creating facts', as it was called, gathered momentum. Dayan talked openly of his designs for the new port of Yamit at Rafah, which was to isolate Egypt for ever from contact with the Gaza Strip. 'Every word spoken about Yamit,' said President Sadat, 'is a knife pointing at me personally and at my self-respect.'

Finally there was, as has already been mentioned, the feeling that this was Egypt's last chance. One day I said to President Sadat, 'I'm afraid it looks as though the détente is going to become a reality and impose itself on us before we can impose

205

Road to Ramadan

ourselves on it. The détente will set conditions for the Middle East problem instead of the Middle East problem setting conditions for the détente.' The President gave a very shrewd answer: 'Maybe we will just be able to catch the last part of the tail of the détente,' he said.

CHAPTER IV

War

The plan for Operation Badr was excellent though the initial successes were not exploited with sufficient energy or imagination. For five days the victory for Arab arms was almost complete, and no praise can be too high for the men of all ranks who made it possible. Then came five days of lull, at the end of which the Israelis took the initiative, and the final five days of the fifteen days of fighting went to the Israelis.

At 1405 hours on Saturday 6 October, 4000 guns, rocket-launchers, and mortars opened up on the Egyptian front and 1500 on the Syrian front. This artillery barrage was supported by strikes from over 300 aircraft. Fifteen minutes later 8000 troops in 1000 rubber boats were crossing the Suez Canal, and the first fortress on the Bar-Lev Line was captured by elements of the Second Army at 1500 hours exactly. Many others fell soon afterwards. Simultaneously the engineers with their water cannons were breaking down the sand rampart on the eastern bank of the canal and in four and a half hours had breached it in eighty places. At 1710 the first officer prisoners were taken by units of the Second Division north of Ismailia. By 1930 hours the first formations of the two Egyptian armies were established on the east bank of the canal along a front of 170 km. Eighty thousand men in twelve waves had penetrated Sinai to a depth of three to four kilometres and were well dug in inside the Bar-Lev fortified area.

In order to secure these positions it was essential that the Israeli armour should not be able to engage them. This, as has been seen, could only be achieved by confronting the enemy armour with mobile anti-tank weapons that could be carried by individual infantrymen. Those officers and men detailed for the

207

task ran without stopping from the moment they landed on the east bank until they had covered the five kilometres which separated them from the positions they were to occupy on the perimeter. Only three or four minutes after they had reached these positions the first units of Israeli armour appeared on the scene. These were astonished by the volume and accuracy of the fire which greeted them and which took a heavy toll of their vehicles. But it was a very close run thing.

On the Syrian front the initial success of Arab arms was hardly less spectacular. Profiting by complete surprise Syrian ground forces negotiated the Israeli anti-tank ditch and advanced at great speed. Many Israeli strong points fell within the first hours of the battle and the observation post at Jebel el-Sheikh, with its wealth of complex electronic equipment, was captured intact, its contents being immediately transported to Damascus for examination and subsequent use. The Israelis quickly counter-attacked with tanks and aircraft, but Syrian anti-tank and anti-aircraft fire took a heavy toll. A diversionary landing by Israeli forces at Latakia, aimed at obliging the Syrians to withdraw troops from the front for protection of vulnerable areas in the rear, was repulsed.

The Syrian attack was mounted along two main axes, both of which were intended subsequently to divide into two. By midnight on Saturday the heaviest of the two thrusts, a pincer movement towards Nafak, Jisr Benat Yacoub and El Al, had almost reached its allotted positions, though the northern thrust, in the general direction of Qala, had not pushed ahead so rapidly.

At 6 o'clock on Saturday evening the Soviet Ambassador telephoned to say he wished to see the President, and at eight he arrived. It was at this meeting that confusion arose over the possibility of a ceasefire which was not cleared up for several days. What had happened was that, before the battle started, President Asad had summoned the Soviet Ambassador in Damascus, Nuritdin Mykhitdinov, and told him that the situation was critical on the Syrian front because of the Israeli threats. Tension had risen to boiling point and he thought fighting might break out within the next few hours. The Ambassador

asked him if there was any assistance that his Government
could give. President Asad had, naturally, some military requests to make, but when these had been disposed of the Ambassador asked if there was anything on the political side that he
could do. 'Do you want us,' he asked, 'to take any action in the
Security Council?' President Asad apparently said that no harm
would be done if a resolution calling for a ceasefire was put
forward. It may be that at the back of his mind was the thought
that if the fighting was going Syria's way the resolution would
not matter; if the fighting went Israel's way the resolution might
come in useful. So Mykhitdinov sent this information back to
Moscow and it was relayed to Cairo. Vinogradov spoke to
Brezhnev on the telephone and the instructions which he got
were:
1. He should give President Sadat the congratulations of the
Soviet Union on the successful and speedy crossing of the Canal.
2. He should inform President Sadat that now that the success
of the crossing was assured the Syrians had no objection to the
idea of a ceasefire being put forward. Contact between the
two super-powers had been continuous all the day and obviously
the Soviet Union was, as always, more concerned with the next
political move ahead, while the Arabs were preoccupied with
the immediate military situation.

President Sadat was astonished when he got this information.
He asked Vinogradov where it came from and was told it came
'from Moscow'. The President said he could have understood if
the proposal for a ceasefire had come from Washington, since
the battle was going the Arabs' way. He protested that it was
impossible for him to contemplate a ceasefire – five divisions
were crossing into Sinai; the armour was on its way. 'We want
peace,' he said, 'but peace can't be contemplated before the last
Israeli soldier leaves Sinai.'

By midnight on Saturday ten bridges had been thrown across
the Suez Canal, the majority being Russian PMP-type. The
crossing – from the demolition of the sand ramparts to the
completion of the bridge-laying – would normally have taken
10–12 hours, but owing to the ingenuity of the engineering corps
and the hundreds of crossing exercises that had been conducted

over the past years, the time was cut down to six hours. These bridges were supplemented by fifteen ferries, all working at full capacity. In addition to the units crossing the canal, paratroops and special commando units were being scattered like salt over Sinai to disrupt enemy communications and control points. The oil installations at Abu Zneima, Sudr and Bellayim were in flames, thus denying Israel the southern Sinai oilfields which she had been exploiting since their capture in 1967. A successful raid was launched against Sharm el-Sheikh, and the Navy began a blockade of Bab el-Mandeb, thus emphasizing the unreality of Israeli claims that control of Sharm el-Sheikh was essential to its security.

In the afternoon of 6 October, while all Israel's attention was concentrated on the threat to the Bar-Lev Line, nearly fifty special commando units had been dropped into Sinai by helicopter, each helicopter carrying thirty men. One of these commando leaders, Ibrahim el-Rifai, was already a legend in the Egyptian army. Between 1967 and 1973 he had taken part in between eighty and ninety raids in various parts of Sinai, and he and his men had been dropped far behind the enemy lines several days before the battle began. He was later to be killed in action while his squad of frogmen were laying explosives under one of the bridges which General Sharon had thrown across the canal at Deversoir in the later stages of the battle. He himself was on one of the roads beside the bridge when he received a direct hit from an Israeli tank. Ibrahim el-Rifai was one of only fourteen men to be posthumously awarded the highest Egyptian decoration for valour, the Star of Sinai.

During these early hours Israel's forces on both fronts were still reeling under the shock of surprise. The Egyptian command heard Israeli tank commanders complaining in a state of total bewilderment of fire which seemed to be coming at them from nowhere in the desert, and it was with great satisfaction that an order from Major-General Peled, the Israeli Air Force commander, to his air crews was intercepted which instructed them to keep fifteen miles away from the canal. This was interpreted as showing that the scale of Israel's losses in the air had become intolerable. For the first time the Israeli command felt that it had certainly lost air domination, had probably lost air superiority, and had perhaps even lost air parity over the battle zone.

Before dawn on 7 October the Israeli Sinai Command ordered all troops manning the Bar-Lev Line fortresses to choose between surrender (after destroying all weapons and equipment) or making their way back eastwards to rejoin the forces in the second and third defence lines.

At 0810 on 7 October the Israeli tactical command post at Mitla reported that Egyptian tanks were completely surrounding the area. This marked the furthest penetration of Egyptian forces during the battle.

So far execution of the plan had gone like clockwork. Credit for this success, which exceeded the wildest dreams of the planners, must without doubt go to the junior commanders, and to the NCOs and men of the infantry, artillery, engineers and armour, many of whom were later to speak of the sense of exaltation they felt when, after the monotony of training had at last been replaced by the reality of war, they found themselves with the opportunity to wipe out the stigma of defeat and humiliation under which the Egyptian army had suffered for six years.

During Sunday the 18th Infantry Division liberated Kantara East. By so doing the divisional commander fulfilled a promise he had made to President Sadat, who was particularly concerned with the fate of a town where he had served as a lieutenant-colonel just before the revolution, in 1950 and 1951. The following day, news came through that the Syrians had entered Kuneitra and were fighting in the suburbs of the town. Now, in Arabic *kantara* means a bridge and *kuneitra* means a small bridge – the Israelis used to boast that they were in occupation from 'bridge to bridge, from Kantara to Kuneitra'. So now President Sadat sent President Asad a message: 'One thousand *mabrouks* (congratulations) for the *kuneitra* and *kantara* . . .' But though this message was sent it was never made public because later it was learned that the news about the Syrians' entering Kuneitra was premature.

In fact on the 7th Israeli counter-attacks on the Syrian front

211

were growing in strength and causing the more successful of the two main Syrian thrusts, that in the South towards Jisr Benat Yacoub and El Al, to lose its momentum. The Israeli high command had already decided to concentrate its main air and ground effort in the north, with the aim of knocking Syria out of the battle and then turning its full force against the Egyptian positions in Sinai.

On Sunday President Sadat had a further meeting with the Soviet Ambassador. Probably on Saturday he had not taken the talk about a ceasefire seriously, but now the ambassador reported that the Syrians had been in touch with Moscow about their heavy tank losses, and Moscow had suggested that, as the delay in shipping new tanks from Odessa (the usual port of loading) to Latakia would be so considerable they should get in touch with the Iraqis and get tanks from them – Russia would make up the Iraqi deficiencies later. He confirmed the correctness of the message which Mykhitdinov had received from President Asad to the effect that he did not object to the idea of a ceasefire if it was proposed. When Vinogradov had left, President Sadat sat down to write a message for President Asad. He said that a ceasefire now would leave Israel in a stronger position than when the fighting started. It would be a mistake, he insisted, to think that the object of the fighting was to gain territory – it was to bleed the enemy, and to do this we must be prepared to accept severe losses. 'I cannot accept your point of view,' he said. 'I would advise you to commit your reserve armoured division to the battle and at the same time, if necessary, withdraw one of the infantry divisions from the front and position it for the defence of Damascus.'

On Monday 8 October, tanks, infantry, artillery, heavy equipment, administrative and medical services continued moving across the canal into Sinai in a continuous stream. Israel's reserves in Sinai had by now begun to be mobilized, and were thrown into the battle in a four-pronged attack. But the Israelis repeated our errors of 1967. The units were committed in driblets and the attack was not co-ordinated, so that the operation was a failure, and the next afternoon, Tuesday 9 October, one tank brigade, the 190th commanded by Colonel

Asaf Yagouri, was annihilated. Israeli forces were withdrawn eastwards to take up defensive positions 15–20 kilometres east of the canal. It was this failure which touched off the quarrel between Generals Gonen and Sharon.

It was also on Monday that a strong detachment from the Third Army was sent off to capture the fort of Ayun Musa – on the east bank opposite Suez – and, in particular, to neutralize the two tank batteries of long-range 175 mm guns which had been responsible for the destruction of the towns of Suez and Port Tewfiq during the War of Attrition.

As the Egyptian command saw the situation, they now had a strong defensive wall on the east of the canal. Israeli forces coming from the centre of Sinai in the area of manoeuvre between the passes and the canal would be obliged to attack this wall, and the more attacks they launched against it the harder we should hit them. This seemed a more profitable tactic than moving to the offensive.

But on the Syrian front the picture was less cheerful. Israel had by now regained the initiative and Syrian troops had been ordered to switch to the defensive and to concentrate on holding on to the territory which they had liberated and on preparing to withstand Israeli counter-attacks that were certain to be launched.

It was on Monday that an answer came from President Asad to the telegram which President Sadat had sent him the day before. The Syrian President denied that he had requested the Soviet Union to ask for a ceasefire and said he was puzzled by Vinogradov's language. The battle was going well as far as Syria was concerned. They were inflicting heavy losses on the enemy and had already liberated more than half the Golan Heights. Their losses were not abnormal and could be replaced from their own reserves without calling on Iraq. He assured President Sadat that anything as important as a ceasefire could only be considered after it had been agreed between the allies.

As I used to do each day, I went that evening to see the President in Tahra Palace and found him in a very happy and relaxed mood. I went upstairs with him. He took off his uniform and put on pyjamas and dressing-gown before sitting down to

213

the *iftar* meal. Before we had begun to eat the telephone rang. It was the Soviet Ambassador to tell him about the airlift of arms which he expected to start shortly. I remember the President saying to Vinogradov (in English – Vinogradov speaks excellent English): 'Yes, yes. Magnificent! Magnificent! Tell Comrade Brezhnev I feel thankful to him from the bottom of my heart. Tell Brezhnev that it is Soviet arms which achieved the miracle of the crossing.' When he had finished speaking I asked him what he thought Russia's real attitude was. He said he thought they saw the situation moving in a very favourable direction and felt this was their chance to regain most or all of their lost prestige in the Middle East. 'I don't think they'll miss this chance,' he said.

I stayed with the President until late at night. He found it impossible to sleep, so he thought he would like to see a film and suggested a Western. He asked me to watch it with him, but I felt exhausted and could hardly keep my eyes open. He laughed, and said: 'All right, go to bed.' But after I left his house I looked in at the *Al Ahram* office to see if there was any news, and heard that President Nixon had asked for a meeting of the Security Council. I called up the President while he was still watching the film to tell him about this, and he asked whether I thought it meant that Nixon was going to begin taking strong action against the Arabs. 'I don't think so,' I said, 'because if he really wanted to get tough with us he wouldn't have gone to the Security Council where he is subject to a veto from the Soviet Union or China, which would tie his hands completely.' The President seemed to accept this interpretation.

By sunset on Tuesday all the divisional footholds on the east bank of the Suez Canal had been consolidated into two army bridgeheads 10–12 kilometres deep. The initial objective of the campaign had been accomplished, and it is fair to say that the Egyptian army and the Egyptian people were enjoying their finest hour since the days of Suez in 1956.

But the next four days were to tell a different story. These were four days during which the initial impetus of the attack was lost and the Egyptian forces in Sinai, though successfully repelling Israeli attacks inevitably missed the opportunity to break out towards the passes in the centre of the peninsula. This was the period of the so-called 'operational pause', which led to a fierce argument between the Egyptian and Syrian political and military commands that has not yet been resolved.

The Syrians maintained that the attack was to continue till the Egyptian forces reached the passes by which time Syrian troops should have reached the Jordan River and Lake Tiberias, ready to exploit success towards Nazareth. Then, and then only, would an 'operational pause' have been justified. The Egyptian claim is that it was agreed there would be an 'operational pause' after the successful crossing of the Bar-Lev Line. This would give the opportunity for regrouping to meet the expected enemy counter-attack, after which the advance towards the passes could continue. In fact an 'operational pause' is not a concept known to military theorists. There can only be a pause when the mission for which the operation was planned has been successfully completed.

It may be that the spectre of previous defeats inhibited those in command from taking anything that could possibly be construed as a risk. The security of the army may have weighed more with them than the exploitation of an unlooked for degree of success. Be that as it may, between 8 October and 10 October an opportunity was missed. It is my belief that had the passes been reached and occupied the whole of Sinai would have been liberated with the incalculable political consequences that would have flowed from such a victory.

Meanwhile Israeli counter-attacks on the Syrian front, both on the ground and in the air, were gaining in strength. The Syrian command appealed to the Egyptians to take quick action to relieve the pressure on them, for by Monday 8 October the Israeli northern command had committed two fresh tank brigades to the battle. Frustrated by the unexpected stubborn resistance of the Syrian troops in the southern sector and by the scale of his own losses the enemy turned the night of 9/10 October into an inferno, while the air force kept up continuous strikes. Damascus and Homs were heavily bombed in an attempt to weaken civilian morale and provoke a collapse of the regime. Kuneitra became the scene of bitter fighting with heavy casualties on both sides. To the Syrians the town was prized as capital of a Syrian province; to the Israelis its value lay in its pivotal position in their defence planning for the occupied Golan area.

By Wednesday the Syrian forces were in a grave plight. The mounting Israeli attacks were inflicting very heavy losses, and the Syrian command had been obliged to commit to the battle the 500 tanks which, constituting the 3rd Tank Division, had been stationed around and to the north of Damascus as the strategic reserve. Another appeal by the Syrian Commander-in-Chief to his Egyptian counterpart asked for retaliation to be carried out on Israel for the bombing of Damascus and Homs. This was difficult for Egypt to accept because of the degree of escalation in the war it would certainly have entailed. The Syrians then approached the Iraqis who, after first consenting, later decided there was insufficient time for their bombers to undertake the necessary action. In these circumstances relations between the two commands, in Cairo and Damascus, became somewhat strained.

On the night of Tuesday 9 October President Sadat was in Tahra Palace, awaiting the results of the big tank battle that had been expected, when he got a message from Vinogradov asking to see him. The meeting took place in the President's office from which the President emerged somewhat tense. Apparently Vinogradov had said that things were going badly on the Syrian front. By now they had lost the staggering total of 600 tanks. A meeting of the Security Council, called by the Americans, was due, and the Russians were in a quandary. They still seemed to think that the Syrians were anxious for a ceasefire, but they knew that the Egyptians were not. If a proposal for a ceasefire was put forward, what should they do? To veto it, or to abstain, would be equally strange.

President Sadat begged the Ambassador to stop telling him about the Syrians' intentions. He said he had had a message from Hafez Asad himself and knew perfectly well what his point of view was. What he (the President) was really concerned about was the promised airlift. The Americans were doing all they could to supply the arms Israel was asking for: what were the Russians going to do? If they wanted to go back on their promises, well and good. Sadat would thank them and not make complaints, because one day the truth about everything was bound to come out.

Vinogradov insisted that he was not trying to put pressure on Egypt for a ceasefire. To this President Sadat replied that he wanted an investigation into the behaviour of the Soviet Ambassador in Damascus. 'I want an official investigation,' he said, 'and I want to be told the result.' Then his mood relaxed, and he once again assured the Ambassador that the Arab victories would greatly enhance the reputation of Russian arms and the position of the Soviet Union in the Middle East.

Soon after this I went round myself to Tahra Palace. It was the time of the *iftar* meal, the breaking of the fast. As soon as the President came in I could see that something had annoyed him, but he made no mention of his interview with Vinogradov. He showed me the draft of a speech he had been thinking of making to the nation over radio and television – something he had been keen on since the outbreak of hostilities but which had been held over until we could be more certain how the battle was going. Now the draft, which he made me read aloud, seemed inappropriate. It began: 'I am glad to be with you all at this glorious hour in our history . . .' The President interrupted: 'What glorious hour? The Syrian front is under very heavy pressure. The situation there is terrible.' He was pacing up and down. 'We shall have to change it,' he said. 'Let's go to the people and tell them that we are going to fight even alone. I can talk to them as Churchill talked to the British in 1940.' Then he called General Ahmed Ismail on the telephone and asked him to come round.

I went out to meet Ahmed Ismail, leaving President Sadat dictating a message to Hafez Asad. Ahmed Ismail embraced me. He said that this was the first time that he had emerged above ground since the fighting started, and told me how one commando unit had succeeded in destroying Bellayim and Abu Rudeis. Then he went on to discuss the role being played by the Iraqis. Apparently the Iraqi Government had sent a special envoy to Moscow who had asked Podgorny to intervene with

217

the Shah of Iran and ask him to relax the pressure on Iraq's eastern border so that Iraqi forces could go to the help of Syria. Podgorny had promised he would, and then had expressed surprise that all Arab states were not hurrying to the aid of Egypt and Syria. 'Why don't they contribute all they've got to the battle?' Podgorny asked. 'What have Iraq and Algeria got all those arms from us for? Is Iraq going to start a war against Kuwait, or is Algeria going to fight Morocco? What are you waiting for?' Podgorny went on to issue the same warning that Vinogradov had given in Cairo – that once Israel had achieved a victory on the Syrian front she would concentrate all she had against Egypt.

I was myself anxious to find out exactly what the position was, so I got in touch with Vinogradov and arranged to meet him later that evening at his house. It was not until 10 p.m. that I reached the Ambassador's house. His secretary was waiting for me in the darkened garden. Inside all was in darkness because of the blackout, but I could hear that somewhere someone was playing the theme from Rachmaninov's Second Piano Concerto. I went through the door which led into a small reception room on the right and saw by the light of a single candle the Soviet Ambassador seated at the piano. For three or four minutes I stood silently listening to him until the Ambassador, sensing someone was near, looked up. 'Bravo!' I said, clapping my hands. Vinogradov smiled. 'This is my relaxation,' he said. 'In times of tension this is the only way I can really relax.' And he started to tell me about the stormy interview he had had with the President. He said that Brezhnev and Grechko had been talking to him on the telephone, and that both of them thought Israel was pressing Syria hard in an effort to knock her out of war, after which they could concentrate their forces against Egypt. 'I have been in almost continuous session today with our military attachés,' he said, 'and to tell you the truth they don't like the way things are developing. I don't see why your troops are not advancing. Why haven't you consolidated your gains and begun to push on to the passes? This is not only the sensible thing for your army to do, but it would help take pressure off the Syrians.' He emphasized that there was only a limited amount of time in which the Arabs could obtain results. The time allowed for fighting was limited, and the Arabs should prepare themselves for the next phase – a political one. He said that one of the questions Brezhnev had asked him on the telephone that day was: 'What is the limit of their limited objectives?' (President Sadat was still assuring the Russians that this was only a war of 'limited objectives'.) He assured me that there was absolutely no reason for the suspicions President Sadat had voiced, that the Soviet Union was holding back through fear. On the contrary, the airlift to Egypt and Syria was already starting. I reminded Vinogradov that from the first day of the war the Americans had allowed the Israelis to take any arms and equipment they wanted from the United States in their own planes – all El Al flights had been halted and the planes diverted to shuttle American war material into Israel. Vinogradov said it would be difficult to carry on the Russian airlift if one Arab government was wanting a ceasefire and the other was opposing it. 'We can do anything,' said Vinogradov, 'but we must know exactly what it is we are being asked to do.'

Vinogradov told me that he and his military advisers were extremely worried about the military situation. They felt that the density of the concentration of Egyptian forces on the eastern front exposed them to considerable danger. 'If the Israelis start area bombing,' he said, 'your losses could be worse than any you had in 1967.' I tried to be a sympathetic listener, because it was plain that the President had given him a rough time that afternoon. Apparently the last thing he had asked the President was what he wanted politically to come out of the fighting, for as always the Russians were thinking of the next move ahead. Upon which the President had looked sternly at him and said: 'You are now talking to the Supreme Commander of the Armed Forces. Your political question I have not heard. If you want to talk about the political situation go and talk to Dr Fawzi.' Vinogradov asked me what I thought. I told him he should certainly see Dr Fawzi as the President had suggested, and the next day he did.

I returned home from the Soviet Ambassador's house in an anxious frame of mind. Some hours before, when I had been discussing the situation with two of our leading military experts, they had assured me that the military situation was 'ideal'. The Israelis, they said, were concentrating their armour in an area between the passes and the canal which gave them only limited room for manoeuvre and enabled us to hit them hard. It was, in fact, only this Tuesday afternoon that Brigadier Hassan Abu Saada, commander of the Second Infantry Division – which first contacted the Israeli forces on a large scale – and one of the best commanders thrown up by the war, had captured the commander of the Israeli 170th Armoured Brigade which was completely destroyed.

What I heard from the Russian confirmed my anxieties about the passes. I had always thought that we should go for these features and hold them; if we let our troops stay in the open country between the canal and the passes they would be exposed to enemy attack.

I telephoned the President in Tahra Palace, and was told that he had gone out with his daughter and her fiancé for an incognito tour of the centre of Cairo to feel the pulse of the people. I left a message asking him to call me back. This he did at 1.30 in the morning. I told him I had seen Vinogradov and gave him an account of how the Ambassador and his staff assessed the situation. The President said he disagreed with them: 'As I told Hafez Asad, territory isn't important; what is important is to exhaust the enemy. I don't want to make the mistake of pushing forward too fast just for the sake of occupying more territory. We must make the enemy bleed.' When I eventually went to bed I found it hard to sleep, for the conflicting concepts of how the battle should be fought were going round and round in my mind.

Early the next morning I called up General Ahmed Ismail and told him of the view held by the Russians that we should go all out to capture the passes. 'You know,' he said, 'that had been my intention. But in view of the deteriorating situation on the Syrian front we must revise our plans. Should the enemy turn and concentrate all his attacks on us we must at all costs avoid being dangerously extended.'

On Thursday 11 October the Syrians were still losing ground

in the northern sector. Israeli attacks were increasing in numbers and intensity, and were penetrating far along the Kuneitra–Damascus road. But by then it looked as if the Iraqis might be coming in. President Sadat received a message from President Bakr saying that he had been trying for two days unsuccessfully to contact Cairo to reassure President Sadat that Iraq was coming to Syria's aid by putting at President Asad's disposal four squadrons of aircraft. The forward air bases in Iraq were also available for use by the air forces of Syria and Jordan.

The same day Yasser Arafat sent a telegram to President Sadat saying that the executive committee of the PLO was trying by every means to rush Fedayin units to the Aghwar area. These would in effect open a third front. Abu Iyad telephoned the President and reported that Yasser Arafat had told him that for 24 hours a thousand Fedayin had been waiting on the frontier seeking permission from the Jordanian authorities to cross into the Aghwar area of southern Israel. This had been refused, and President Sadat was asked to intercede with King Hussein. However, the President doubted whether there was much he could do. He suspected that King Hussein would probably enter the battle only after he was quite certain that the Israelis had been so severely weakened that they were in no position to give him much trouble.

There was still some friction with Ghadaffi. President Sadat was irritated with Ghadaffi for publicly saying that he disagreed with the overall plan of attack. Now came a telegram from Ghadaffi which did little to improve matters: 'Greetings. I am sending you all the anti-aircraft missiles we have, also the garrison of Tobruk. An armoured brigade has been ordered to move to Cairo immediately. Our oil is at your disposal; consider it your oil. We are despatching as many convoys of provisions and medicines as we can. Markets and warehouses have been stripped of their contents. I hear that you are annoyed at some of the things I am reported as saying. What in fact I said was: "Even if the battle goes against us, which God forbid, this would be due to enemy superiority and weapons and not to any shortcomings by our troops. It is sufficient that now the Israeli soldier is fleeing before the Egyptian soldier. This is not only a great triumph for Egypt but has enormous significance outside Egypt. (I cannot imagine anything otherwise at this time)." But I would tell you, my dear President, that our people take it somewhat amiss that their political contribution to the battle is being ignored in all broadcasts from Cairo while Feisal's contribution is magnified. There is no mention of Libya. I am sorry about this, my lord President, but now the most important thing is the will to fight. God be with you at this time. Ghadaffi.'

I was in Tahra Palace on the afternoon of the 11th, waiting for the President, when his wife came in. She played a gallant part throughout the war, constantly with the soldiers in the hospitals, bringing their cheerful letters and messages to the President which did much to encourage him. We were talking about the situation with Fatah Abdullah, Minister of State for Presidential Affairs, when General Ahmed Ismail came out of the President's office. There was a plate of fruit on the table beside us, and General Ismail, who had hardly had time to eat for the last five days, picked up a bunch of grapes and began munching them as he strolled round and round the room, talking about the battle – going over again the capture of the Bar-Lev Line, and telling us of the reported collapse of General Gonen. I got a summons from the President to join him. I went into his office and found him very tired, taking off his uniform and putting on a pair of grey striped pyjamas. He said he thought the situation on the Syrian front was getting a bit better. Reinforcements were going there, including some from Iraq, and he had told the Soviet Union that if there were any arms for Egypt which could be made use of in Syria they should be diverted there. He had received a message from King Hussein via an emissary, the former Jordanian Chief of Staff, General Amer Khammash, to the effect that the King was against opening up the Jordanian front because his country lacked air defences. He preferred to send units of his army to give support on the Syrian front.

General Ismail came into the room, looking cheerful. He had received a message that the Syrians were successfully containing the Israeli attack. 'I knew it was good news as soon as I saw the expression on your face,' said the President. Then the telephone

222

rang; it was President Boumedienne of Algeria. He mentioned Monday's speech by David Elazar in which he had said: 'We shall strike them, we shall beat them, we shall break their bones.' 'It seems to me,' said Boumedienne, 'that when they start talking like this they are losing their nerve.' Another bit of good news which came in was that the Sheikh Zaid of Abu Dhabi, who was then in London, had transferred $100m. to Egypt.

The President was in a good mood. He told me that he was going to pray in a small mosque in which he had prayed when he was only four years old when he came with his father to Cairo for the first time. He said he had prayed there the week before without being noticed. 'The mosque is just the same as it was fifty years ago,' he said, 'except that it used to be lit by candles and now it has electric light.' The atmosphere in Tahra Palace was optimistic, and the talk was about what we were going to do when the battle was over. I felt, however, that there were many questions that required an answer and I was also anxious about the international scene.

The Americans, as I was later told by Dr Kissinger, originally thought that within forty-eight hours of the opening of hostilities the Israelis would be in a position to deliver a devastating counter-attack against the Egyptian forces in Sinai. They therefore thought that by proposing a ceasefire and withdrawal by both sides to the pre-October 6th lines they would be helping us. If there was no ceasefire and Egypt received the crushing military defeat they expected, they foresaw two possible developments, neither of which could they contemplate with any satisfaction – either they would have to intervene to restrain Israel, or the Egyptians would have to ask the Russians to rescue them which would mean Russia being once again installed in Egypt, and in a far stronger position than before. Then the picture changed. The Americans realized that Egypt was not in danger of another sudden catastrophic defeat – that in fact the Egyptian armies had put up a very impressive show. Kissinger, even before he became Secretary of State, was maintaining contact with Hafez Ismail through the American and Egyptian intelligence networks. So on Tuesday 9 October he sent Hafez Ismail a message along the same lines as his message to Zayyat in Washington: 'All right; you've made your point. But where do we go from here? We can't expect the existing situation to hold for long, and when it changes it's going to change against you.' Next day Hafez Ismail sent him an answer which had, in fact, been dictated by President Sadat. This answer made five points:

1. There should be a ceasefire followed by a withdrawal within a specified period under UN supervision, of all Israeli forces to behind the pre-5th June 1967 lines.

2. Freedom of navigation in the Straits of Tiran should be guaranteed by a UN presence in Sharm el-Sheikh for a specified period.

3. Following the complete withdrawal of Israeli forces outlined in para. 1 the state of belligerency with Israel would be ended.

4. Following the withdrawal of Israeli troops from the Gaza Strip the area would be placed under UN supervision pending an opportunity for its inhabitants to exercise the right of self-determination and to decide their own future.

5. Within a specified period after the ending of the state of belligerency a peace conference would be convened under UN auspices, to be attended by all interested parties, including the Palestinians, and all members of the Security Council. The conference would deal with all questions concerning sovereignty, security and freedom of navigation.

On the night of Friday 12 October, the day after the cheerful meeting in Tahra Palace, the British Ambassador in Cairo, Sir Philip Adams, asked to see the President. He was received shortly after midnight, and handed over a message from Heath which asked Egypt to agree to a standstill ceasefire on existing positions, pointing out that this was a concession the Israelis had already been compelled to agree to. Heath's message was discussed the following morning and the consensus was that Egypt could not accept a standstill ceasefire at a moment when we were advancing, especially as a big offensive was due to begin on the Egyptian front the next day. The British Ambassador was told by Ismail Fahmy that we could not accept a ceasefire unless the Israelis made some positive gesture to prove that they were beginning to evacuate the territories occupied in 1967. He was told of the five points that had been given to Kissinger.

The 'operational pause' lasted throughout 10, 11, 12 and 13 October, and by the evening of the 13th what may be considered the first phase of the battle, in which Egypt had won an astonishing victory, came to an end. Fourteenth October was to be the day for unleashing the Egyptian armour in a drive towards the passes.

Opinion about the offensive among staff officers at GHQ and in subordinate commands was divided. Some felt that, though the ideal moment had been missed, there was still a good chance for going forward, and if the attack was pressed it might be possible to make up for lost time. Others thought it was too late for this, and that it would be better to concentrate in defensive positions on the east bank of the canal.

The Israeli forces, badly knocked off balance during the first forty-eight hours, had recovered themselves. It was now the Egyptians who were uncertain, while the position on the Syrian front was giving rise to grave anxiety. By the 13th messages from Damascus calling on Egypt to draw off Israeli pressure took on a sharper note.

It was partly in response to these appeals that on the 14th the commanders of both the Second and Third Armies were ordered to mount offensives eastwards with their armour, while at the same time holding the bridgeheads over the canal with their infantry. The situation was in some ways analogous to that of another October battle when another cautious commander, General Montgomery, after he too had taken nine days to crack the enemy's defences, unleashed his armour while keeping his infantry back to maintain the strategic balance in the theatre of operations. Montgomery's caution may have reflected his concern to avoid the disaster which befell Ritchie, just as General Ismail's caution reflected his preoccupation with Field-Marshal Amer's disaster in 1967.

The intention was that the two armies' armour should penetrate thirty kilometres to the western exits of the Sinai passes, capturing the lateral road constructed by the Israeli army and thereby neutralizing the Israeli reserves which were deployed round the road. The armour was to prevent the forward movement of Israeli armour from the reserve areas to the operational area, and thus create favourable conditions for the final advance of Egyptian forces eastwards. But what had been open for Egypt to accomplish on 7 October was no longer there to be achieved on 14 October.

As soon as the Egyptian armour started its forward movement in the early hours of Sunday, and left the cover of its air defences, it became an easy prey to Israeli strikes from the air. The anti-tank weapons and helicopter-borne missiles caused severe damage among our tanks. Very many tank commanders and crews fought their way forward with great gallantry against the varieties of French SS-anti-tank missiles that the Israelis had now been given time to deploy on the battlefields. Never for a moment was the fighting spirit of the troops below the highest.

Like the Israeli counter-attack on 8 October, the Egyptian attack on the 14th was delivered in four prongs and in the same piecemeal and unco-ordinated manner. To reinforce this offensive, elements of the two tank divisions deployed on the west bank of the canal as general reserve – the core of the First Army – were brought into Sinai, a step which was to have grave consequences in the future. The mounting of this offensive was interpreted by the Israeli Government, as also by Washington, as an indication that the final Egyptian thrust was under way. The airlift of arms to Israel continued with increasing momentum, American tanks and artillery being flown direct to the battle area. By now the Americans and the Israelis knew that Egypt's strategic reserve had been committed to the battle. The 21st Armoured Division, which was behind the Second Army, had crossed the canal; so had one brigade of the 4th Armoured Division, which was behind the Third Army.

Accurate fire from anti-tank missiles newly arrived on the battlefield brought the Egyptian advance to a halt twelve to fifteen kilometres from its starting point, after suffering heavy losses. Later the elements of the Egyptian attacking forces received the order to draw back to their start line.

Ironically the situation on the Syrian front, which was in part at least responsible for the ill-conceived Egyptian offensive, had by the 14th begun to show some signs of improvement. During the night of 12/13 October Israel had been preparing the knock-out blow against Syria promised by General Elazar. All available forces had been concentrated for the kill, and they received from the Israeli Chief of Staff an order similar to the 'Good hunting, gentlemen' order given by Montgomery to his armour at Alamein. But the Syrian forces had been regrouping and they were helped by the fact that at this opportune moment the Iraqi 12th Tank Brigade arrived on the scene and immediately entered the battle in the region of Nawa. The Israeli advance in the south was slowed down and twenty tanks and four APCs were knocked out. Fortunately, back in the days when the Unified Arab Command was active, the 12th Tank Brigade had taken part in exercises here and many of its officers and men were familiar with the terrain in which they had to fight.

On 13 October the Israeli drive towards Damascus continued. Syrian airfields and missile sites were subjected to heavy bombardment. But when it was most needed another fresh formation made its appearance to support the regrouped Syrian units: this was the crack 40th Tank Brigade of the Jordanian army. This brigade, which was also familiar with the battle area, deployed rapidly on the left of the Iraqis. Now a really unified Arab command was seen in action – Iraqis, Jordanians, and Syrians fighting side by side. Moroccans had been in action on this front from the beginning, and a Saudi Arabian mechanized regiment was to join in on the 15th. These reinforcements threatened the right flank of the Israeli drive towards Damascus, and the Egyptian army's Sinai offensive was also successful in drawing Israeli units from the Syrian battle. All the same, during 17 and 18 October Israeli air strikes increased, and early on 19 October another push along the road to Damascus was attempted. This was repulsed with the loss of fifty-two tanks and seventeen APCs destroyed or damaged.

Damascus had been saved. Whether in fact the Israeli army, had the way remained open, would have entered and occupied Damascus must be a matter for conjecture. It would, of course, have been a dramatic political triumph of precisely the sort that many Israelis had for long been advocating, but great numbers of troops would have been required to control this fiercely nationalist city of some 700,000 inhabitants. Explosions in Arab countries and the probable reaction of the rest of the world, particularly of the Soviet Union, to such a situation would have caused the Israeli Government to hesitate, even if such a target had been aimed at by them or been genuinely within their reach.

So the Egyptian offensive of 14 October failed, the two armies east of the canal being ordered to take up defensive positions, hold the ground they had captured, and resist enemy attacks. In the higher ranks of the Egyptian command it now seemed better to go back to the alternative plan of letting the Israelis beat their heads against the wall of fire presented by the bridgeheads than to risk a mobile battle in the interior of Sinai in which Israel would in all probability have the upper hand.

From the foundation of the state of Israel it had been accepted doctrine that the best way to protect it was to carry the war into enemy territory. This doctrine did not automatically apply after 1967 to the occupied territories because, if the Egyptians chose to fight in Sinai, Israel felt it would be happy to meet them there. But Israel was determined that if it detected signs of a build-up by Egypt on the west bank of the canal it would launch a pre-emptive strike to nip such an attack in the bud. Egyptian planners had taken this possibility into account, and a plan for dealing with an Israeli assault on the west bank of the canal had been prepared: Plan 200. Deversoir had been identified as one of three likely crossing places and troops for executing the plan had been earmarked.

General Sharon, who had been GOC Sinai Command for three years before 1973, had given plans for Israel's pre-emptive strike across the canal final shape and had trained troops to execute it. The plan envisaged the penetration of Egypt's defences at the meeting point between the two armies, and a crossing of the canal by sufficient troops and equipment to disrupt Egyptian communications and to destroy enough missile sites to open a gap in Egypt's air defence cover and so enable Israeli aircraft to join in the battle. Once a foothold had been secured on the west bank, Israeli forces would divide into small units moving rapidly over a wide area, thus resuming the traditional role of the Israeli army of 'being everywhere and nowhere'.

It required no great subtlety on the part of the Israeli command to reckon where the meeting point between the two Egyptian armies would be, as this had been fixed since 1969 in the defensive positions adopted on the canal and remained at the same point when Egypt moved to the offensive. This was verified by high altitude American reconnaissance planes based in Greece and so was confirmed to Israel. The area behind Deversoir and Fayid offers plenty of cover for an invading army. The country is fertile, with many trees and contains extensive entrenchments built for the Egyptian army after 1967. The airfields of Deversoir and Fayid, and further west those of Kabrit and Qasr Farid, would, if captured, greatly assist the speed of the Israeli assault.

Sharon's plan, if successfully carried out, could act as a tonic to flagging Israeli morale. Moreover, should the air force be able to knock out the remaining Egyptian missile sites, the whole front would be exposed to attack from the air. In this case, the Israelis hoped, panic might well set in, and the Egyptian armed forces once again, as in 1967, turn in headlong and disorganized flight westwards.

Generals Sharon and Tal acted on Napoleon's dictum – as had their predecessors Dayan and Yadin in 1948 – that 'he who controls the cross-roads of the battlefield will be master of the ground'. The most important cross-roads in the area west of the canal were one east of Ismailia, one known as the Ahmad Osman cross-roads at the back of Fayid, and two conspicuous 101 Km cross-roads to the west of Suez. All three were to be captured by Sharon's forces. When the Israelis were certain that Egypt's strategic reserves had been committed to the battle, Sharon was finally given permission to initiate the attack across the canal for which he had been pleading, and it was launched on 15 October. In the region of Deversoir-Abu Sultan a gap of about forty kilometres between the two Egyptian armies was virtually unguarded at that time, and Israeli amphibious troops, crossing the Great Bitter Lake, quickly gained a footing on the west bank. Astonishingly there was still, at the point of

Sharon's main crossing, an Israeli strongpoint on the Bar-Lev Line which had not been liquidated or abandoned, and this was able to give great assistance to the crossing Israeli troops. Pushing north on the morning of the 16th these troops expanded their corridor, and by the afternoon of that day many complete units were across the canal. Some Egyptian units on the spot did report what was happening, but communications between the front and GHQ were extremely poor.

Under pressure from the Russians, and in the light of his exchanges with Kissinger and Heath, President Sadat came to the conclusion that the time was coming when the search for a political solution ought to be stepped up. He doubted whether Israel would be prepared to accept the five-point plan which had been submitted to Kissinger, so he decided to address the National Assembly on Tuesday 16 October and to use this opportunity to present a more comprehensive peace plan. His speech would be given to the Egyptian nation, and so to the world, by television and radio.

Egypt, said President Sadat, would continue to fight to regain the land which had been seized by Israel and to restore to the Palestinian people their legitimate rights. But they were prepared to accept a ceasefire on condition that Israel withdrew forthwith from all the occupied territories to pre-5 June 1967 lines, under international supervision. Once these withdrawals had been carried out, Egypt was willing to attend a peace conference convened by the UN, and he would do his best to persuade the other Arab leaders involved and the representatives of the Palestinian people to take part in it. Egypt was willing, said the President, to start work on clearing the Suez Canal immediately, so that it could be open for international shipping.

Golda Meir was due to speak in the Knesset at exactly the same moment as the President spoke to the Assembly – midday Cairo and Tel Aviv time. Shortly before Sadat's speech, however, it was learned that the Israeli Prime Minister had postponed her speech till 4 p.m., presumably so that she could hear what the Egyptian President had to say and reply to it. When she did speak she said, among other things, that Israeli forces were now fighting 'east and west of the Suez Canal'. I telephoned the President as soon as I had reports of Golda Meir's speech, but he said he had no information that would bear out her claim. He called up Ahmed Ismail who said he had been told 'three infiltrating Israeli tanks' had managed to cross the canal. This failure in communication was the biggest mistake Egypt made in the whole war. By the time everybody realized what was happening the Israelis had a full brigade across the canal.

It was put to the President that this talk about 'three infiltrating tanks' was probably not the whole picture as it stood now; there must have been more solid ground for Golda Meir to speak as she did in the Knesset. But, from the information available to him at the time, President Sadat felt such suspicions only showed that we were falling victim to Israeli psychological warfare. When a little later I spoke on the telephone to General Ahmed Ismail he said there was no need to worry: 'It's a psychological move. We're going to burn up the area they're in tonight.' But nobody had any exact information about the situation at that time.

After President Sadat had made his speech to the Assembly, President Asad sent a message which reflected the strains, political as well as military, that were beginning to show between the two allies 'I would have preferred,' he wrote, 'while we are still in the middle of the battle, to have seen the proposals outlined by you to the People's Assembly before they were made public. I do not wish to follow the example of others and take a position for or against these proposals, but I feel that each of us has the right to know of the ideas and intentions of the other before hearing about them in a broadcast. It gives me no pleasure to write these words, but I wish to hide none of my thoughts and opinions from you since we are engaged together in a battle of life and death.'

President Sadat's reply read: 'Brother Hafez: The proposals I put forward yesterday were based on the policy we agreed together. There was nothing new in them that called for consultation, since they were concerned with an Israeli withdrawal and with the rights of the Palestinian people. I was prompted to make this speech by the knowledge that Golda Meir was about to address the Knesset and by my conviction that we must conduct the political and the military battle side by side. I believe that we can move forward and that we have no room for manoeuvre within the formula I proposed. Should anything new arise, then of course we must consult together. I am glad that your feelings towards me have not changed . . .'

It was at 5 p.m. the same day – Tuesday 16 October – that Kosygin came to Cairo, and he was almost immediately in consultation with President Sadat. By then the Russians were in favour of a ceasefire, and were obviously in close touch over this with the Americans, who had been advocating a ceasefire since the 10th. Kosygin said that the battle with its current scale of losses in material was very risky. Discussions went on the next day and until Kosygin left to go back to Moscow on Friday, 19 October.

On Wednesday the 17th a delegation of Arab Foreign Ministers, most of whom were in New York for the General Assembly of the UN, saw President Nixon in Washington. The delegation, which had been chosen to exclude representatives of countries directly involved in the fighting – and, as Mohammed Masmoudi, the Tunisian Foreign Minister, said, so that 'the smell of oil should be present without being overpowering' – consisted of ministers from Saudi Arabia, Kuwait, Morocco and Algeria. As the Moroccan and Algerian were more familiar with French than with English they asked for an interpreter to be present, but after some debate the Americans ruled against this. They said they would prepare a transcript of the proceedings and let everyone present have a copy, but in fact this never materialized.

The Foreign Ministers were received by Kissinger who took them in to see the President. After their meeting with Nixon they had another talk with Kissinger which was also attended by Sisco. Nixon they found very affable. He said that the United States had been obliged to go to the help of Israel, and talked at length about the airlift. The Arabs complained that as soon as Egypt and Syria had shown signs of winning the American airlift had started. Nixon said that America had only started after the Russians had begun their airlift. 'I want to tell you', he said, 'that the security of Israel is something we can't compromise over. We aren't in favour of the expansion of Israel, but we want her to have secure frontiers.' He said that the United States was ready to play a constructive role. 'In 1967,' he said, 'you accused us of collusion with Israel. This time you came to talk to us: that makes a lot of difference. I have with me here my Foreign Minister. You will be talking to him. Some of you may accuse him of being a Jew: he is, but he's an American too and he serves me well. I'm sure his feelings as a Jew won't interfere with his loyalty to America or his loyalty to me. You will find him constructive. Mrs Meir once told our ambassador in Israel: "Now you and we both have Jewish Foreign Secretaries, the only difference being that our Foreign Secretary talks better English than yours does." ' He described Mrs Meir as being 'very efficient' but said her strength was based on her feeling of military superiority. Now, he said, the situation was different. But again he stressed that he was determined that the present crisis should not be allowed to precipitate a confrontation with the Soviet Union.

The Ministers then discussed the question of a ceasefire with Kissinger. The Algerian Foreign Minister, Bouteflika, said that if the Algerians or Vietnamese accepted a ceasefire their political negotiations would never have ended in success. Kissinger said the Middle East war was not a guerrilla war; it could be stopped, and if negotiations failed it could be started up again. Bouteflika asked what would happen if Israel broke the ceasefire. Kissinger said that Israel could not fight alone for more than nine days; after that she would be entirely dependent on the US and, if she broke the ceasefire, the US could withhold supplies. Discussion then moved on to Resolution 242, which both Nixon and Kissinger said they were prepared to use all their efforts to see implemented. The Minister asked why in fact it had not yet been implemented. Kissinger said that, quite frankly, the reason was the complete military superiority of Israel. The weak, he said, don't negotiate. The Arabs had been weak; now they were strong. The Arabs had achieved more than anyone, including themselves, had believed possible. Kissinger was asked if it was possible for Israel to withdraw to the pre-June 1967 lines or to give a pledge to do so. He said he was afraid he could give no promises on that. A return to the 1967 lines would leave Israel facing the same dangers it had faced before the June war. The Foreign Minister of Saudi Arabia, Omar Saqqaf, said that the Arabs could not accept a demilitarized Sinai. Nor can Israel, said Kissinger, because she intends to stay in Sinai. On the rights of the Palestinians, Kissinger was very blunt. What you are proposing, he said, means either the destruction of Israel or the destruction of Jordan. He too stressed his determination to avoid any confrontation with the Soviet Union and said that there would be no actual intervention by America in the fighting unless there was 'violation of the territory of Israel proper.'

Kissinger gave the impression that he was in no hurry to do anything about the Middle East. He was due to go to China in ten days and said that when he came back he would ask for the files and start to work in his own style. He said his style was not making speeches or roving around foreign capitals. Here he looked at Sisco and added, 'with all respect to Sisco'. Bouteflika asked him if China had priority over the Middle East even while there was a war going on there. Kissinger said priorities could always be re-adjusted. Saqqaf mentioned that, when he had met Kissinger alone, Kissinger had told him that it would be better to wait for three or four weeks until the combatants had exhausted each other, after which time some settlement might be possible. Finally, Kissinger said he thought Sadat's speech on the 16th had some constructive points in it, though he could not agree with all of it. 'We don't consider President Sadat our enemy,' he said.

After the Israeli forces had established their bridgeheads they laid down a bridge over which the armour crossed, supported by long-range and medium-range artillery and aircraft. Several missile sites were destroyed in this first wave of the offensive. A first target of the attackers was Ismailia, but stiff resistance was met and the attackers turned south and west, rapidly gaining more ground until on 17 October a highly efficient formation, the Egyptian 182nd Parachute Brigade, which included volunteers and commandoes, was rushed in to hold the situation. Elements of this brigade had almost reached the

Israeli crossing points, and frogmen acting in co-ordination with it were poised to blow up the bridge, when the order was received to draw back and maintain a front in line with that of the division next to them in order to avoid creating a salient. The colonel commanding the brigade found it hard to believe that this order came from Egyptian headquarters, and asked for confirmation. This was given by an officer whose voice he recognized, but in an effort to gain time, and so give his mission a chance of success, he appealed to Cairo GHQ for confirmation of the order. This too was given, and with reluctance he withdrew his hand from the Israeli windpipe on which it had been about to close.

The artillery of the Second Army, concentrated under the efficient control of Brigadier Abdel Halim Abu Gazala, and clements of the artillery of the Third Army, under the no less efficient control of Brigadier Munir Shaash, began bombardment of the enemy bridges, scoring more than one direct hit, before they too received the order to withdraw to avoid creating a salient.

The resumed Israeli drive on Ismailia, aiming at the capture of the vital cross-roads of Nefalia, which, had they been lost, would have placed the entire Second Army in grave danger, was checked by the combined efforts of the military and the civil population. Some of those who saw the fighting there said it was as if President Nasser's often repeated slogan of the need for unity between civilians and soldiers had come alive. But by the evening of 19 October Israel had established a formidable bridgehead on the west side of the canal which included four tank brigades, one mechanized brigade, and a parachute brigade.

It was probably the day before this, on Thursday, 18 October, that President Sadat saw the extent of Israel's thrust across the canal, because that day Kosygin was able to produce aerial photographs of the battle area which had been flown to him. Kosygin left next day, convinced that Egypt was ready for a peace conference, provided it included all fourteen members of the Security Council, the Secretary-General of the United Nations, and all interested parties including the Palestinians.

He was told we were ready to discuss this at once, as well as methods of arriving at a ceasefire.

During these days there was more trouble with King Hussein. When President Sadat was first told about the thousand Fedayin who wished to attack Israel through Jordan he thought the time was not right for such a move. Now, however, he had come to the conclusion that they would be able to perform some useful functions, such as attacks on Israeli communications. He sent a message to King Hussein requesting him to give favourable consideration to the project. The King's entourage stalled for two days, on the excuse that he was 'outside Amman'. The President insisted. He got the answer that 'they would try to contact the King', and another two days passed. Eventually a long message came from the King in which he explained that Jordan's frontier with Israel was almost completely denuded of troops as one armoured brigade had already been sent to the Syrian front and another was guarding lines of communication with Syria. Would the operation suggested by the Fedayin, he asked, produce results that would justify such an adventure, or would it simply expose the Jordanian front to the dangers which it lacked the resources to meet? He then asked some more questions. What was the maximum force the Fedayin could mount? What assurances could be given that the population of Jordan living close to the border would not be subjected to Israeli retaliation? Could the Fedayin move into those areas, taking into consideration the lines of communication with Syria? Finally, the King said he did not want either himself or the command of the Jordanian Army to be given any details of the operations which the Fedayin were planning. By the time this message was received the delaying tactics in Amman had been successful and a ceasefire was imminent.

This is perhaps the point to mention a curious domestic footnote to the battle. A day or two after the crossing of the canal, the army information services had a leaflet printed which was distributed to all serving soldiers. This was couched in the most flowery language of piety: 'In the name of God, the merciful, the compassionate: the Prophet is with us in the battle. O Soldiers of God . . . etc. etc.' It went on to say that 'one of the good men' had had a dream in which he saw the Prophet Muhammad dressed in white, taking with him the Sheikh of el-Azhar, pointing his hand and saying 'come with me to Sinai'. Some of the 'good men' were reported to have seen the Prophet walking among the soldiers with a benign smile on his face and a light all around him. So it went on, ending up: 'O soldiers of God, it is clear that God is with you.' I felt this sort of exhortation to be inappropriate. By implying that the success of the crossing was due to a miracle, it diminished the part played by the troops who had been engaged in the battle and who had behaved with such conspicuous bravery and enterprise. There were signs of growing religious fanaticism as war fever mounted, so that eventually the President felt obliged to announce publicly that the commander of the first infantry brigade to cross the canal was a Copt, Major-General Fuad Ghali – who later, incidentally, became the successful commander of the Second Army.

I had for some time been worried because it appeared we were losing the information war. After the first days of the Canal crossing when, if anything, our reports underestimated our achievements, the information services seemed to have suffered a sort of heart attack. Almost nothing came out of them. People lost confidence and went back to their old habit of listening to foreign broadcasts. I discussed this problem with the President when I went to see him late on the evening of Friday the 19th, or perhaps by then it was the morning of the 20th. I found him sitting on the balcony at Tahra Palace – it was so dark that the officer who brought me in failed to see him. While we were talking the telephone rang and they said it was the Commander-in-Chief on the line. The call had been put through to the President's bedroom, so we went in together. 'Yes, Ahmed,' I heard him say. 'Yes. We must take a chance and see what Kissinger is going to produce in Moscow. [The Russians had told Sadat of the visit a couple of hours before.] 'Do you want me to come over to Number Ten? Well, all right then. I'll come.' 'What's happened?' I said. He said that General Shazli was back from the front with a full picture and General Ahmed Ismail thought the President ought to go to

237

Number Ten. So he went there, taking with him Abdul Fatah Abdullah, Minister of State for Presidential Affairs. Those he found waiting there included General Ahmed Ismail, General Gamasy, General Said el-Mahy, Commander of the Artillery, General Husni Mubarak, Commander of the Air Force, and General Mohammed Ali Fahmy, Commander of the Air Defence.

At this vital meeting a difference of opinion showed itself. General Shazli, who had seen the situation on the spot, realized its extreme gravity. He felt that some of the reinforcements that had been sent to the east bank should be withdrawn, in particular the armoured brigade which had been sent to join the Third Army, so that they could face enemy infiltration on the west bank. He also advocated withdrawing some tanks and anti-tank missiles from the east. Unless these measures were taken he feared that the Third Army might be encircled and the Second Army threatened.

General Ismail's view was that even a partial withdrawal from the east would be certain to weaken the morale of the troops and might result in a collapse comparable to that of 1967. The President agreed with him. He thought that any weakening of Egypt's forces on the east bank would adversely affect Egypt's position in the political negotiations that could not now be long delayed. After the meeting was over Ismail had a few words alone with President Sadat in another room. He said that he was now speaking for history and as a patriot, and if the President saw a way open for a ceasefire on acceptable terms he would support this decision. 'I'm not pessimistic,' he said. 'Our army is still intact. But in no circumstances should we get involved in any military development which will again face our armed forces with the threat of destruction.'

The same day President Sadat sent a message to President Asad: 'We have fought Israel to the fifteenth day. In the first four days Israel was alone, so we were able to expose her position on both fronts. On their admission the enemy have lost eight hundred tanks and two hundred planes. But during the last ten days I have, on the Egyptian front, been fighting the

United States as well, through the arms it is sending. To put it bluntly, I cannot fight the United States or accept the responsibility before history for the destruction of our armed forces for a second time. I have therefore informed the Soviet Union that I am prepared to accept a ceasefire on existing positions, subject to the following conditions:

1. The Soviet Union and the United States to guarantee an Israeli withdrawal, as proposed by the Soviet Union.

2. The convening of a peace conference under United Nations auspices to achieve an overall settlement, as proposed by the Soviet Union.

My heart bleeds to tell you this, but I feel that my office compels me to take this decision. I am ready to face our nation at a suitable moment and am prepared to give a full account to it for the decision.'

President Asad's reply came next day. 'I received your message yesterday with deep emotion. My brother, I beg you to look again at the military situation on the northern front and on both sides of the canal. We see no cause for pessimism. We can continue the struggle against enemy forces, whether they have crossed the canal or are still fighting east of the canal. I am convinced that by continuing and intensifying the battle it will be possible to ensure the destruction of those enemy units that have crossed the canal. My brother Sadat, for the sake of the morale of the fighting troops it is necessary to emphasize that although the enemy have as a result of an accident been able to break our front this does not mean that they will be able to achieve victory. The enemy succeeded in penetrating the northern front several days ago, but the stand we then made and the subsequent heavy fighting have given us greater grounds for optimism. Most points of enemy penetration have been sealed off and I am confident that we shall be able to deal with those remaining in the course of the next few days. I consider it imperative that our armies should maintain their fighting spirit. My dear brother President, I am sure you appreciate that I have weighed my words with the utmost care and with full realization that we now face the most difficult period of our history. I felt it incumbent on me to explain my thinking to you, especially in

239

relation to the military situation on the southern front. God be with you . . .'

A ceasefire was agreed to on 22 October and the Sinai battle entered its final phase. No Arab politician or commander had any excuse for being surprised that, immediately the ceasefire came into effect, Israel began to break it. This was the traditional Israeli practice. In the first round of fighting, in 1948–9, Israel only accepted a ceasefire when a lull was necessary for the reception of smuggled arms from Europe or for regrouping for the next attack. In the second round, in 1956, after Eden and Mollet had accepted the ceasefire and the general Egyptian order for withdrawal from Sinai, Ben-Gurion deliberately delayed Israel's acceptance until he received confirmation of the capture of Sharm el-Sheikh by the 9th Brigade, despite the confusion which he knew his delay would mean for his allies. In the third round, in 1967, Israel again deliberately held up acquiescence in the ceasefire ordered by the UN until the Syrian campaign had been settled to its satisfaction with the upper reaches of the River Jordan in its hands.

In October 1973 Israel never had any intention of respecting the ceasefire, and the Egyptian command should have allowed for this. Israeli strength in the bridgehead west of the canal was quickly raised to five tank brigades, two mechanized brigades, and one parachute brigade. Counter-attacks on the Third Army gained ground daily, the aim being to seize as much ground as possible to be used as a bargaining counter in the ensuing negotiations. The Israelis also took as many prisoners, both civilians and military, as they could in this period, to be used as hostages later. They were also busily occupied in carrying away anything portable – crops, cattle, factory equipment, and so on – but this was plunder pure and simple.

During this final phase of the battle the real issues were being decided in the dialogue that was going on between the two super-powers – a dialogue that was to culminate in the American declaration of a state of nuclear alert.

Certain aspects of the operational plan and its execution call for comment.

1. This was the first time that the Arabs made proper prepara-

tions for a war. Planning on both strategic and tactical levels, thanks to the work of General Ahmed Ismail and General Gamasy, was meticulous; General Shazli, with the exact attention to the minutest detail instilled in him by his career as a paratrooper, had ensured that training was more than thorough; the arms were the best available and our forces were fully acquainted with their use. On previous occasions Arab commanders had acted – or, more often, reacted – on the spur of the moment, with disastrous results.

2. If anything the operational plan and its execution by the Egyptian command erred on the side of over-caution. This was exemplified in the fears of General Ahmed Ismail, who was entirely justified in his determination not to be another Field-Marshal Amer, responsible for the destruction of another Egyptian army.

3. The balance of political and military requirements in planning the operation was correctly kept. Credit for this on the Egyptian side must largely go to the late President Nasser, President Sadat, Generals Riad, Fawzi and Ismail, and on the Syrian side to President Asad, who played a decisive role in reconstructing the armed forces of Syria. He was the first President of Syria to combine real with nominal power.

4. For the first time the Arabs made a thorough study of the enemy they would have to fight. Our previous deficiencies in this respect now seem almost incredible. Because Israel was a country that we felt ought not to exist we behaved as though in fact it did not exist. All references in printed literature coming from abroad about Israel were liable to be seized by the customs, who even tore passages referring to it out of publications such as the *Encyclopaedia Britannica* and *Larousse*. A lecturer at the Egyptian Staff College who, before the 1967 war, tried to analyse the Israeli war machine, was discouraged from doing so. It was only after the 1967 defeat that, with the backing of President Nasser, a thorough assessment of the Israeli military establishment – its methods, traditions, and personalities – was undertaken.

All the same, though by 1967 our knowledge of the enemy had improved out of all recognition, we still made very serious miscalculations of the forces that would be opposed to us. It was inexcusable, in view of modern reconnaissance techniques, that the Egyptian operational plan should have allowed for only ten to eleven Israeli tank brigades, whereas in fact Israel proved, when the fighting started, to be able to put seventeen in the field.

5. Though Egypt had planned the military operation with great exactitude insufficient consideration had been given to the political situation which the operation might be expected to generate. Hence the hesitations and misunderstandings over the timing and scope of the ceasefire.

CHAPTER V
A Nuclear Alert

On 25 October, nineteen days after the fighting had started and three days after an internationally agreed ceasefire was supposed to have come into effect, the United States Government ordered a state of nuclear alert – a move which astonished rather than frightened its enemies and appalled many of its friends. Was so grave a step justified? How did it come to be taken?

From the outset of the crisis, and even before the first shot had been fired, the two super-powers had been in continuous touch with each other through the White House–Kremlin hot line. To begin with, the Americans thought that any Arab attack would be in response to the Israeli build-up following the growing tension on Syria's border after the air battle of 13 September, and their aim was to clear away any misunderstandings which might spark off an unnecessary war. Once the fighting had actually started they were puzzled as to how well informed the Russians had been about it in advance. Obviously, if the Russians had been party to Arab plans and had said nothing to the Americans, this would have had implications for the working of the détente, though there was little in the super-power 'rules' which would have obliged the Russians to pass on such information to Washington. In fact, as we have seen, the Russians were in an unenviable dilemma. They knew that something was in the wind, but had been told nothing about the timing or scale of the coming attack. President Sadat had given Vinogradov a vague hint on 1 October and President Asad had given an equally imprecise hint to his Soviet Ambassador on 5 October. If the Russians had passed on these warnings to the Americans, and the fact of their doing so became known (as, of course, it would) they would have lost all credibility with the Arabs. On the other hand, supposing there was an explosion, their silence might be misconstrued by the Americans.

As it happened, things worked all right. Any suspicions the Americans might have had about Russia's collusion with the Arabs did not last long, and agreement was quickly reached between the super-powers that all their efforts would be directed towards trying to contain the conflict and, above all, to avoid getting entangled in it themselves. As early as 7 and 8 October the two super-powers were jointly exploring ways and means of arranging a ceasefire, but were unable to agree whether or not this should include a demand for withdrawal of the combatants to their positions before the outbreak of hostilities. The Americans thought it should; the Russians thought that, in view of the Arabs' early successes, such a demand was unrealistic, more especially since it was not a demand that had been made of Israel when a ceasefire was negotiated in 1967. It was after talking to the Kremlin on the hot line, and failing to reach agreement, that Nixon called a meeting of the Security Council. But this attempt at a purely American initiative was unproductive.

After the failure of the Security Council to meet, attention began to move to the question of the airlift of arms to the combatants. The Israelis had organized an airlift from the first moment of the war, diverting as many of their own civilian planes as they could to the United States where they were enabled, with the express sanction of President Nixon, to load up with arms and ammunition. It was when the Egyptians and Syrians heard of this Israeli airlift that they increased their pressure on the Russians to organize a corresponding airlift for themselves. Once this Russian airlift to the Arabs had started, the Americans stepped up their airlift to Israel, making open use of American planes for the purpose. There was, however, a conflict between the State Department and the Pentagon, with some fearing that if the United States rushed to Israel all the arms that were being asked for (and the Israeli demands for, above all, anti-tank guns and missiles had become urgent and almost hysterical) there would be an adverse reaction on the Arab side and even the implementation of the much feared 'oil weapon'.

By the middle of the first week America had gained a clearer appreciation of the extent of Arab successes on the ground and was beginning to favour the call for a standstill ceasefire, rather than a ceasefire combined with a withdrawal. Some pressure was put on the Israelis to accept the idea. The British Prime Minister, Mr Heath, was used as the channel for conveying a proposal along these lines to President Sadat and President Asad. The British Ambassador in Cairo, Sir Philip Adams, conveyed the message to President Sadat in Tahra Palace shortly after midnight on 12 October. The President gave him his immediate reactions, and the next day Ismail Fahmy received the ambassador in his house and enlarged on the President's message. This initiative achieved nothing concrete, but by then the Russians were themselves even more interested in the idea of a standstill ceasefire. They were horrified at the unprecedented speed with which equipment was being used up in this new type of war, particularly at the number of tanks destroyed on the Syrian front, and their intelligence was reporting the imminent launching by Israel of a massive counter-attack in Sinai.

The Politburo met on 12, 13 and 14 October. One outcome of these meetings was the decision to send Kosygin to Cairo. He arrived at 5 p.m. on Tuesday 16 October. He met President Sadat for the first time immediately after his arrival, and argued in favour of the standstill ceasefire which the Russians had been discussing with the Americans. President Sadat, however, was still insisting on an Israeli withdrawal linked to a definite timetable and for an enlarged peace conference. Kosygin said that the Egyptians had proved themselves in battle and thereby created an entirely new factor in the search for a political solution. But the military tide, he warned, might be turning against them. There was also the risk, if the fighting continued, that the super-powers might be dragged into the conflict by the accelerating demand for arms made on them by the combatants.

245

President Sadat asked Kosygin: 'Are you afraid of Israel?' Kosygin said: 'We are afraid of nobody, but we have an obligation to world peace and are committed to search for a just and durable solution of the Middle East problem on the basis of Resolution 242.'

Kosygin's conversations in Cairo continued on Wednesday and Thursday, and he was naturally all the time in direct communication with Brezhnev in Moscow. He had brought with him an officer specializing in the interpretation of aerial photography, and at one meeting in Kubba Palace he gave the President pictorial evidence of the extent of the Israeli crossing to the west bank of the Suez Canal – no fewer than 270 tanks and armoured vehicles were identified there. Some disagreement emerged over the nature of the peace conference which, in his speech to the People's Assembly, President Sadat had said should be the consequence of a ceasefire. We thought such a conference should be attended by all the members of the Security Council plus the interested parties – that is, Egypt, Syria, Jordan, the Palestinians, as well as Israel – though we accepted that there might have to be a sub-committee of the conference on which only the five permanent members of the Security Council and the interested parties would be represented. The Russians wanted a small conference, mainly because they were concerned about the role China might choose to play at a larger meeting. Kosygin left Cairo in the morning of Friday 19 October.

While Kosygin was in Cairo, President Nixon had been in hot-line contact with Brezhnev, and after Kosygin's return to Moscow these contacts multiplied. There was pressure to arrange a standstill ceasefire to be effective the same night – the night of the 19th. The points which had to be settled before this could be finalized included the link there should be between a ceasefire and the implementation of Resolution 242; composition of the peace conference; how and when to stop the airlift to the two sides. By 10 p.m., after ten hours of hot-line negotiations, Brezhnev said that as time was so important it would be better if they could move to direct talks and suggested that Kissinger should come to Moscow immediately with authority from the President to reach binding agreements.

Kissinger arrived in Moscow on the evening of Saturday, 20 October, and talks between him and the Soviets started immediately. One controversial point which came up straight away was Kissinger's insistence that there should be direct negotiations between the combatants, once the ceasefire had come into effect. He argued that, in view of the Arabs' early successes and with Egyptian armies still on the east bank of the Suez Canal, the Arabs' former refusal to sit down with the Israelis was no longer valid. A condition of 'No Peace: No War,' he said, had given place to a condition of no victory, no defeat. Each side had got something of what it wanted, and now was the time for them to get together and talk about it. It was not possible, he argued, for the super-powers to impose a settlement on the combatants – this was something they would have to work out for themselves: all the super-powers could do was to provide guidance and supervision.

While these negotiations were going on in Moscow the reports reaching Cairo from the battle front were increasingly alarming. General Shazli had been sent to the front in the afternoon of the 18th with orders for the encirclement of what was still thought to be a 'pocket' of Israeli infiltrators across the canal. As soon as he arrived on the spot he saw that the true position was very different from the one which had been painted in Cairo. It was no 'pocket' with which he had to deal, but a major breakthrough. There were also signs that on the east bank of the canal the Israelis were planning an outflanking movement to the south of the Second Army.

These alarming reports had to be balanced by the President against the broader picture of the battle. The outstanding fact was that the Egyptian army had really proved itself. The Israeli theory of security, which had dominated not only Israeli thinking but also the thinking of a great number of foreign governments, had been shattered; the Egyptian people as a whole had shown their will to fight, and suffer, and endure. But now it was no longer a case of Egypt against Israel but of Egypt against Israel and the United States, and in these circumstances it would be foolish to expose a gallant army to unnecessary trials. A ceasefire made sense.

President Sadat went back to Tahra Palace, asked the Soviet Ambassador to come to see him, and told him to pass a message to Brezhnev that he was prepared to accept a ceasefire on the basis of the terms which Kosygin had offered when he came to Cairo. This message reached Brezhnev while he was engaged in talks with Kissinger, and from that moment things began to move. The text of the Resolution calling for a ceasefire to be presented to the Security Council was drafted on the Sunday and transmitted to Egypt at 6 p.m. Cairo time. We were told that the Security Council was going to meet later that evening.

It was decided that Kissinger should return home via Israel to give an account to the Israelis of what he had been doing in Moscow and to explain the text of the Security Council resolution to them. Many Israelis were by then opposed to the idea of a ceasefire, feeling that victory was within their grasp. I think this calculation was faulty, because by then both sides were stretched to the utmost and would have found it impossible to keep up the momentum required to achieve a decision on the battlefield. From what we learned afterwards, Kissinger was at pains to point out to the Israelis that, though they might have regained the initiative, the first days of the fighting had proved many of their strategic assumptions to be false: they had been surprised; the Arabs had proved themselves capable of concerted action; and the energy crisis was providing the Arabs with a political bonus. He emphasized the significance of the word 'negotiations', in the resolution: here was promise, he said, of something the Israelis had been demanding for twenty-six years. And of course he reiterated America's concern to avoid a confrontation with Russia.

When the President heard that Kissinger was going to Israel, he thought we should ask him to break his journey in Cairo as well. An invitation from President Sadat was sent, which reached him while he was in Israel (the intelligence or 'invisible' link with Washington was working all the time). However, many Israeli leaders, Golda Meir in particular, strongly objected to the idea of a Cairo visit. They feared that if Kissinger went straight from Jerusalem to Cairo, it would look as if the United

States was trying to play the part of an honest broker in the struggle which, if the Soviet Union continued to back the Arabs, would tilt the balance of power in the Arabs' favour. So Kissinger's answer to President Sadat was that it was unfortunately impossible for him to come at that particular moment but that he hoped to visit Cairo very shortly.

The Security Council session was duly convened at 10.00 p.m. on Sunday evening New York time (4 a.m. Monday in Cairo and Tel Aviv), all the delegates being dragged back to New York from wherever they were enjoying their weekend holidays. The Chinese, persuaded by the Americans and some other delegates, had agreed to abstain in the voting, so Russia's fear that they might be tempted to use their veto was removed. The text of a resolution which had been hammered out while Kissinger was in Moscow was formally presented to the Council and approved *nem con* – China keeping its promise to abstain. Resolution 338 called for a ceasefire to become effective in not more than twelve hours, all forces remaining in the positions which they then occupied. Immediately after the ceasefire all parties should undertake the complete implementation of Resolution 242 and, concurrently, 'negotiations should start between the parties concerned under suitable auspices for the establishment of a just and durable peace in the Middle East'.

The ceasefire was supposed to become effective at 1852 hours, Cairo time, on 22 October; but from the outset the Israelis paid no attention to it. This was the moment when General Sharon began to conduct what he called 'a guerrilla operation by tanks' on the west bank of the Suez Canal. It was later confirmed that he was acting on the orders of General Dayan. Sharon succeeded in occupying the cross-roads on the Suez–Cairo road, though he failed in his attempt on the cross-roads on the Ismailia–Cairo road. He then drove on down towards Attaka. On the morning of the 23rd he pushed south, surprised the naval base at Adabiyah and occupied it. Other Israeli units were despatched in boats across the canal to give support to tank formations in an assault against the coastal defence post at Sukhna. The Israeli aim was clearly to complete the encirclement of the Egyptian Third Army, to disrupt communications along the Cairo–Suez road and to cut off the town of Suez.

Although the Egyptian Second Army was intact and standing firm, and the Third Army under General Ahmed Bedawy was resisting heavy enemy pressure, they could not be left indefinitely as they were. President Sadat was sending urgent messages almost hourly to both Brezhnev and President Nixon pointing out that the ceasefire was being systematically violated by Israel. By Tuesday 23 October the super-powers had come to realize that some further action on their part was required, and they called a fresh meeting of the Security Council.

Egypt's criticism of the first Security Council Resolution, 338, had always been that it made no mention of UN troops being sent to supervise the ceasefire on the spot. We were making the mistake, as I said at the time, of accepting 'a law without a judge'. The new resolution, which America and Russia now put forward, and which was adopted as Resolution 339, was some improvement on the first, but was still very far from meeting Egypt's requirements. Above all, it did not order a return to the lines of the first ceasefire – the lines of 22 October – and so left Israel in possession of the gains obtained by her violations. When Vinogradov showed President Sadat the text of the proposed resolution the President pointed this out. Vinogradov demurred: making amendments now, he said, would complicate matters. The President said that as it stood the resolution was inadequate. 'Mr President, do you want us to veto it then?' Vinogradov asked. The Ambassador's question annoyed the President. Of course he did not want the resolution vetoed. His only aim was to get the ceasefire to stick and not to give the Israelis any excuses for going on fighting. So he was obliged to accept the text of the resolution as it stood. Resolution 339, after reaffirming Resolution 338, requested the Secretary General 'to take measures for the immediate despatch of UN observers to supervise the observance of the ceasefire, using for this purpose first of all the UN personnel now in Cairo.' This resolution was also passed *nem con*, China again being cajoled into abstention.

Yet on the day after Resolution 339 had been adopted,

Wednesday 24 October, the Israelis were still moving their troops forward. President Sadat sent identical messages to Brezhnev and Nixon: 'You must,' he said, 'be in force on the ground to witness for yourselves Israeli violations of the ceasefire.' I think that by this time Brezhnev was beginning to suspect that perhaps the Americans were deceiving him. Though he trusted Kissinger and the mechanism of détente, he could not understand how Israel could go on with such flagrant violations of a ceasefire which was supposed to have been partly sponsored by the American Government itself – especially after Kissinger had made a personal visit to Israel – unless there were some connivance with Washington. But there was not on this day – nor on any other day, for that matter – any suggestion by us or the Syrians that the Russians should move their forces into the area. The only demand ever made or contemplated was that Russians and Americans should come to observe.

Nixon sent President Sadat two messages on 24 October. In the first he said: 'Immediately on receipt of your message I instructed Secretary of State Kissinger to make urgent representations to the Israelis that the continuation of offensive military operations will have most serious consequences for the future of United States – Israel relations. The Israeli Government have replied that the attacks are being initiated by the Egyptian Third Army, that Israeli forces are on the defensive and have been ordered only to fire back if attacked. From here the true facts are impossible to determine. I want to assure you that the United States is unalterably opposed to offensive military actions by Israel and is prepared to take effective steps to end them. In the meantime you should ensure that all military action by your forces is also stopped. Secretary Kissinger is getting in touch with Mr Ismail later today about the possibility of direct talks between our two sides about post-war diplomacy.'

The President's statement that 'from here the true facts are impossible to determine' was not very convincing and was calculated to reinforce Russian suspicions that Israel was being deliberately allowed to get away with its violations of the ceasefire. The Americans, as well as the Russians, were photographing

251

the battle areas every hour or so. It was perfectly possible for the Pentagon to compare the situation on the 22nd, when Suez was not encircled and Adabiyah not occupied, with the situation that had developed by the 24th. Israeli protestations that nobody could tell where the lines of the 22nd had run were not to be taken seriously. If anyone wanted to know they had plenty of ways of finding out. Some years before Gromyko had told Mahmoud Riad about the amazing precision of the new techniques of satellite photography. 'If you like,' he said, 'we can give you a picture of Sinai which will enable you to identify all the snakes that are there.' It is not to be supposed that the Americans were behind in this department.

The second message from Nixon to Sadat, received shortly afterwards, read: 'We have just been informed by the Israeli Prime Minister that strict instructions have been issued to Israeli armed forces to stay in defensive positions and not to fire unless they are fired upon. In response to your proposal for US ground observers the Israeli Government has also agreed to permit US military attachés to proceed immediately to the area of the conflict in order to observe that these orders are being carried out. It would be very helpful if you could instruct your forces accordingly.'

It is at this point that the attitude of the Syrian Government becomes of vital importance. The Syrians were, as we have seen, annoyed at our acceptance of the ceasefire, and were more than annoyed at the way in which they learned about it. They said that the first they heard about its timing was when Egypt's representative at the Security Council signified his acceptance on 22 October. Subsequently Dr Aziz Sidqi was sent as special envoy to President Asad to try to persuade him of the necessity for Syria to accept it too. He found President Asad in a very bad mood. He was convinced that the Israeli counter-attack on Mount Hermon had been successful only because the Israelis knew that a ceasefire was imminent and were therefore able to throw all their resources into this final operation. On the other hand, a major tank assault, in which the Iraqis were to take part, which had been planned for 23 October, had had to be cancelled. Eventually, however, President Asad realized he had no option but to accept the ceasefire. He was told that Egypt was asking the two super-powers to send observers and personnel to come to the area to see for themselves what was going on. The Syrians had no direct contact with the Americans: they could only communicate through Egypt or through the Russians. On the 24th President Asad sent for the Soviet Ambassador in Damascus and asked him to arrange for Soviet forces to come to Syria immediately. President Asad sent a message to President Sadat asking him if the Soviet Union was going to send 'personnel' – but the same word in Arabic (*quwat*) can mean 'personnel' or 'forces', and though it was in the first sense that President Asad used the word the authorities in Cairo thought it possible that President Asad might be using it in the larger sense. Egypt knew the Syrians were complaining that the Iraqis were refusing to accept the ceasefire and threatening to withdraw all their troops, and thought it conceivable that the Syrians might be wanting some Soviet forces to plug the gap left by the Iraqis. So President Sadat's reply was: 'The Soviet Union has told me that they have sent seventy observers. I understand your position, and accept that you may think it necessary to request Soviet troops if you think the situation calls for them.'

Exchanges between the two Presidents continued as follows – President Asad: 'When I asked you to inform me about Soviet forces coming to the area, I thought these were as a result of a request by you. I called the Soviet Ambassador in Damascus and informed him about the Soviet forces to be sent to Egypt, but I have never requested a Soviet force for Syria.' President Sadat: 'I understood from your message that the demand for Soviet troops was for Syria and I accepted this as far as it was made necessary by the situation on your front. We ourselves have never requested Soviet forces but only Soviet observers to take part in supervision of the ceasefire. The Soviet Union has already sent seventy observers. I have so informed Waldheim.'

Undoubtedly all these coded messages between Cairo and Damascus, exchanged during a space of not more than two to three hours, were intercepted by the Americans. It is possible that they gave the impression that somebody was asking for Soviet forces to be sent to the area. The consequence, as we know from what Kissinger said afterwards, was that there was a meeting of the 'Special Action Group' of the American National Security Council at which it was said that there was 'concrete evidence' that the Russians were about to intervene by force in the Middle East. There could be no other conceivable source for such a statement apart from these Sadat-Asad exchanges. It is of course probable that, as a purely precautionary measure, some Warsaw Pact units would have been put on standby. This would be normal practice in America or Western Europe in such a period of tension, and could not have provided the sort of evidence the Americans were talking about. Another possible element in the misunderstanding was the despatch of observers from the Soviet Union. President Sadat had told Nixon that these were coming, though when it was learned they were on their way Washington may have jumped to the conclusion that these were the advance party for some much larger force, particularly since it was known to the Americans that Waldheim had only asked for thirty-five observers from the Soviet Union.

It was while these exchanges between the two Presidents were going on that Brezhnev sent a message to Nixon on the hot line, drawing attention to Israel's continued violations of the ceasefire and adding: 'If the Israelis are not going to adhere to the ceasefire let us work together to impose a ceasefire, if necessary by force.' This was felt in Washington to be very tough talk. According to Kissinger, it reminded them of the 1956 'ultimatum', on the Suez intervention by Britain and France, sent by Bulganin to Eisenhower, in which he said the Soviet Union was prepared to intervene 'either bilaterally or unilaterally' to impose respect for that General Assembly ceasefire resolution. It was this message of Brezhnev's which was shown by the Administration to several senators to justify the alert.

Whatever evidence may in fact have been laid before the National Security Council, it decided, according to Kissinger on his initiative, to declare a Grade 3 emergency. President Nixon joined the council at the end of its deliberations and approved the decision. The Defence Secretary passed the necessary instructions on to the Chiefs of Staff.

To give the Americans the benefit of the doubt there may have been some excuse for their misreading of the situation, though the fact that we and the Russians were in constant contact with them should have enabled them to avoid so dangerous a miscalculation. Kissinger was later to admit that the nuclear alert had been an error. 'Let us concede,' he said, 'that we had an American President who found himself in a difficult position and who decided to take the maximum precautions in order to reassure himself and to reassure others.' It may equally have been a case of a President who was conscious of his own prestige, for domestic reasons and was anxious to have a Cuba crisis of his own – and a Secretary of State who was conscious of his reputation for forceful diplomacy.

The Russians were predictably astonished by the American alert. Brezhnev told Boumedienne and Asad that he thought it was all a false alarm resulting from an American desire to over-dramatize the crisis. If, he said, it was meant as a warning to the Soviet Union, the message had the wrong address on it. West European leaders were horrified. When Kissinger came to Cairo a little later he was particularly bitter about the re-action in Europe. He went so far one evening in conversation with some of us to say: 'I don't care what happens to Western Europe. They can all go to hell as far as I am concerned. They are on their knees to us when they think they need us; but when they think they can do without us they behave completely irrationally.' Some of his language was even stronger.

The incident of the 25 October alert was revealing in many ways. It demonstrated how the two super-powers have become at the same time partners as well as antagonists. It demonstrated their determination at all costs to avoid being dragged into a real confrontation with each other, and their willingness to exchange all relevant information to achieve this end. It showed that each is prepared for a realistic acceptance of the other's interests in a particular geographical area (in this case the Middle East), and that they always find it easier, when it comes to the stage of making concessions, to put pressure on their friends rather than to do it themselves. The question of the rival airlifts provides a particularly illuminating commentary on the working of the super-power relationship. When the airlifts were finally halted it was found that the amount of arms which America had supplied to Israel almost exactly balanced, ton for ton, the amount which the Soviet Union had supplied to Egypt and Syria.

CHAPTER VI

A New Type of War

The fourth round between the Arabs and Israel, fought during the month of October 1973, produced a new type of war, not only unlike the three previous rounds but different also in some respects from any previous combat in any other part of the world. Worth studying as indicators of the possible shape of things to come, the characteristics of the October War may be listed as follows:

1. It was a war fought above the conventional level but below the nuclear level. Perhaps the best name to give it would be 'electronic war', because of the extensive use made of guided missiles and electronic reconnaissance. The operations room in such a war is like the control room in a power station – a matter of computers and press-button dials.

2. In spite of the great developments in technology this was a war in which the human element was of the greatest importance and in which numbers counted. Neither side had any secret weapons which the other did not know about. It was the proliferation of these weapons on the Arab side and the competence with which they were handled that came as a surprise to the Israelis.

3. This was perhaps the first true example of a limited war – a war deliberately limited in its objectives and in its duration. It was also limited in the size of the battlefield and in that the number of participants on either side did not increase as the fighting went on – those who did enter were solely members of the joint Arab command. On the western front, the battlefield never extended more than twenty kilometres west or twenty kilometres east of the Suez Canal. The northern front was similarly confined to an even narrower area.

4. The October War showed that, even if the two super-powers are not actually dragged in as combatants, an electronic war cannot be fought without their involvement. Kissinger said that Israel could not fight a war for more than nine days without coming begging to the United States for replacement of equipment. A similar degree of dependence governs relations between the Arabs and the Soviet Union. Losses of material on both sides in the October War were on a staggering scale. The overall number of tanks destroyed during fifteen days of fighting was estimated at 3000. By comparison the losses in one of the biggest tank encounters in World War Two, that between Montgomery and Rommel in North Africa over a period of six months, was no more than 650. It is this dependence by the combatants on the super-powers which not only limits the duration of the war but also the extent to which either side can impose its will on the other.

5. The war showed that defence, properly organized, can be as decisive a factor as offence. All the important battles after the assault across the canal were planned as defensive. Even the storming of the canal and the Bar-Lev Line was in a sense a defensive action in that it could not have succeeded had the missile wall not been there. In the initial stages, Egypt did not propose to advance beyond the protective range of the missiles, and so waited for the Israelis to come and attack on the east bank of the canal. When they came Egypt hit them hard; when they came again they were hit hard again. Israel succeeded in crossing the canal to the west largely because Egypt's forces remaining west of the canal had been stripped of their anti-tank missiles for the benefit of the units which had crossed. On the other hand the Israeli army, as General Elazar admitted, suffered because its commanders thought of it as essentially an offensive force. When they went shopping in the United States it was the tanks they were interested in, not the anti-tank weapons – until, that is, the fighting started, when their priorities became dramatically reversed.

6. The war marked the rehabilitation of the infantry arm. With Molutka and Strella, an Egyptian infantryman could stop tanks and aircraft.

7. Complementing the rise in status of the infantry was the overturning of aircraft and armour from the position they had held on the battlefield since World War Two. Their role became that of victim, not of master. It was a matter of great psychological importance to pilots and tank commanders that they found themselves unable to locate their enemy. An anti-aircraft gun or an anti-tank missile is usually a fixed object, capable of being located and so destroyed. But a single Egyptian soldier, armed with his Molutka or Strella, is mobile and invisible, moving in the desert under the cover of sandhills and thorn-bushes.

8. The successful crossing of the Suez Canal and the over-running of the Bar-Lev Line proved the vulnerability of static defence lines and shattered the Israeli doctrine of the efficacy of 'secure natural frontiers'. The closure of Bab el-Mandeb and the 'oil weapon' added their own commentary on this doctrine.

9. The fourth round emphasized the vital necessity in limited war of having a political strategy to take over when the fighting ceases.

10. The war showed that, from the planning point of view, a decision about when the war might be expected to end was no less important than the decision about when it was to start. The super-powers are not going to permit a war, for which they have to supply the equipment, to drag on indefinitely. At a certain point they will step in and freeze it. The intervention of the UN has also to be reckoned with. India correctly appreciated this in 1971. She calculated that it would be fifteen days before a ceasefire was imposed on her and Pakistan, and managed to complete her operations in fourteen.

11. In an electronic war, speed and agility are likely to be the decisive factors. Because of the inevitably limited span of the war, as well as the sophistication of the weapons employed, a sensitive and flexible human response is essential. Information from the front must be rapidly received and no less rapidly processed. Some military thinkers, like the French General André Beauffre, even suggest it should be possible to manipulate all forces in the field from a central control room in the same

way that operations in the air are already controlled. During the October War, Egypt had some successes and some failures in this respect. Quick utilization of a captured Israeli code-book enabled Egypt to locate the position of the headquarters of the Israeli command in Sinai, with the result that it was destroyed and the Israeli armoured commander in Sinai, General Abraham Mendler, killed. On the other hand, had the information passed back by our advanced commando patrols, which reached Gifgafa on the 7th, that the way ahead was open, been properly appreciated, Egyptian forces could have moved directly to the passes.

12. The war showed that numbers once again counted. Israel had always said that numbers could be a burden and that the size of the Arab armies could never make up for the quality of the Israeli army. On the other hand Nasser, in one of his talks with Brezhnev, had spoken of building up an army a million strong. We did not do that, but from among her 36 million inhabitants Egypt was able in 1973 to find a sufficient number of properly qualified troops to make the battle area a forest of missiles. The manpower reserves at Egypt's disposal were also useful to enable quick re-crewing of tanks and aircraft. For the first time, Arab quantity did something to offset some of the advantages of Israeli quality.

13. The war showed surprise to be possible still, in spite of all the apparatus of electronic equipment available to both sides, and available of course in still more elaborate forms to the super-powers. The super-powers and the world at large were just as much surprised by Egypt's action as was Israel.

14. Finally, the war emphasized once again the importance of the historical dimension. The simple explanation of why it happened is that the Egyptian people were determined to rid themselves of the acute sense of inferiority which had burdened them since the defeat of 1967. Israel suffered from an exaggerated self-confidence and from total blindness to the obstinacy of the Egyptian and Arab character. Israelis and Americans have always been at fault in approaching situations in what they believe to be a strictly pragmatic way. They have dealt only with what they could see, concentrating on the present to the

almost total exclusion of the past. How often in talks with Rogers, Kissinger, Sisco and others has Egypt heard the Americans say, in effect, 'We're not interested in raking over the past: let's look at the situation as it is today.' But today's situation is the creation of yesterday.

CHAPTER VII

Oil

One consequence of the war was that the Arabs used the so-called 'oil weapon' for the first time. This was something the many people in the Arab world had for a long time been demanding and that many people in the West had been dreading. However, as will be seen, the first application of it did little to harm those it was meant to harm, or to benefit those it was meant to benefit.

Why the weapon was successfully defused cannot be understood without a look at the background of the energy situation in the Middle East and the West, and in particular at the attitudes of one government in each of these two camps – those of the United States and Saudi Arabia – which between them held the keys to the equation. In the winter of 1972 the United States had experienced what the papers called an 'energy crisis', when gas stations closed and homes and offices went unheated. In fact this was not an energy crisis in any true sense of the word but a crisis in the petroleum market. The United States, with its vast reserves of coal, uranium, petroleum and shale oil, has greater energy resources than any other country in the world. The United States' trouble was its inability to formulate a co-ordinated policy for energy. This was a dilemma from which, ironically enough, it was eventually to be rescued by the October war.

For several years there had been a conflict in the United States between the oil companies and the environmentalists – a conflict which, at the beginning of the 1970s, the environmentalists appeared to be winning. Congress passed the Clean Air Act in 1970, the National Environmental Policy Act in 1970, and the Clean Water Act in 1972. In April 1973 the

Supreme Court blocked the construction of the Alaska pipeline. The oil companies – which, because they own 30 per cent of American coal mines and 40 per cent of America's uranium deposits, ought to be seen as energy companies – were unable to develop the new oilfields off the Californian coast or to construct new refineries. The building of new nuclear plants was postponed, and in the eastern coalfields, which are those nearest to the centres of industry, production was cut back. The vigorous pleas by the companies to be allowed to raise the price of oil were rejected by the Federal Government and opposed by public opinion, which felt strongly that the companies' profits were already quite big enough. The companies, on the other hand, argued that without higher prices for oil it would not be economic to exploit the new sources of energy in the United States. What they feared was that the quota of permitted oil imports might be increased and that this would mean an actual reduction in the price of domestic oil to match the price of imported oil.

The Federal Government hesitated between two alternative policies – allowing a rise in energy prices inside the United States, and at the same time making available for exploitation new lands containing untapped energy resources and modifying the environmental laws; or lowering prices by increasing the flow of cheap oil from abroad. The result of this hesitation was a shortage of fuel oils in the winter of 1972. This shortage was to some extent alleviated when President Nixon ordered an increase in import quotas, followed by a complete abolition of quotas in May 1973. He simultaneously gave the oil companies a major concession by his ruling that oil for newly built refineries could be imported free of tax for five years. But in 1972 imported oil represented only 5 per cent of the total energy requirements of the United States, and of this only 18 per cent came from Arab countries.

The situation in the other two areas which are main markets for Arab oil, Western Europe and Japan, was very different. Western Europe is much less favourably placed as regards energy than the United States. It has no uranium; only Britain and West Germany have any considerable stocks of coal. Much is hoped for from North Sea oil and gas, but even if the most optimistic forecasts prove correct imported oil is expected to make up an even greater proportion of Western Europe's energy supplies in 1980 than in 1973 – 80 per cent instead of 60 per cent.

Japan is even worse off than Western Europe, importing 90 per cent of its energy requirements, and of this again 90 per cent consists of oil from the Persian Gulf. Nor do Western Europe and Japan have another advantage enjoyed by the United States for, whereas American companies own 60 per cent of the oilfields in the Arab world, Western Europe and Japan, except for Britain and France, have no direct access to Middle East oil. American companies are thus the principal beneficiaries from the oil sold by the Arabs to Western Europe and Japan.

The American aim has been to form a common front between the main consumers of Middle East oil and so ensure that supplies of crude oil continue to flow at the right rate and at the right price. The Americans also wish to finance the development of future energy resources inside their own country from the profits made by the energy (oil) companies and by encouraging the oil-producing Arab countries to invest much of their profits in these future developments. At present the companies are spending $16,000m. on development; this will rise by 1980 to $50,000m., and the balance of $34,000m. will have to come from higher profits and from foreign (Arab) investment.

To turn from the West – the consumer of energy – to the Arab countries, the producers of energy. In 1959 the Western oil companies reduced the price paid for Arab crude. This action resulted in the formation of the Organization of Petroleum Exporting Countries (OPEC), designed to protect the producing countries against what they regarded as arbitrary action by the foreign companies which exploited and marketed their oil. It must be confessed that for a long time OPEC could boast only very limited achievements. For ten years the price of Arab oil remained stationary. OPEC's only real success was to get a reduction in the marketing expenses of oil and to get agreement on the 'expensing' of royalties (the companies could no longer show the royalties paid to governments as part of their working expenses). One of the reasons for OPEC's lack of success was that during the late 60s and early 70s the world appeared to be facing a glut of oil. Major producing countries in the Middle East, particularly Iran and Saudi Arabia, were in need of extra revenue and had been pressing the companies to increase production. So had countries just starting out as oil exporters, like Nigeria. In 1972 all the major multinationals were urging on the governments of the oil-producing countries the need for a cutback in production. At the beginning of 1973 there was talk of 'large potential surpluses' of oil, and even Iran, the champion of accelerated production, was growing worried.

The key country in the shaping of oil policy for the Arab world is Saudi Arabia. The rate of production in Kuwait and Abu Dhabi must be limited for some time to come. If there is to be a marked step-up of production in the Gulf to meet the ever expanding needs of Western Europe and Japan, it must come from Iran and Saudi Arabia, but Iran's reserves are small compared with those of Saudi Arabia (55,000m. barrels compared with at least 150,000m. – or, some experts would say, anything up to 450,000m. barrels).

King Feisal had always said that the Arabs should not use oil as a weapon, and his Minister of Petroleum, Shaikh Ahmed Zaki el-Yamani, elaborated this view in an address to the Middle East Institution in April, 1973 and in evidence before a Senate Investigating Committee. Saudi Arabia, he said, was to supply the United States with all its requirements of oil provided the oil companies were prepared to accept Arab participation in the companies at a rate rising to 50 per cent by 1980, and provided they would also give preference to Arab oil entering the United States. He promised that Saudi Arabia would invest considerable sums in the United States, especially in oil projects, refineries, and in distribution systems inside the United States.

The American authorities, however, were not particularly impressed by this offer. They were reluctant to become too dependent on one form of energy or on supplies from the country. They regarded all talk by the Arabs of using oil as a political weapon as being so much hot air. After all, there were the repeated statements by King Feisal that it would not so be used. Moreover, it was always thought that, if the worst came to the worst, the Arabs could be forced to supply their oil in the required quantities to the rest of the world. The Americans believed that the Israeli army was not only perfectly capable of marching on Cairo but could also, if required to do so – as Senator Fulbright revealed in the Foreign Affairs Committee – occupy virtually without opposition Kuwait and the adjacent oil-producing areas of Saudi Arabia.

The first change in the situation on the Arab side came with the Libyan revolution of September 1969. In July 1970 Muammar Ghadaffi ordered production at one Libyan field, that being worked by the American company, Occidental, to be lowered by 300,000 barrels a day. He chose Occidental because it was an independent company with no resources elsewhere to fall back on. If it was to meet its contractual obligations, it could only do so from Libya. Occidental, however, was not unduly perturbed because there was plenty of oil elsewhere and there was a clause in its contracts that any increase in the price of crude could be passed on to the consumer. It agreed to the production cut. Later it was the turn for most of the other foreign companies operating in Libya.

Ghadaffi was playing his cards shrewdly. He benefited from the fact that in 1967 the Suez Canal had been closed and a year later the TAP oil pipeline from Saudi Arabia to the Mediterranean had been cut by the joint action of Palestinian guerrillas and a Syrian bulldozer. There was also a world shortage of tanker tonnage, so that the oil companies had neither the time nor the capacity to compensate for losses in Libya by lifting increased supplies from the Gulf. So fortunate indeed was this combination of circumstances for Libya that it was widely rumoured that the bulldozer which sliced into TAP line was no accident but was deliberately planned between Ghadaffi and Atassi, the President of Syria at that time. However, there was never any proof of this.

*

Arabs had for years been talking about the 'oil weapon' in a desultory way, and I had myself been one of the first to advocate the need to put the Arabs' unique position as a main supplier of the world's energy to a practical use. Various suggestions as to how this could best be done were made. Some favoured nationalization of foreign operations in Arab countries, but this was never a real solution. The Iraq Government nationalized the IPC's Kirkuk operations in June 1972, but this did not affect the company's downstream operations – the transporting, refining and marketing of oil, from which the component companies of IPC derived most of their profits. When their concessions are nationalized all that the international companies lose is the profit on the production of crude, and this can easily be made good by higher profits from their other operations. In fact, Iraq had difficulty in disposing of its nationalized oil, and there were reports that it used the 1973 embargo as a screen behind which to unload some of it.

After the war of June 1967 the oil weapon came increasingly to the fore, because to the Arabs in their hour of defeat this seemed almost the only card they had left to play. The first opportunity to formulate a united Arab policy on oil came with the Khartum summit conference at the end of August 1967, but in a curious way both governments and companies were then almost equally scared at the implications of the new weapon. The companies feared that really crippling cuts in production might be made, as there had been a good deal of talk about cutting off all supplies of oil until such time as Israel had evacuated the Arab lands occupied in the war. The Arab governments, with few facts and figures to guide them were uncertain of the consequences of their actions, and none of them wanted to see a repetition of the disastrous Mossadeq experience.

Nasser went to the conference thinking that if he could get half what he had lost as a result of the war and the closure of the Suez Canal made good by the oil-producing countries he would be quite content. Pride prevented him from spelling out his exact financial needs, and nobody was more surprised than he when, at Khartum, King Feisal opened the bidding – for bidding

267

is what it was – with the announcement that Saudi Arabia was willing to contribute £50m. a year to help the countries which had suffered in the war; Kuwait, he recommended, should contribute £60m. and Libya £30m. Egypt's share of this aid was £100m. a year, which was in fact 10 per cent more than our estimated losses. This decision was quite extraordinary. Whether in fact it was King Feisal's own idea, or whether it was suggested to him by some others who were anxious to avert a damaging use of the oil weapon, it is impossible at this stage to know. What is certain is that it gave Egypt and Jordan a vested interest in the continuing free flow of oil, and so had the effect of silencing any further serious discussion of the oil weapon for some time to come.

King Feisal remained opposed to the idea of using oil as a weapon in the battle until shortly before the October war. As late as July 1973 he was on record as saying 'Oil is not a military weapon: it is an economic force with which we can buy weapons which can be used in battle.' When the TAP-line was cut he expressed strong disapproval and said that the subsidies promised at Khartum to Egypt and Jordan would have to be delayed for a month because the cutting of the pipeline meant that Saudi Arabia was losing money. In fact it was Egypt who asked the Syrians to mend the TAP-line and the Fedayin not to interfere with it again.

Then something made King Feisal change his mind. The Saudi family, we know, was divided on this question, with some of the princes in favour of using oil as a weapon and some against it. But, whatever the reason, the last time King Feisal saw President Sadat before the October war, which was at the end of August 1973, he told Sadat that if he wanted to use the oil weapon this time he could. 'But,' Feisal said, 'give us time. We don't want to use our oil as a weapon in a battle which only goes on for two or three days and then stops. We want to see a battle which goes on for long enough time for world public opinion to be mobilized.' This fitted exactly the thinking of the Egyptian Government.

*

268

So by 1973 there were two parallel crises: there was an energy crisis of a sort – an essentially economic problem – which was looking for a detonator; and there was the old Middle East crisis – an essentially political and military problem – which was looking for some new catalyst. Both found what they wanted in each other: the energy crisis found a detonator in the Middle East crisis, and the Middle East crisis found a catalyst in the energy crisis. But the energy crisis owed more to the Middle East crisis than the Middle East crisis did to the energy crisis.

When the October war started no precise plan for the use of the oil weapon had been drawn up. Neither Egypt nor Syria, after all, are oil-exporting countries; and, as we have seen, President Sadat had rightly thought that it would be a mistake to ask other Arab governments for pledges of action in advance, though he hoped that once the fighting had started they would rally to help the combatants.

There had been a task force in the Egyptian Ministry of Foreign Affairs studying possible courses of action, but nothing definite had come out of it. On the other hand, by a most fortunate piece of timing, a document came to hand a few days before the war which was to play a considerable part in guiding Arab oil policy. This originated in a project in the spring of 1973 in *Al Ahram's* Centre for Strategic Studies. I had invited Dr Mustafa Khalil, a former Deputy Prime Minister for Industry and Mineral Resources and a brilliant administrator, to make a study of the energy crisis in the United States and its implications for the Arab states. After some hesitation he accepted the task and on 1 October had telephoned to me to say that his report was finished. He handed it over to me and I showed it to the President.

It will be recalled that Sayed Marei, Assistant to the President, had been appointed head of a committee to co-ordinate policy with other Arab governments. At 8 o'clock in the evening of 6 October, Sayed Marei rang up Mustafa Khalil saying that the President had asked him to prepare a memorandum on how oil should be used in the war and asked him to get a copy of the Khalil report from me: could they talk about it? They did, and

Mustafa Khalil volunteered to make a twelve-page summary of his report and its recommendations. This he did the next morning. At 2 p.m. on the same day, 7 October, there was a meeting at the Ministry of Foreign Affairs between Mahmoud Fawzi, Sayed Marei, Mustafa Khalil and myself for a discussion on oil policy. Dr Fawzi accepted the Khalil report without suggesting any changes, and later the same day it was decided to send Mustafa Khalil with Sayed Marei to Saudi Arabia and the Gulf states to explain Egypt's attitude to the war. The two of them left on the morning of 8 October in an Egyptian Airways Ilyushin – evacuating Czech and East German advisers caught by the war who were being repatriated via Jiddah. From Jiddah a special plane took them to Riyadh.

The point of view expressed in the Khalil report was that oil should be regarded as a strategic and economic commodity and not as a weapon in itself, since oil by itself can never win a war. It can be used as a sort of political lever, and of course oil has always played a dominant part in the politics and diplomacy of the consuming countries, so there is nothing new in the Arabs' making political use of it. On the other hand, it is important that the producing countries should not make enemies of the consuming countries, though they have the right to ask for reasonable reciprocity. If the Arabs are supplying any country with one strategic commodity – oil – and are getting another strategic commodity – armaments – in return, they have a right to expect that the flow in both directions will continue whether there is a war with Israel or not. If the arms are withdrawn, then the oil would have to be withdrawn too. The report also said that we should take note of the attitude of other countries and base our conduct accordingly. If they were opposed to our war with Israel, which we regarded as a lawful act to liberate Arab territory, we should be entitled to take a stand against them. We had a right to expect Europe, if not to come to our support, at any rate not to show hostility towards us. We could reasonably expect the governments of Western Europe and Japan to exert pressure on the Americans to remind them of the importance of Arab oil in these areas.

Moreover, there should be reciprocity over prices and production. As an economic commodity, the price of oil should conform to the price of other sources of energy, and not be permanently lower. Nor should the producing countries be expected to raise their production beyond a rate at which they could make reasonable use of their profits. The holding by Arab governments of an excess of paper currency could only in the long run damage the Western economies, besides bringing no real benefit to the Arabs. Agreement and understanding between producers and consumers must be the aim, and not sudden or unilateral action by either of them.

This was the gist of the argument which the Egyptians put to King Feisal. The first meeting took place in the King's private office in the royal palace in Riyadh. On the Saudi side as well as the King, were Prince Fahd, the Minister of the Interior, and Doctor Rashad Faraoun, one of King Feisal's closest advisers. On the Egyptian side were Sayed Marei, Mustafa Khalil, and Colonel Saad el-Qadi, who had been sent with maps to demonstrate the progress of the battle. King Feisal listened in silence to the exposé by Sayed Marei and Mustafa Khalil, only nodding his head from time to time. The analysis by Colonel el-Qadi obviously interested him greatly, and he asked many questions: were we going to advance to the passes? why did we not occupy southern Sinai? and so on.

There was a second meeting at eight o'clock in the evening, after the *iftar*, the breaking of the Ramadan fast. On this occasion the King was much more forthcoming. 'You have', he said, 'made us all very proud. In the past we could not lift our heads up; now we can. You have done your duty and suffered in doing it. Your cities have been destroyed. The least the other Arabs can do is to help you financially and with whatever military equipment they have.' It was then that he promised an immediate gift of $200m. He also said that units of the Saudi army were leaving for the Syrian front. 'What we are giving you,' said the King, 'is not charity. What we offer in money is much less than what you are giving in lives and other sacrifices.'

The King said he accepted completely the policy outlined by Sayed Marei and Mustafa Khalil. The Egyptians emphasised

271

that they were not trying to force any policies on the oil-producing states. If Saudi Arabia did follow the recommendations of the report, it should do it in the way best calculated to benefit its own national interests and the interests of the Arab world. They stressed the need to prevent the formation of a common front by the United States, West Europe, and Japan, and with this in view suggested a declaration guaranteeing the continuation of supplies to West Europe and Japan provided that no action harmful to the Arabs was taken. At the same time a warning should be given that any country taking harmful action laid itself open to an embargo. They thought that the production of oil should be frozen at its current rate as a general warning that the oil weapon was being considered and that a small reduction in the rate of production should be adopted if it seemed that the warning was not being heeded. More drastic measures were discussed, including certain economic measures against the United States such as nationalizing their assets in Arab countries and making direct arrangements between Arab oil producers and consumers in West Europe and Japan (thus cutting out the American role as middle-men). Mustafa Khalil said that an oil embargo would mean nothing to the United States now, though it would be an increasing threat up to 1980 when alternative sources of American fuel became available.

King Feisal asked the Egyptians what immediate practical steps they recommended. They suggested he should summon the American Chargé d'Affaires – the ambassador, James Atkins, ironically one of the State Department's energy experts and a persistent prophet of Arab action on the 'oil weapon', was away for some reason – and give him a résumé of the points just discussed, while the Saudi Foreign Minister, who was about to arrive in Washington, should be instructed to see President Nixon and present the same case to him. The King acted on both suggestions. 'What about our Libyan friends?' he asked. What have they given you?' Sayed Marei said that Ghadaffi had offered $40 million and four million tons of crude oil. 'That is not enough,' said the King. 'It would be better if they had spent their money on the battle instead of on stirring up trouble in other Arab countries.'

Next day the Egyptian mission went on to Kuwait, where it saw the Ruler. He listened attentively and said that the matter of financial aid would have to be considered in the Council of Ministers. Qatar, Abu Dhabi and Oman, which the mission visited next, were all equally interested.

In Bahrain the mission first met the Ruler and then the Council of Ministers, in which a lively debate of over two hours ensued, the Bahrainis being obviously keen to understand all the implications of the new situation.

Soon after the Marei-Khalil mission had completed its work the Arab oil ministers met in Kuwait on 17 October to co-ordinate oil policy for the war. The first reports we had were that, at the instigation of Saudi Arabia, the ministers were going to impose a 15 per cent cutback in production. President Sadat thought this represented a great sacrifice by the producing countries (which in fact it did not), and asked them to be content with a cut of 5 per cent. At the same time they called for a huge increase in the price of crude oil, which was something we had never asked them for. None of the other options Egypt had recommended were considered. The only outcome was a staggering increase in price and a moderate cut in production – a programme which could not have been better designed to suit the wishes and fill the coffers of the American oil companies.

Even though a cutback of only 5 per cent had been agreed to, some of the Arab governments temporarily reduced their output by as much as 25 per cent. This caused a great deal of alarm in the West, as did the embargo imposed on countries which were regarded as having acted in a manner hostile to the Arabs, notably the USA and the Netherlands. In fact the embargo had little effect, apart from a psychological one, on the countries it was aimed at. I remember asking Shaikh Yamani, the Saudi Oil Minister, how the embargo worked. He said that every tanker captain was required to give a pledge that he would not discharge his cargo in any of the embargoed countries – that was all. 'But what else can we do?' he asked. Naturally some captains gave the pledge and broke it, while others discharged their oil at, say, London, whence it was transferred in another tanker to Rotterdam. They also adjusted supplies so that the embargoed countries got their oil from producing countries where the embargo was not being applied, like Nigeria. This may have been a bit more expensive but did not worry the oil companies which, as usual, passed on the extra cost to the consumers.

Paradoxically, it was at a moment when there was supposed to be an energy crisis and when the USA lay under an Arab oil boycott that the profits of the American oil companies reached unprecedented heights. It has been estimated that the Arabs' share of the rise in the price of oil will amount to $60,000m. for 1973. The oil companies, because of the profits they derive from downstream operations in addition to their share of the profits on crude get approximately seven dollars for every dollar that goes to the producing countries. That gives some idea of the fantastic affluence of the concessionary companies today.

So the American companies had never had it so good. The doubling of the price of oil by the oil-producing countries – encouraged by the companies and uncalled for by Egypt – sent their profits rocketing. They were able to offer us the golden fetter of 'participation'. For them it meant that the price of oil inside the United States could now rise to the point where, as these energy companies had always wished, the exploitation of other sources of energy became economic. Public opinion in the States, bewildered by the atmosphere of crisis, was prepared to swallow price rises and sabotage of the environmental legislation which, before October, it had found unacceptable. For many of the Arab countries this meant still more swollen incomes, which they could either use up on expensive and unnecessary gadgets, like elaborate defence systems against unspecified enemies, or plough back into the American economy by investing it there. Either way it was the USA which scored.

The embargo came at exactly the right moment for the USA. But it, and the doubling of the price of oil by the oil-producing countries, dealt a crippling blow to the economies of America's

274

rivals – Western Europe and Japan. Before, the United States had a balance of payments problem and the dollar was weak; after, the balance of payments improved and the dollar was in a much improved position. The United States had exported its inflation to Western Europe and Japan by obliging them to buy oil at inflated prices and to pay dollars for it.

If the timing of the start of the embargo suited the Americans, so did the timing of its calling-off. The resolution imposing the embargo had been quite explicit: it was to remain in force until a timetable for evacuation of all occupied Arab territories, including Arab Jerusalem, had been internationally agreed. Now all this was forgotten. President Sadat and King Feisal were bombarded with telegrams and letters day after day from President Nixon and Henry Kissinger. It was impossible, they were told, for the American Government to do anything with Congress, the press, public opinion – or with Israel – unless the embargo was unconditionally lifted. Eventually they felt obliged to comply, but before any of their aims had been achieved.

The American attitude is by now quite clear, and may be expected to reveal itself in all future oil diplomacy. It starts from the premise that the Arabs are an emotional and unstable people who cannot be trusted. It is essential therefore for the countries which depend on Arab oil to maintain a common front in negotiating with them. Another advantage of this common front is that it will discourage the Soviet Union, itself in as strong an energy position as the United States, from attacking a weakened Western Europe, or a weakened Western Europe from looking to the Soviet Union for help in its energy problems.

The Arabs, as has been seen, played their cards badly. They ordered a cut in production which was indiscriminate and a rise in price which benefited the concessionary companies more than the producing countries. Having imposed an embargo with precise political objectives they withdrew that embargo before any of those objectives had been met, even partially. All that can be said on the credit side is that the world saw the Arabs acting for once in unison and oil being used, even if clumsily, as a political weapon. Oil has thus become a credible element to be reckoned with in the Middle East dispute. This was not the case before the October war.

There are certain things that the Arabs should aim at in the future. They should prevent at all costs the formation of a united US-Western Europe-Japan front, and the best way of doing this is to guarantee the future energy requirements of Western Europe and Japan. It is entirely contrary to Arab interests to make enemies of the principal consumers of their principal product – oil. There must be permanent, mutually beneficial arrangements covering levels of production and prices between the producers and consumers of oil, just as there are for other basic commodities.

The Arabs should not be distracted by side issues like participation. If, instead of doubling the price of oil, the oil-producing countries had imposed an export tax or altered the rate of the profit split between governments and companies, they would have found a more satisfactory formula. Another possible formula would have been a 65 per cent increase in price coupled with a freeze on the revenues of the concessionary companies, such as had been imposed in Venezuela. The Arabs should always work towards direct arrangements between the oil producers and the oil consumers, which would cut out the American middlemen and so end the fantastic profits reaped by the oil companies and the continuing drain on Western Europe's dollar reserves.

So if we ask who came victorious out of the first use of the oil weapon the answer must be the United States. Before 1973 we had been thinking of a world in which the domination of the two super-powers, the United States and the Soviet Union, was being challenged by three newcomers, Western Europe, Japan and China. After 1973 the challenge from Western Europe and Japan faded out completely, while China remained as much on the sidelines as ever. In the end the Americans were to decide that the best oil price for them was one somewhere between the pre-war price and the price to which the oil-producing companies and countries had pushed it, so they stepped up their attempts to bring Europe into line with them. It will be an unfortunate outcome for the Arabs if Europe is taken over, where oil is concerned, by the American camp. But whatever happens there can be no doubt that it was the two energy giants, the United States and, to a much smaller degree, the Soviet Union, which stopped the war and formulated the peace – if peace is in fact ever to come.

Index

Abdullah, King of Jordan, 143
Abdullah, Abdul Fattah, 222, 238
Abdullah, Saad, 101
Abdul Meguid, Dr Ismet, 37
Abu Dhabi, 223, 265, 273
Abu Iyad, *see* Khalaf, Salah
Abul Ezz, General Madhkour, 53
Abul Nur, Abdul Muhsin, 128, 131
Abul Said, *see* Hassan, Kahled el-
Abu Lutf, *see* Qadumi, Farouk
Abu Saada, Brigadier Hassan, 219
Adabiyah, 8, 249, 252
Adams, Sir Philip, 224-5, 245
Adham, Kemal, 119-20, 167, 183
Agranat Commission, 27, 31, 36, 38
Al-Ahram, 32, 69, 78, 91, 107, 112, 114, 115, 127, 145, 164, 177, 183, 188, 214, 269
Alamein, 16, 19, 196, 229
Algeria, 75, 188, 218, 232, 233
Allon, Yigal, 32, 120-1
Amer, Field-Marshal Abdul Hakim, 22, 49, 62, 179, 225, 241
Amman, 31, 91
Arabs, 46, 61, 96, 115, 248, 249, 267, 275
Arab Socialist Union, 20, 114, 122-3, 128, 131, 134, 135, 196
Central Committee, 93, 122, 128, 129, 130-1, 167, 197
Higher Executive Committee, 52, 106, 113, 126, 127, 128, 130-1, 135
Arafat, Yasser, 62, 63, 64, 65, 66, 82, 96, 97, 99, 101, 103, 121, 140, 221

Aref, President Abdul Rahman, of Iraq, 48, 59, 61
Asad, President Hafez, of Syria, 12, 14, 23, 30, 31, 32, 140, 160, 172, 208-9, 212, 213, 216, 217, 221, 231-2, 238, 239-40, 241, 243, 245, 252-5
Aswan High Dam, 52, 89-90, 117, 204
Ata, Colonel Hashem el-, 141
Atassi, Dr Nureddin, 98, 266
Attrition, war of, 13, 28, 56, 60, 67, 72, 97, 180

Baathists, 69
in Iraq, 61
in Syria, 61, 128
Baghdad Pact, 92, 136
Bahrain, 273
Bakr, President Ahmed Hassan el-, of Iraq, 41, 221
Bar-Lev, General Haim, 36
Bar-Lev Line, 40, 41, 44, 133, 207, 210, 211, 215, 222, 230, 258, 259
Beauffre, General André, 259
Beaumont, Sir Richard, 103
Beirut, 78, 91
Ben Gurion, David, 240
Bergus, Donald, 95-6, 116, 139, 140, 141, 145-6, 148, 149-50
Boumedienne, President Houari, of Algeria, 41, 48, 68, 223, 255
Bourguiba, President Habib, of Tunisia, 41, 68
Bouteflika, Abdul Aziz, 233, 234
Bou Yasir, Saleh, 191-2
Brandt, Willy, 21, 200
Brezhnev, Leonid, 21, 24, 34, 35,

279

Index

Brezhnev, [*contd.*]
38, 44, 48, 65, 72, 81, 84-9, 93,
94, 95, 109, 119, 137, 144, 158-9,
163, 169, 170-7, 209, 214, 218,
219, 246, 248, 250, 251, 254-5,
260
Britain, 54, 74, 157, 166, 186, 188,
254, 263, 264

Central Intelligence Agency, 39, 99,
139, 140
in Egypt, 18, 148-50, 199
Chaban-Delmas, Jacques, 107
Chazov, Dr Evgeni, 67, 74-5, 81,
98
China, 43, 72, 76, 77, 144, 199, 201,
214, 234, 246, 249, 250, 276
Chou En-Lai, 77
Cyprus, 32, 58

Daoud, Diaeddin, 128
Daoud, General Mohammed, 102
Dayan, General Moshe, 15, 22, 24,
27, 32, 36, 37, 44, 45, 54, 96, 141,
160, 229, 249
De Gaulle, President Charles, 59,
204
Douglas-Home, Sir Alec, 36-7, 103,
107
Dulles, John Foster, 92, 198

Eban, Abba, 38, 39, 58, 60
Egypt, 12, 27, 39, 52, 54, 64, 75,
76, 84, 91, 121, 140, 146, 160,
184-5, 240-2, 258-61, 268, 269
armed forces, 43, 44, 46, 48-55, 93,
147, 162-3, 179, 182, 204-5
economy, 20, 52, 204
front in October war, 207-8, 209-
223, 225-6, 228-31, 234-5, 238, 247
internal situation, 20, 44, 46, 84,
86, 94, 122-3, 129-37, 168, 177,
188, 194, 204-5, 236-7
Egyptian-Syrian joint command,
11, 12, 16, 215, 257

Eisenhower, General Dwight D.,
166, 198, 254
Elazar, General David, 36, 37, 223,
227, 258
Eshkol, Levi, 47, 54, 58
Ethiopia, 60

Fahmy, Admiral Abdul Rahman,
180, 181
Fahmy, Ismail, 34-5, 224, 245
Fahmy, General Mohammed Ali,
238
Faiz, Dr Mansur, 106
Farouk, King of Egypt, 23
Fateh, 28, 62-4, 120
Fawzi, Dr Mahmoud, 22, 25, 122,
126-8, 132, 157, 166, 170, 198,
199, 219, 270
Fawzi, General Mohammed, 48-9,
51, 55, 56, 68, 69, 72, 73, 74, 79,
83, 85, 97, 104, 105, 107, 108,
110, 112, 125, 129, 130, 134, 136,
178, 241
Feisal, King of Saudi Arabia, 52,
53, 59, 75, 77, 78, 79, 80, 99, 139,
140, 157-8, 159, 183-4, 188, 222,
265, 267-8, 271-2, 275
Fikki, Ahmed Hassan el-, 145
France, 54, 166, 168, 254, 264
arms supplies, 59, 61, 81

Gabon, 132
Galili, Israel, 32, 36
Gamasy, General Abdul Ghani el-,
12, 183, 238, 241
Gandhi, Mrs Indira, 21
Gaza, 22, 54, 91, 121, 132, 155, 160,
177, 205, 224
Germany, West, 71, 166, 263
Ghadaffi, President Muammar el-,
of Libya, 12, 23, 70, 71, 76, 79-81,
99, 102, 103, 159, 160, 162, 184-
198, 221-2, 266, 272
Ghaleb, Murad, 84, 163
Ghali, Fuad, 237

Index

Ghorbal, Ashraf, 37, 152, 199
Golan Heights, 10, 213, 215
Goldberg, Arthur, 53, 174
Goldman, Nahum, 59
Gomaa, Sharawy, 73, 104, 105, 107, 108, 109, 110, 122, 124-5, 128-31, 134, 135, 136, 144, 145
Gonen, General Shmuel, 27, 213, 222
Gorshikov, Admiral, 163-4, 180
Grechko, Marshal Andrei, 85, 86, 93, 151, 156, 161, 163, 164, 168, 169, 173, 175, 218
Gromyko, Andrei, 56-7, 89, 94, 252

Habash, George, 79, 96
Haile Selassie, Emperor of Ethiopia, 60, 71
Hamadullah, Farouk Osman, 141
Hashim, Dr Zaki, 199
Hassan, King of Morocco, 68, 77, 79, 80
Hassan, General Abdel Qader, 162, 178, 181
Hassan, Khalid el (Abul Said), 62, 121
Hatem, Abdul Qader, 35
Hawatmeh, Naif, 96
Hawaz, Col. Adam el-, 69
Heath, Edward, 21, 144, 145, 200, 224, 230, 245
Heikal, Mohamed Hassanein, 127, 164, 174, 189-90, 199-200, 218-20
  acting Foreign Minister, 95-6; and Ghadaffi, 187, 189; and Palestinians, 62-4; and Soviet leaders, 143-5; independence of, 78-9; Minister of Information, 93, 97, 106, 135; resignation, 109-10, 114; visits Libya, 69-71, 185
Hoffi, General Itzhak, 28
Homs oil refinery, 13, 30
Hussein, King of Jordan, 41, 49, 56, 57-8, 61, 64, 67, 68, 97, 120-1, 140, 143, 160, 221, 222, 236
  and Palestinians, 81, 96, 98-103, 140
Huwaidi, Amin, 73, 74, 107, 108, 109

Idris, King of Libya, 68-9, 71
India, 76, 167, 168, 259
  war with Pakistan, 157, 168
Indonesia, 75
Iran, 90, 218, 265
Iraq, 41, 59, 61, 67, 81, 99, 118, 188, 212, 216, 217-18, 221, 222, 227, 252, 253, 267
Ismail, General Ahmed, 11, 14, 16, 29, 30, 31, 32, 33, 34, 37, 40, 41, 136, 149, 150, 178, 181-3, 193, 217, 220, 222, 225, 231, 237-8, 241
Ismail, Hafez, 21, 29, 34, 39, 107, 155, 163, 171, 175, 200-3, 223-4
Israel, 21-2, 24, 26, 27, 29, 31, 32, 33, 34, 36, 38, 39, 42, 43, 44, 46, 47, 48, 51, 58, 60, 64, 72-3, 74, 76, 79, 81, 82, 88, 89, 91, 96, 113, 115, 116, 117, 118, 120, 129, 132, 136, 141, 145, 150, 153-4, 160, 162, 164, 167-8, 169, 177, 191-3, 200, 201, 205, 209, 233, 234, 236, 240, 243-52, 254-6, 257, 267, 270
  armed forces, 15, 27, 33, 43, 44, 45, 61, 207-31, 234-5, 241-2, 266
  direct negotiations with, 36, 53-4, 92, 247
  emigration of Soviet Jews to, 28, 169
  espionage organization (Mitkal), 33
  occupied territories, 53-4, 205, 275
  raids on Egypt, 55, 67, 73, 82, 84, 87
  withdrawal, 53, 54, 91, 92, 116, 117, 132, 133, 153-4, 203, 209, 224, 225, 230, 233-4, 239, 244, 245, 275

281

Index

Jackson, Senator Henry, 120, 167
Jalloud, Major Abdel Salam, 23, 24, 76-7, 159
Japan, 263-4, 265, 270, 272, 275-6
Jarring mission, 56-7, 58, 65, 91, 92, 116, 132, 153, 165, 174
Jerusalem, 54, 275
Jobert, Michel, 36, 37, 205
Johnson, President Lyndon B., 67, 165
Jordan, 31, 33, 52, 64, 67, 75, 81, 104, 121, 143, 160, 221, 222, 227, 234, 236, 246, 268
army, 49
civil war, 98-103, 113, 121
June 1967 War, 12, 22, 33, 42, 43, 44, 45, 46, 49, 50, 53, 54, 58, 84, 136, 167, 169, 178, 185, 188, 199, 204, 219, 225, 229, 233, 234, 238, 240, 241, 260, 267

Kamil, Ahmed, 135
Katyshkin, General I. S., 83, 85, 112, 119, 161
Keating, Kenneth, 38, 39
Kendall, Donald, 199-200, 202
Khalaf, Salah (Abu Iyad), 27, 28, 63, 81, 121, 221
Khalil, Dr Mustafa, 269-73
Kharubi, Mustafa, 70, 159-60
Khartum conference (August 1967), 52, 53, 58, 59, 78, 121, 267, 268
Kholi, Hassan Sabri el-, 69
Kissinger, Dr H., 25, 36-7, 38, 39, 41, 140, 141, 155, 184, 187, 199, 200-2, 223, 225, 230, 232-4, 237, 246-9, 251-2, 254-5, 261, 275
Kosygin, Aleksei N., 65, 72, 83, 88, 93-4, 107, 109, 111, 112, 113, 160, 176, 187, 232, 235, 245-6, 248
Kreisky, Dr Bruno, 28, 35
Kuwait, 63, 75, 121, 140, 158, 218, 232, 265, 266, 268, 273
ruler of, 104, 273

Ladgham, Bahi, 99, 103
Lashinkov, General, 51, 83, 112, 179
Libya, 12, 23, 68-73, 76, 80-1, 82, 93-4, 102, 121, 127, 128, 130, 131, 141, 157, 158, 159, 160, 176, 184-97, 266, 268, 272
Louis, Victor, 145

McCloskey, Robert, 152
Macovescu, Gheorghiu, 60
Mahjoub, Abdul Khaliq, 142-3
Mahy, General Said el-, 238
Marei, Sayed, 22, 35, 122-3, 269-73
Masmoudi, Mohammed el-, 232
Mazurov, Kyril, 65, 82
Meir, Mrs Golda, 28, 32, 36, 38, 39, 40, 92, 145, 201, 203, 230, 231, 233, 248, 252
Mohieddin, Khaled, 142
Montgomery, Field-Marshal, 6, 49, 225, 258
Morocco, 218, 227, 232
Middle East News Agency, 30
Mortagi, General, 178
Mubarak, General Husni, 44, 238
Muslim Brotherhood, 62
Mykhitdinor, Nuritdin, 208-9, 212, 217, 243, 253

Nassar, General Fuad, 4, 5
Nasser, President Gamal Abdel, 23, 44, 45, 55, 73, 91, 108, 122, 125, 136, 147, 165, 183, 197, 198, 204, 235, 241, 260, 267
achievements, 136; aftermath of June war, 46-57, 179; and mediation attempts, 53-4, 56, 58-60; and UN resolution 242, 54; attitude to PLO, 63-4, 82, 96-7, 121; to Rogers plan, 92-3; and Ghadaffi, 76, 79, 80-1, 185-9; and Libyan revolution, 68-72; and Jordanian civil war, 98-103; and Arab states, 57-8, 61, 67-8, 75,

Index

Nasser, [*contd.*]
77-80, 130-1; relations with USSR, 48, 57, 62, 65-7, 83-8, 90, 93-4, 113, 117-18, 131, 137, 144, 156, 162, 165-6, 174, 177-9; rebuilds army, 43-52; resignation, 46, 147, repression under, 136; health, 62, 65, 66, 67, 73-5, 83; death, 104-5, 106, 122, 190; funeral, 107, 110-12, 199; posthumous influence, 123, 129
Nassif, General El-Leithy, 105, 134, 135
National Assembly, Egyptian, 114, 116, 122, 127, 129, 230, 231
Netherlands, 273
Nimeiry, President Jaafar el-, of Sudan, 67, 72, 81, 82, 99, 100, 101, 141-3, 188, 189
Nixon, President Richard, 38, 91, 92, 116, 117, 139, 140, 162, 166, 169, 170, 171, 172, 173, 174, 184, 198, 199, 200-2, 214, 232-3, 244, 246, 250-2, 254-5, 263, 272, 275
Nofal, General Bahieddin, 11, 29, 30, 31
Nur, Babakr el-, 141

October 1973 War, 43, 61, 190, 197-198, 205, 207-42, 244, 257-61, 262, 268, 269; outbreak, 40, 207; ceasefire, 209, 212, 223, 224, 230, 232, 239, 240, 244, 245, 246, 277
Oil-producing countries, 35, 53, 188, 264-77
Oil weapon, 26, 35, 52, 115, 205, 245, 262-76
Okunev, General V. V., 119, 156, 175
Oman, 273
OPEC, 264-5
Osman, Ahmed, 148, 149
Oufkir, General Mohammed, 80, 259

Pakistan, 75, 76, 168, 186, 259
Palestinians, 54, 96, 201, 203, 224, 230, 235, 246; and King Hussein, 98-103, 121, 140; PLO, 62, 169, 221; resistance movements, 17, 28, 63, 64, 65, 81, 82, 120, 236, 266, 268
Peled, General M., 210
Podgorny, President Nikolai, 65, 83, 94, 104, 158, 160, 166, 175, 217-18; in Egypt, 46, 50, 117, 138, 143
Pompidou, President Georges, 21
Ponomarev, B. N., 141-7, 158

Qadumi, Farouk (Abu Lutf), 28, 62, 63, 81, 97, 121, 140
Qatar, 14, 196, 273

Rabat Summit Conference (Dec. 1969), 77, 79-80, 82, 189
Rabin, Yitzhak, 26
Rafael, Gideon, 60
Randopolo, Tanashi, 147-50, 152
Riad, General Abdel Munim, 45, 46, 49-50, 51, 57, 66, 178, 241
Riad, Mahmoud, 22, 53-4, 56, 58, 89, 92, 95, 107, 130-1, 132, 140, 148, 152-5, 165, 252
Riad, Mohammed, 146
Richardson, Elliot, 107, 199
Rifai, Abdul Munim, 102
Rogers, William, 90, 92, 117, 132, 133, 140, 141, 146, 152-5, 166, 173, 261; Rogers Plan, 90, 92-3, 95, 96, 97, 115
Rumania, 32, 59-60

Sabri, Ali, 105, 109, 112, 115, 116, 118, 122-31, 134, 136, 138, 139, 147, 151, 173
Sadat, President Anwar el-, 12, 14, 18-22, 23, 24-7, 28, 29-30, 34, 35, 36, 37, 38, 39, 40, 41, 73, 74, 93, 104-7, 109-10, 112, 114, 115,

Index

Sadat, [contd.]
121, 128, 133, 138-9, 142, 143, 144, 151, 152, 154, 159, 160, 161, 166, 190-8, 205, 209, 211-14, 216-24, 230-2, 234-41, 243, 245-54, 268-75; succeeds Nasser, 114, 122, 126-7; and Ali Sabri group, 122, 126-31, 134-7, 147; in Moscow, 65, 66, 118-19, 156, 157, 158, 167, 168; and withdrawal of Soviet advisers, 120, 165, 169-76, 180, 183; relations with USA, 114-16, 118, 140, 141, 150, 184, 199-202; Heikal's opinion of, 117-18
Sadat, Mrs Jihan el-, 221
Sadiq, General Mohammed, 98, 99, 103, 117, 120-1, 134, 135-6, 151, 155, 158, 160-1, 169-71, 175, 177, 178, 180, 181, 204
Saiqa, 17
Salem, Mamduh, 22, 134, 135
Saqqaf, Omar el-, 234
Saud bin Abdel Aziz, ex-King, 59
Saudi Arabia, 14, 58, 75, 77, 78, 79, 119-20, 140, 158, 184, 196, 227, 232, 234, 262, 265-8, 270-2
Schonau camp, 17, 28
Scocroft, General, 200, 202
Scranton, William, 198, 199
Shafei, Hussein el-, 22, 101, 105, 109, 112, 125
Shakur, General Yusuf, 12, 30, 31
Shalev, General Arye, 32
Sharaf, Sami, 73, 74, 78, 103, 105, 107, 108, 109, 110, 112, 122, 124-126, 129, 131, 134, 136-7, 144
Sharm el-Sheikh, 54, 91, 132, 210, 240
Sharon, General Ariel, 210, 213, 228-30, 249
Shazli, General Saad el-, 12, 14, 15, 27, 150, 181-3, 237-8, 241, 247
Sheikh, Shafie Ahmed el-, 142
Shelepin, Aleksander, 67

Shuqair, Dr Labib, 125, 127, 128
Siad Barre, President Mohammed, of Somalia, 94
Sidqi, Dr Aziz, 35, 157, 161, 176, 180, 252
Sinai, 11, 15, 27, 28, 32, 33, 36, 44, 60, 90, 91, 97, 116, 132, 153, 155, 196, 207, 209, 210, 212-23, 225-230, 234, 237, 240, 245, 252, 260, 271
Sisco, Joseph, 53-4, 91-2, 132, 133, 141, 152, 154, 166, 198, 232, 234, 261
Sterner, Michael, 140-1, 145-6, 147
Sudan, 72, 81, 82, 141-3, 144, 188, 189
Suez Canal, 52, 58, 60, 82, 84, 85, 93, 116, 132, 136, 152, 153, 179, 181, 230, 257, 259, 266, 267; British and, 133; 1956 campaign, 54, 55, 119, 177, 185, 198, 214, 240, 254; Egyptian crossing of (1973), 15, 16, 17, 40, 41, 42, 153, 155, 207, 209-10, 214, 237; Israeli crossing of (1973), 48, 198, 228-230, 234-5, 246
Sultan bin Abdel Aziz, Prince, 158, 170-1, 183
Syria, 12, 13, 27, 29, 52, 54, 57, 61, 64, 67, 75, 94, 121, 127, 130, 131, 140, 157, 185, 188, 189, 191, 196, 203, 232, 243-6, 251, 252, 266, 269; and Jordanian civil war, 98, 99; Syrian front in October war, 28, 31, 32, 33, 207, 208, 211-12, 213-22, 225, 226-8, 236, 239, 245, 252, 253, 271

Tal, General, 229
Talhouni, Bahjat el-, 64
Tallal, King of Jordan, 143
Tel, Wasfi, 99
Tito, President Josip Broz, 21, 59
Tlas, General Mustafa, 11, 14, 30
Tripoli pact, 81, 82

284

Index

Turkey, 71

UN, 17, 20, 21, 37, 56, 132, 133, 153, 159, 182, 224, 230, 239, 240, 259
General Assembly, 21, 25, 42, 157, 232, 254
Security Council, 21, 29, 42, 51, 92, 209, 214, 216, 224, 235, 244, 246, 248, 249-50
Resolution 242, 51, 53, 54, 58, 64, 75, 116, 132, 153, 159, 173, 174, 233, 246, 249; Resolution 338, 249, 250; Resolution 339, 250-1
Upper Volta, 132
USA, 18, 24, 35, 42, 56, 74, 81, 86, 87, 89, 90, 91, 92, 96, 98, 113, 136, 139, 160, 162, 164, 167, 170, 172, 173, 181, 183, 186, 187, 188, 216, 223, 234, 243-56, 258, 261, 262, 270-7
relations with Egypt, 18, 114-15, 147-50, 152-5, 166-7, 199, 201
Middle East policy, 47, 91-2, 146, 184, 201, 203
energy crisis in, 262-3, 269, 274
arms supplies to Israel, 92, 112, 115, 120, 132, 150, 201, 203, 216, 219, 226, 232, 239, 244
Sixth Fleet, 47
USSR, 21, 24, 34, 35, 39, 43, 46, 47, 48, 56, 58, 72, 76, 77, 90, 93, 94, 98, 100, 114, 115, 128, 137, 142, 145, 146, 147, 148, 150, 155, 164, 187, 203, 214, 217, 219, 222, 228, 230, 233, 234, 237, 239, 243-256, 258, 275-7; advisers in Egypt, 51, 85, 86, 88, 112, 119, 151, 160-164, 167-76, 179-80, 190, 201; evacuation of (October 1973), 33, 34, 35, 36; arms supplies to Egypt, 47, 48, 50, 52, 53, 59, 62, 67, 81, 84-90, 112, 117, 118, 119,

156-7, 158, 159, 162, 171-81, 214, 216-17, 219, 222; to Palestinians, 64-5, 81-2; to Syria, 212, 219, 222; relations with Egypt, 112-13, 117, 118, 119, 120, 129, 137, 138, 141, 151, 155, 156, 160-5, 166-81, 183, 184, 187, 190, 202, 223; Soviet-Egyptian friendship treaty, 25, 138, 139, 141, 175; facilities for fleet, 47-8, 138, 164, 166, 175; détente with USA, 24, 86, 159, 164, 165, 169, 170, 173, 174, 175, 199, 202, 203, 205-6, 243, 255
U Thant, 56, 92

Vienna, 28, 32, 34
Vinogradov, Sergei, 81, 82, 83, 112
Vinogradov, Vladimir, 24-5, 34, 35, 38, 39, 40, 41, 94, 111-12, 117, 128, 137, 138, 142-5, 151, 161, 163, 171-5, 208, 209, 212, 213-14, 216-19, 243, 248, 250

Waldheim, Dr Kurt, 235, 253, 254

Yadin, General Y., 229
Yamani, Sheikh Ahmed Zaki el-, 265, 273
Yamit, 22, 24, 160, 205
Yariv, General A., 17
Yemen (YAR), 52, 58, 204
Yugoslavia, 157

Zafarana, 29, 39, 73
Zakharov, Marshal Matvei, 46, 50-51, 56, 84, 112, 179
Zayyat, Dr Mohammed Hassan el-, 25, 29, 36, 37, 39, 41-2, 152, 199, 224
Ze'ira, Major-General E., 17, 32, 36, 40
Zionism, 43, 139, 201

285